Reading Descartes Otherwise

Reading Descartes Otherwise

Blind, Mad, Dreamy, and Bad

Kyoo Lee

For Kelsi,
who thinks,
reads,
writes,
with extraordinary
insight & clarity.

Best wishes,
Yours, Q
Summer 2014
NAROPA

FORDHAM UNIVERSITY PRESS

NEW YORK   2013

Fordham University Press has no responsibility for the persistence or accuracy of URLs for external or third-party Internet
websites referred to in this publication and does not guarantee
that any content on such websites is, or will remain, accurate or
appropriate.

Fordham University Press also publishes its books in a variety of
electronic formats. Some content that appears in print may not
be available in electronic books.

Library of Congress Cataloging-in-Publication Data is available
from the publisher.

Printed in the United States of America

15 14 13   5 4 3 2 1

First edition

CONTENTS

ACKNOWLEDGMENTS

Special institutional thanks are due to the Department of Philosophy and The Office for the Advancement of Research, John Jay College, The City University of New York.

For the last few years while drafting this book, I have also benefited greatly from some extra time and space provided by the following institutions:

Faculty Research Fellowship, The Andrew W. Mellon Foundation
The Center for the Humanities, The Graduate Center, CUNY
Wertheim Study, The New York Public Library
PSC-CUNY Research Award (PSCOOC-39-142), Research
    Foundation of CUNY
Visiting Professorship, Wuhan University

Countless personal thanks are also due, but more personally.

All references to the works of Descartes are to the *Oeuvres de Descartes*, abbreviated in this book as AT. The English translation I have used (unless otherwise noted) is *The Philosophical Writings of Descartes*, abbreviated as CSM. For ease of reading, I have used the following system throughout the text: M, 7:19/2:13 (usually formatted as AT VII 19/CSM II 13) refers to *Meditations on First Philosophy*, as printed in *Oeuvres de Descartes*, volume 7, page 19, translated in *The Philosophical Writings of Descartes*, volume 2, page 13.

For the *Geometry*, *Optics*, and part of the *Correspondence*, different translations were used, as noted here, but the citation format remains the same. For example, O, 6:141/108 refers to *Optics*, as printed in *Oeuvres de Descartes*, volume 6, page 141, with a translation elsewhere as noted on page 108. When the non-CSM translation of the *Correspondence* is used, the citation is provided in a regular note.

When AT alone is used, it is indicated accordingly: (Pt, 10:181), for example. When a passage from AT is used from a part that is not included in this listing, such as from the biographical notes (AT XII), it is indicated accordingly: (12:305), for example.

Abbreviation	AT/CSM	Drafted	Published	Title (English Translation, Where Available)
AT			1964–74 (ed.)	*Oeuvres de Descartes,* rev. ed., 11 vols., ed. Charles Adam and Paul Tannery (Paris: Vrin, 1964–1974); first published as 12 vols. (Paris: Cerf, 1897–1913).
CSM			1985 (trans.)	*The Philosophical Writings of Descartes,* 3 vols., trans. John Cottingham, Robert Stoothoff, Dugald Murdoch, and Anthony Kenny (Cambridge: Cambridge University Press, 1985).
C	I-V/III	1619–50	1657	*The Correspondence*[1]
Cc	VIIIB/I	1647	1647	*Comments on a Certain Broadsheet*
D	VI/I	1637	1637	*Discourse on the Method*
Dh	XI/I	1647	1647	*Description of the Human Body*
G	VI	1637	1637	*Geometry*[2]
M	VII/II	1641	1641	*Meditations on First Philosophy*
O	VI	1637	1637	*Optics*[3]
Or	VII/II	1642	1642	*Objections and Replies*
P	VIIIA/I	1644	1644	*Principles of Philosophy*
Ps	XI/I	1649	1649	*The Passions of the Soul*
Pt	X/I	1618–22	1859	*Private Thoughts; Olympica*
R	X/I	(1628)	1701	*Rules for the Direction of the Mind*
S	X/I	(1641)	1701	*The Search for Truth*

Abbreviation	AT/CSM	Drafted	Published	Title (English Translation, Where Available)
Tl	XI/I	(1633)	1664	*Treatise on Light* (Part II of *the World* as projected)
Tm	XI/I	(1633)	1664	*Treatise on Man* (Part I of *the World* as projected)

[1]Andrea Nye, *The Princess and the Philosopher: Letters of Elisabeth of the Palatine to René Descartes* (Lanham, Md.: Rowman & Littlefield, 1999).

[2]René Descartes, *Discourse on Method, Optics, Geometry, and Meteorology*, rev. ed., trans. Paul J. Olscamp (Indianapolis: Hackett, 2001).

[3]Ibid.

We must acknowledge the weakness of our nature.

—RENÉ DESCARTES (1596–1650), *Meditation VI*

I should like it best if you never put forward any new opinions, but retained all the old ones in name, and merely brought forward new arguments. . . . What is done cannot be undone. Now you must try to defend as moderately as possible the truths you put forward, and to correct without any obstinancy anything you may have said which is untrue or inexact. Remind yourself that there is nothing more praiseworthy in a philosopher than a candid acknowledgement of his errors.

—RENÉ DESCARTES (1596–1650), *Letter to Regius, January 1642*

If Descartes Remains Overread and Underexplored . . .

It has been almost a decade—or two if I keep counting.

Reading, or otherwise sitting on, the work of René Descartes (March 31, 1596–February 11, 1650) with the quiet pleasure I see in a g(r)azing cow, I have been savoring, and saving somewhere, this nagging thought: His philosophy—his "Cartesianism," his "rationalism," his "methodological" doubt, his theoretical "self-centeredness," his historicized him-ness—seems to remain overread and underexplored. I have been sensing that something else is going on, too, in those usual pages, in that familiar picture. And here, I am inviting you, my readers, to read with me this strangely intimate distance that the Cartesian "I" appears to maintain with and from itself: this marginal, magical void within the Cartesian ego filled with phenomenological energies and voices, which I have come to see as not only irreducible but also liberating in some ways. I have begun to realize that I might have been in a string of sporadic side talks or small talks with a cast of minor Cartesian characters and unforeseen associates including, perhaps, myself or someone like myself.

If so, so be it, as in *"larvatus prodeo"* (I advance masked) with the "cheeks flaming"—mark that mask and those cheeks:

> Fear of God is the beginning of wisdom. The actors, called to the scene, in order to hide their flaming cheeks, don a mask. Like them, when mounting the stage in the theatre of the world, where, thus far, I have only been a spectator, I advance masked [*Larvatus prodeo*]. (Pt, 10:213/1:2, trans. modified)

This mode of self-presentation, the figural indirection or suspension of as-if that frames and tones most of Descartes' oeuvre, also coheres with the Ovidian low-profile lifestyle he assiduously duplicated, namely, *"Bene vixit qui bene latuit"*—One who lives well, keeps himself well hidden—or to paraphrase it into an imperative, "Go through life without drawing attention to yourself"[1] (C, 1:286). In the 1634 letter that contained this thought, Descartes was expressing his urbane taste and desire for privacy and anonymity to one of his most supportive and trusted confidants, Marin Mersenne, who was the information hub of the post-Renaissance early modern Europe, an intellectual diplomat par excellence who knew and kept an archive of many closeted characters of Paris. A host of other free-thinking young things such as Galileo Galilei, Thomas Hobbes, and Pierre Gassendi were among Mersenne's close friends; to that man on an unofficial yet unwavering mission we owe much of our intimate knowledge of how (the mind of) Descartes worked and evolved. So, partly thanks to him, we have some sense of Descartes the person as well, of the private, mobile man of plural voices. What sustains my curiosity is not the thinker's quirky little (auto)biographical details or (socioenvironmental-)psychological realities per se, although they remain relevant. Of primary interest to me is, in a sense more simply, the subject position of that person intricately subject to objectification including self-thing-ification, as indexed in such philosophically inflected traces of "I," including "I" vis-à-vis "You." What I want to figure out, while working through such Cartesian codes of selfhood, is what happens in and around such acts of mediated self-reflection or more broadly self-introspection and dialogue.

Take this curious little passage that follows *larvatus prodeo*, another fairly well-known fragment from that *Praeambula* (preliminary) section of Descartes' notebook:

Science is like a woman: if she stays faithful to her husband she is respected; if she becomes common property she grows to be despised. (Pt, 10:214/1:2)

As Descartes' biographer, Adrien Baillet also wondered, "Why this double game, which resembles a drama?"[2] Yes again, why this masked privacy? And who, or what, is murmuring underneath or behind it? What is this thinking thing that appears to itself like a veiled woman in the face of God, God the gaze of truth that neither trembles nor moves? How should we read this double space in which the dual masking of the object of repre-sentation (e.g., me or sciences as an object of study) and a representative (e.g., I or the scientist who studies such) is staged at once? What necessitates, compels, and sustains such a non-flat, simplex figuration of the subject of thinking?

At this point, I can neither find nor forge any definite answer to that question, which is part of what I will be searching for as I proceed. At this point, I hope you, too, will at least be open to this hypothesis split open here, namely, that something is not right about the very assumption of fixed or cloistered Cartesian subjectivity itself. That image, as we will see shortly, needs some shaking and diversifying from within, this pervasive myth of Descartes' "abstract" or "disembodied" ego, which historically and mostly has been masked, marked, merged into "Western, white, male, single, bour-geois." At this point, we only need remember that, whatever the case, what-ever or whoever Descartes the thinker, the writer, the wanderer is, or whatever or whoever we think he is, he says he is not *that*. If anything, he remains a thing, "a thinking thing" (Or, 7:246/2:171), to recall that bit he says about himself as a case in point.

Perhaps, then, the Cartesian "cast" is temporal first and foremost. The mask of philosophical narrativity or fabulation Descartes wears would function as a temporal anchor or switchboard for the *cogito*, stabilizing the very temporal malleability and diversity of self-identifications; what "fills" that cast or what appears masked, although inseparable from the mask it-self, would become secondary, seen from the perspective of the ego's cogi-tative progression. Like Michel de Montaigne, for whom time is "a mobile thing, which appears as in a shadow together with matter, which is ever running and flowing, without ever remaining stable or permanent,"[3] Des-cartes is keenly aware of such a liquidizing passage and power of time that the senses, typically, register through matter; the difference is that the latter also desires to arrest time, to keep a certain moment flash-frozen such as the singularized time of the *cogito*. So Descartes' larval mask, nominally, maintains the structurally elastic and even esoteric relationship that I, a thinking thing, would have with myself each time anew. If I thought I knew I was a genius but now see I was mistaken simply or even doubly, what still makes me me, what sustains myself, is that reflective recognition, that very "*relation*, not object" (Or, 7:473–4/2:318–319, emphasis added), the mediated self-relation observed as such—that is to say, regardless of whether I am a genius, which, after all, does not *matter*. I could think of myself as anything, even an unwitting secretary for an evil genius, but the point, roughly, is that thinking undeniably happens and happened. On a related note, even if I, "a man who adds two and three together," think of you as that evil genius by whom I "can be deceived" (Or, 7:467/2:320), insofar as my self-distrust will "not affirm or deny anything" (Or, 7:467/2:320) except noting the occurrence of that thought, we both will receive the benefit of the doubt. True, practically at the end, it is mainly about me, my time here and there, but at least one thing that deserves a special recognition from the start is that this self-preservative prudence remains structurally relational, relational in some peculiarly (un)systematic ways that are not exactly dialectical or just rhetorical or primarily psychological—or all of that perhaps *and*, curiously, something other and more than that . . .

Such Janus temporality, but not necessarily figurality, of the Cartesian mask is most dramatically illustrated in the "Seventh Set of Objections and Replies," especially at the beginning (Or, 7:451–454/2:302–304) where Father Bourdin and Descartes exchange warnings and agree on ground rules before the quiet shouting match starts. Overall, Bourdin's dismissal there of the *Meditations on First Philosophy*, "this little pamphlet of yours" (Or, 7:469/2:315), is a little obsessive, and Descartes' moves are appropriately schizophrenic. No less than four times, the Jesuit Father attempts to find "a way into the method" (Or, 7:488–508/2:329–345) by drawing the risk-taking philosopher's attention to the fundamental flaws of his discursive orientation: The priest interrogates the experimental skeptic's starting point, his methodological reliance on subtractive doubt as the analytical apparatus for (re)constituting and reinforcing his faith. The Father senses that, contrary to the intention, this eliminativist strategy would end up forwarding the atheist energy forever rather than leaving the good faith eternally re-warded. The irreducible atheist streak there unnerves the Father. And Descartes knows his time. So what does Descartes do? Or rather, what *did* he do? Before engaging Bourdin point by point, he *unveils* himself as a true believer, old and new:

> [He makes] . . . a mask which will not so much cover as distort my features. But here I hereby pull off the mask and throw it away, because in the first place I am not used to play-acting, and in the second place it is quite out of the place here, when I am debating a very serious issue with a man who belongs to a religious order. (Or, 7:454/2:304)

Recall: Was it not "the fear of the Lord" that led Descartes to mask himself in the first place? So should he not keep the mask on? Whence and whither this flipping? And which mask is he talking about?—the one he has been wearing, or the one put on by the heavily editorializing Father? What philo-sophical bra is he claiming that he is taking off, right here, right now?—the veil of the unveiled face? Such knotty contradictions and expansive ambi-guities aside, is the Cartesian cast something one can take off? Rather, per-haps it is something that can be revived, with its heuristic role recast, in a similar way that Descartes flips the argument of the inner skeptic without, that is, destroying it.

Descartes Needs Rereading

Let me flip open Descartes again.

My mind seems to have been actively suspended by certain constantly slippery gaps and cinematic interplays between the memory of my own first unschooled encounter with Descartes, the shock of the *Meditations* (1641) on the one hand, and the usual scholarly scenes of interpretation, or scholastic "filters" around that philosophical time bomb, on the other. As John Carriero put it,

> CAN SOMEONE today take up a work of philosophy written over 350 years ago and engage with it on its own terms? This book is an attempt to do so with Descartes' *Meditations concerning First Philosophy*. My goal is to work through the text as it appears and to confront it in an unfiltered way.[1]

As someone who is trying to do something similar, "to engage with the *Meditations* on its own terms," I am on the same page, more or less. However, rather than "confronting" the text, as Carriero did in his recent, splendid book of line-by-line commentary, I am inclined to go along with it instead, as far and slowly as I can. I would like to read the thinking of Descartes in addition to thinking it, while doing justice, at least minimally, to both the idiosyncrasies of my own philosophical childhood and the adult idioms of advanced Cartesian scholarship. What happens if we go off with or even against Descartes for a while, that manifold Descartes? How about following some minor leads, voices, and characters as well as major ones in this quasi-biblical drama of the self-fashioning "modern" mind at work? Why not vibrate a little with this vibrant material, a phenomenological text par excellence?

A further analogy might help. I am thinking of the Academy Awards, annually aired on television, where supporting actors are also recognized on stage—if not, by definition, centralized. Now, imagine this: You, an outside viewer, are about to cast a decentralized look at those modern engineered edges of reality and illusion, facts and fables. You, an alternative viewer, are focusing on those structurally transitory intersections of presence and absence, the ghostly stream of images on live television, themselves being the living allegory here. That deconstructive, distracted *you*, folded, molded, into that dualized space-time, is me, the other reader of Descartes. Most of the viewers would usually look, anxiously, forward to that last moment of triumph: "I appeared (at long last), therefore, I am (the star of the year)." But we, otherwise distracted, would not necessarily do that; we would witness something else, should keep looking elsewhere. We, the other minor viewers, understand that it is as if the narrative build-up were there only to be forgotten, those relatively unimportant moments. From the start, they appear almost as objects of necessary forgetting, fading out; they appear in order to *be* such. So here is just my little experimental idea: What if we reverse the order, play it back and retrace the process in a slower motion? Where and when can we revive—rediscover and hear back from—those minor characters and extras? How can we support their subversive, otherwise inscribed centralities, and recognize their alternative credentials?

Why not read the *Meditations*, too, this way, this "other" way? My suggestion is that we watch the process, its cinematographic temporality, up close, more intimately and meditatively, by exploring the phenomenological textuality of its poses and pauses—not just or against but including the backdrop of its ideational contents, normalized objectivity, and discursive marches we often call, quite rightly, the "argument." We will be following the *Meditations* microcosmically and microscopically, immanently and otherwise, focusing on such inaugural figures and forces of necessary alterity as appear in the *First Meditation* and reappear in the opening passages of the *Second:* I count at least four: the blind, the mad, the dreamy, and the bad(ly cornered).

More specifically, we will trace a way in which such subjective figurations of blindness, madness, dreaminess, and ultimate deviousness are followed to but not eclipsed by their common nominal destination, the "ego" of the (*ego*) *cogito:* how the first is inscriptively pressed into the second, which thereby retains the first in some ways, even if repellently. I am interested in that multi-elastic void that, I am again saying, should not be avoided. Why? Again, I believe, "Descartes," the inaugurally "modern" name canonically associated with all such startlingly surreal meditations on the self and the world, remains rather overindexicalized and underexplicated. Something in the dramaturgical reality and psychosomatic dynamism of Descartes' *Meditations* escapes, hauntingly, the history of reading and "rationalizing" him, his paradigmatic and disciplinary legacy thus fashioned.

Certainly, I am not alone in detecting this (an)other Descartes in "Descartes." Susan Bordo, among others, has already tracked it rather clearly and intriguingly, making it easier for someone like me (and you) to pursue further this (an)other line of reading Descartes:

> In the *Meditations*, the epistemological insecurity of the Renaissance—which had been philosophically crystallized in the sixteenth-century revival of Pyrrhonian skepticism—remains powerfully alive in the form of Cartesian doubt. More than merely a lingering, hollow vestige of an earlier intellectual fashion, that doubt, presented to us through the imagery of madmen's delusions, evil geniuses, and hallucinations, appears in the text as invasive, vertiginous. The most vivid moments of the *Meditations* occur in the first two *Meditations*, and they create a nightmare landscape not easily dispelled from the imagination. Looking freshly at the *Meditations*, one cannot help but be struck by the manifest epistemological anxiety of the earlier *Meditations*, and by how unresolute a mode of inquiry they embody: the dizzying vacillations, the constant re-questioning of the self, the determination, if only temporary,

to stay *within* confusion and contradiction, to favor interior movement rather than clarity and resolve.

All that, of course, is ultimately left behind by Descartes, as firmly as his bad dreams . . . were conquered by the vigilance of his reason. The model of knowledge that Descartes bequeathed to modern science, and of which he is often explicitly described as the father, is based on clarity, certainty, and detachment. *Yet* the transformation from the imaginary of nightmare to the imagery of objectivity remains unconvincing.[2]

Likewise, I remain unconvinced, arrested there, somehow glued. I, too, am drawn to all that transformative or at least transitory inner mess that was "ultimately left behind by Descartes as firmly as his bad dreams." That, again, leads me to look into another Descartes, or at an "other" Descartes.

Like the memories of a bad (or good) wine archived on the tongue, such fibrous dimensions and matters of doubt are "not merely lingering" but are stirring, sprawling. Although less visible if not completely invisible, such shadowy "I"s, the phenomenological residua of consciousness including self-consciousness, remain hyperactive in the quiet corners and frames of the Cartesian legacy of modernity that support *and* subvert the ideational project, its face value, its surface tautology: I = I, I am what (I think) I am, no matter what I have been or will have become. Again, focusing otherwise, I am here to observe and preserve the other minor, interior, and seemingly inferior dramatic forces, moments, scenes of the *cogito*, the "haunted, hidden, stamped, inscribed"[3] Descartes, the Platonic cave turned inside out. I would describe, as simply and closely as I can, what I see in the other mirror, the other side of "Cartesian rationality," some perky, allegorical ambiguities of modernity that appear to outlive this postmodern cliché, "Descartes, the abstract modern subject, the father of modern philosophy" projected as such, now abjected or rejected, who perhaps, I am saying, was not there in the first place—except in those very images of modern philosophical virility gone viral.

Richard Rorty, too, is not too far from saying "something like"[4] that, when he lays this out:

If we look in Descartes for a common factor which pains, dreams, memory-images, and veridical and hallucinatory perceptions share with concepts of (and judgments about) God, number, and the ultimate constituents of matter, *we find no explicit doctrine.* Descartes tells us that we have a clear grasp of the distinction between the extended and the non-extended, and so we do (in the same trivial sense in which we might claim a clear grasp of the distinction between the finite and the infinite), but this does not help with the *borderline cases* (sensory grasp of particulars) which are, as it happens, *the heart of the matter.* For it is just the status of the *"confused* ideas of sense and imagination" which makes the difference between mind-as-reason and mind-as-consciousness.[5]

Once . . . second-generation Cartesians . . . had purified and "normalized" Cartesian doctrine, we got the full-fledged version of the "'idea' idea."[6]

It seems plausible to say that Descartes's insight was merely a recognition of the difference between parts of persons or states of those parts (e.g., cramps of their stomachs) on the one hand and certain states of the whole person on the other. . . . By thus making the possible intruders among bodies less easily identifiable, he made them more philosophical.[7]

I agree: The borderline cases of psychosomatic disorder unfolding in the inaugural pages of the *Meditations* concern the *confusing* differences between various senses of the I "in a single inner space."[8] Materializing through the serial appearance of figures of blindness (dumbstruckness), madness, dreaminess, and (moral) badness, all such irreducible differences function as allegorical indexes to allergic complications at "the heart of the (Cartesian) matter," Cartesian idealism or rationalism. In that regard, Rorty's surgically iconoclastic, Cartesian attention to differences, which makes him sound almost like a deconstructive Cartesian, remains instructive. However, I do not entirely share the dismissive tone with which Rorty readily reduces Descartes' philosophy to a "mere" point that has been historically "normalized" and normatively inflated into "Cartesianism"; Rorty's subsequent move toward "anti-Cartesianism"[9] completes his epochal trashing of such a myth of "the mental," the mirror of nature. If, as he suggests and as I happen to agree, the whole classical and scholastic business of philosophy, of "soulful" intellection, should be structurally redescribed into problems and significances of "thinking," of "thinking (in) the present" in particular, what I also sense in the rescaled move Rorty is making is not so much an anti-Cartesian impulse as, on the contrary, certain paradigmatic forces of Cartesian modernity at work again—dare I say, a new style of doing philosophy or being philosophical. Rorty, the self-declared anti-Cartesian, does not see much of Cartesian compulsion, but I do or am inclined to. What I am keen to see reworked today is a certain lucidity of the epochal failures of historical Cartesianism, of its imaginative forces, realized and radicalized as such. Cartesian rationality does not, cannot, unify the world of differences and multiplicities under "thinking," and yet, the very ghostly, holistic spirit of Cartesian philosophy will not simply evaporate, either. Again, we have already tasted Descartes in the casket, masked or not.

True, philosophers, those "conceptual housekeepers"[10] or (un)veilers of (un)realities, generally busy themselves tending to the infinite riches of mess left behind by the scientists and company, sometimes to the neglect of their own. This housecleaner should not be an exception. But this other sort of cleaner would spend some time looking through the modern philosopher's room in its prototypical form, in some nooks and crannies in particular, looking for some invisible dust set in between—without cleaning it up, as it were. The figure of the, say, post-Cartesian philosopher I envisage, also in light of Rorty's *Philosophy and the Mirror of Nature*, is not a dust buster but a dust collector, one who merely shows how the dirt has become an irreducible part of the body, or masked:

> In many different academic arenas, from history of science to literary theory, we find fewer and fewer open adherents to the Cartesian dream; more and more have begun to critically objectify it: to historicize it, to psychoanalyize it, to deconstruct it. The pivotal philosophical texts of modernity, however, have remained untouched by this deconstruction. The *Meditations* are still read by most philosophers as a series of disembodied philosophical arguments, with all the most cherished and historical clichés and sedimented emphases intact. The time seems overdue.[11]

Overdue, indeed, are "some fresh approaches to the *Meditations*, reading which will incorporate and reflect our changed understanding of the modern scientific project and the new insights made available as a result of our growing critical detachment from that project."[12] Specifically, the micro-sweeping reading that follows seeks to explicate the text itself, zooming in on the transitorily elusive architecture of the now, of the "clear and distinct," the enduring intricacy of it. The task, in other words, is to reattach Descartes to "Descartes" with that lovingly "critical detachment."

The Flight to Objectivity by Susan Bordo, excerpted previously, has already incisively touched on that issue of the historical monumentalization or foundational banalization of Descartes, by alternatively spotlighting the "instability and transitional quality"[13] of Cartesianism in the "*psycho*cultural framework"[14] of the sixteenth and seventeenth century. I am miniaturizing the same through reflective footnoting, while magnifying a few, fascinatingly literalized blind spots in Descartes' text. My "reading" question, the guiding concern, is what happens *between* clear and distinct ideas or, literally, paragraphed thoughts, between those thoughts thus *cut*, cuttingly joined. If we presuppose almost nothing, as little as possible, about the *Meditations* but start reading it as if for the first time, if we delve into it while reopening it as a phenomenological drama or cinema of un-unified voices and scenes, if we therefore follow its sequential threads more descriptively than prescriptively, running through it immanently rather than teleologically, which, or what kind of, Descartes would survive—or reemerge?

Another spidery route of Cartesian rediscovery I have set out to draw mirrors Descartes' preontotheological nightmare, the interminable, roughly Kafkaesque intertextuality of it. As what I will demonstrate in turn is an exercise in orchestral use of interdisciplinary reason rather than a linearly analytic or historically layered study of the philosophy of Descartes, I am hoping that this close but not closed reading merits its own liminal and sonorous space. If, however, my alternative attention to elements of alterity in the Cartesian discourse of subjectivity alters the original beyond recognition, I hope it does so at least to the effect of prompting readers to see it anew; Descartes' inventive thinking itself, as I see it, engenders such self-altering potentials. That is, I am hoping that my mistake or excuse, however fundamental or colossal, will not be entirely mine. As I already seem to be hoping too much, let me then just ultimately hope that such a textured probe into signs of vibrantly spectral alterity, "X-factors" lodged at both the core and the edge of the Cartesian text, will turn out significant enough to signal something beyond itself. At stake is a revitalized reframing and rewriting of the inaugural legacy of Cartesian modernity and its proto-phenomenological tracks.

A tiny step here: If I can communicate at least to a couple of readers my ongoing experience of facing Descartes' reflective text, often of being in and out of "it" at once at various stages of my philosophical apprenticeship and rehabilitation, I will at least know I may not be alone in being this odd. Looking farther ahead, if this neo-Cartesian minority report connects a few good readers of philosophy to feeling excited about rediscovering Descartes with or despite Kyoo Lee, I will have fulfilled my modest aim in this little pamphlet of residual thoughts, of post-Cartesian reflections.

Reframing *"Jeux Descartes"*

> For it was you alone who roused me from my state of indolence, and
> reawakened the learning which by then had almost disappeared from my
> memory. . . . [*Tu enim revera solus es qui desidiosum excitasti jam è memoriâ
> pene elapsam eruditionem revocasti. . . .*]
>
> —*Descartes' letter to Isaac Beeckman, April 23, 1619 (C, 10:162/3:4)*

Why Should One Think (Descartes) Again?

Where is René Descartes today—one who "lived, thought and died"?[1]

"DESCARTES"

"Descartes, a French national icon,"[2] once an epochal *wunderkind* and now
nearly indistinguishable from the history of reading him, is for many scholars
today a poster boy or a whipping boy, a hero or a villain: a "solipsist," "narcis-
sist," "rationalist," "idealist," "reductionist," "deductivist," "dualist," "closeted
skeptic/atheist/materialist," and so on. Biographically, compositionally, geo-
graphically, historically, politically, psychoanalytically, scientifically, theologically (etc., etc., etc.), he remains a fascinatingly troubling source for and a
manifold index to modern philosophy and beyond. Everyone, thinker or not,
as long as he or she is thinking, readily has something critical to say about

that bite-size thought attributed to the author of the *Meditations on First Phi-losophy:* "cogito, sum" (I think, I am). "There is something about him that invites familiarity, and we know what that breeds. . . . The conclusion that Descartes spoke nonsense often arrives with no signs of an inner tussle at all."[3] Truly, this Cartesian code seems one of the most deceptively obvious and obviously quotable lines of all time, open to interpretative mutations and compositional variations, especially one-liner possibilities and parodies: "I Broadway, therefore, I am," which I saw while "iPlodding" my way in here. Where is that I of I-think (or even iThink) today? Is it already very dead? Is it yet to come? It is still vitally relevant, I think.

Writing in 1870, Aldous Huxley of *Brave New World* (1932) describes Descartes, the man of novel dis-coursing (*running about*), as someone whose thoughts "magically touch" a certain "future":

> There are some men who are counted great because they represent the actuality of their own age, and mirror it as it is. Such an one was Voltaire, of whom it was epigrammatically said, "he expressed everybody's thoughts better than anybody." But there are other men who attain greatness because they embody the potentiality of their own day, and magically reflect the future. They express the thoughts which will be everybody's two or three centuries after them. Such an one was Descartes.[4]

I probably cannot make it to 2070 but can certainly ask this again: What are those "thoughts" that contempo-futurize themselves through this seem-ingly "potential," "Cartesian" thinker? Again, why is Monsieur Descartes still a potent figure? Apart from the fame or notoriety, praise or blame, appropriation or abuse, what else does that Cartesian "I" deserve or indeed attract?

THINKING ALL AND NOTHING

The idea of Descartes or Descartes as an idea has long become such a cli-ché, a caricature, although "the problem is not Descartes himself, but the appropriation of Cartesianism."[5] Perhaps, Descartes should not have made it so portable, so techno-friendly, after all.

"Cogito, sum" (I am thinking, I am), this conceptual condensation and compositional compression of thoughts to which children, not to mention gentlemen and "even women," can relate "naturally" and "natively" in their generically "fine" and independent mind (C, 1:560/3:86; Dis, 6:4/1:112, 6:9/1:115, 6:77/1:151), was, in its practical spirit, a careful yet radical experiment with the democracy of thinking, of universal pursuit. "You will be amazed that I am taking such a long time to write a discourse which will be so short that I reckon it will take only an afternoon to read" (C, 1:137–8/3:21), said Descartes to his pal Mersenne in 1630, seven years before the publication of the *Discourse on Method.* Surely, good writers, certainly Descartes among them, know that "the one-sentence paragraph should be used sparingly, if at all. . . . If a writer is going to draw attention to the stand-alone sentence, the sentence had better be worth it. That is, the sentence should have enough content—enough resonance—to justify this slightly unusual, attention-grabbing device."[6] Imagine all the efforts that went into the crafting of "it," this formulation, "cogito, sum."

I often wonder, nevertheless, whether the snappy minimalism of that line, "I am thinking, (therefore) I am," is too spot-on, too successful—like an instant classic no one really reads. On reading or hearing it, as if "punched," one forgets almost immediately where that punch-line came from and leads to; it is like a fish caught in a net, becoming the instant memory of its own struggles, its life and death. That ontological snapshot of the Cartesian "Vita Activa" (the life of the mind) does seem to carry such a "striking(ly)" performative quality, "as though no one had touched the matter before me" (as Descartes proposed in his introductory remarks to *Les Passions de l'âme*)![7] If indeed "no one wants to get punched,"[8] still that punch line appears immediately appealing to many. What should then one make of the absorbing vacuity, agility, and elasticity of this "thinking degree-zero"[9] "manifest in sounding-out or written-down speech"[10] of all sorts?

As Descartes repeatedly stressed, this stamp of Cartesian cogitation that he says everyone carries within himself or herself, this *cogitare* serially inflected and stretched by the philosopher who tried to think of everything by eliminating all, means not only "to reflect, deliberate, or introspect" but consciousness or conscious activities most broadly conceived, including and especially self-consciousness, "everything which we are aware of as happening within us, insofar as we have awareness of it" (P, 8A:7/1:195, Article 9), such as "doubting, affirming, denying, un/willing, imagining or sensing or feeling" (M, 7:27/2:18; 7:28/2:19; 7:34/2:24). Descartes is thinking of inner/outer realities in, of, and around selfhood: "As for the fact that there can be nothing in the mind, insofar as it is a thinking thing, of which it is not conscious, this seems to me to be self-evident" (Or, 7:246/2:171).

That seemingly "self-evident" "fact" that "there can be nothing in the mind . . . of which it is not conscious" is the origin of the problems, however. That "thinking thing" carries within its tissues many intricate issues not quite evident to itself. The very nominal inclusivity and perceptual vivacity of Descartes' concept of thinking would, precisely by virtue of its own theoretical ambition, immediately generate its own tautological aporia, however dialectical: Can consciousness "think" (of) its outside? When a corner is reached, does not another corner within it react? For instance, what does "I," a (wo)man, this particular gentle(wo)man cogitator, *want?*— *wanting* itself being notably absent from the list above, "doubting, affirming, denying . . . ." At stake is the other (side) of consciousness, the unconscious, for want of a better term. The enduring question generated otherwise, simmering, trembling, even shimmying, around the mind's edgy attention to itself, concerns the embodied soul or ensouled, soulful, matter.

It is about certain gestures of thought that still matter, no matter what. As Maurice Merleau-Ponty quips in a similar vein (abruptly, while minding the legacy of Karl Marx): "Are you or are you not a Cartesian? The question does not make much sense, since those who reject this or that in Descartes do so only in terms of reasons which owe a lot to Descartes."[11] What and where are those "reasons" for still thinking of and even thanking Descartes every now and then, even when not exactly thinking of him? Why is "Descartes" still taken as a foundational sort of figure?

As for the source of thoughts itself, we now know that to find it we must seek beneath statements, and especially the famous statement of Descartes. Its logical truth ("in order to think one must exist") and its signification as a statement betray it as a matter of principle. For they relate to an object of thought at the moment when access must be found to the thinker and his inborn cohesion, for which the established meanings of things and ideas are only the cue. Descartes' spoken word is the gesture which reveals in each of us that thinking thought to be discovered; it is the "Open Sesame" of fundamental thought. "Fundamental" because it is not borne by anything, but not fundamental as if with it one reached a foundation upon which one ought to base oneself and stay. As a matter of principle, fundamental thought is bottomless. It is, if you wish, an abyss. This means that it is never *with* itself, that we find it next to or setting out from things thought, that it is an opening out—the other invisible extremity of the axis which connects us to ideas and things.

Must we say that this extremity is nothing?

Rather than nothing or all, this Cartesian extremity is (something that links) all *and* nothing. It relates to a certain, infinitely open source of the mind most broadly conceived; with Mearleau-Ponty, I see *cogito, sum,* this unit, rather sympathetically as the "'Open Sesame' of fundamental thought," an endless opening out, an interminable performance of the mind that other minds, too, can hear wherever they are. As often is the case, a clue, a "cue," for that fundamental "nothingness" that is the flesh and blood of philosophic thoughts lies in "the great book of the world" (D, 6:9/1:115), the countless layers of embodied voices of life and death. Again, the world of Descartes, of the Cartesian abyss of self-reflection punctuated by its own movements, is the case in point I am exploring here; the embryonic, if not emblematic, aspects of Descartes' *cogito,* its jazzy temporality, its utterly butterly bottomless openness, remains rather overlooked, as I will show.

OPENLY, EMBRYONICALLY

This materially potent—con-fused or con-fusing—nothingness of pure cogi-tation, the mind playing itself off against its objective "other" such as the "body," is the other, ironic side of the very Cartesian paradigm of thinking, to which Descartes himself seems to have become sensitive toward the later years of his life. Perhaps aging has something to do with it, growing pains that are felt not just by the adolescent. Self-awareness seems to get duplicated in the aging body in the form of a growing awareness of one's own strangeness, the other-hill-over-there-ness, that outsideness unlocatable yet undeniable. Time begins to matter, finally.

Read this curious note on "confused thoughts" (C, 4:605/3:309) that Descartes sent in 1647 to Pierre Chanut, another close friend who was also a pen pal. In the previous year, he had sent Princess Elizabeth a draft of the *Passions of the Soul* (1649), where he, upon reflection, categorized all the passions into six (and *only* six) "primitive" ones: "wonder, love, hatred, desire, joy and sadness" (Pr, 11:380/1:353, article 69). He had been pushed to think hard through them by the relentlessly inquisitive princess asking how the body can affect the mind in that reverse direction, as it obviously does. This purportedly exhaustive list he came up with in response would, in turn, "ensure that readers are not confused [*embarasse*] by the multiplicity of the passions" (Pr, 11:380/1:353). In that letter, Descartes, now an old man, begins to wonder about prenatal "sentimens ou des pensées fort confuses" (sentiments/sensations or very confused thoughts) (C, 4:605/3:309). Perhaps he is also thinking—without necessarily being aware of his thinking—of his mother who had died just about three months after his birth (cf. C, 6:220/3:250), from whom he inherited "a dry cough and a pale color which stayed with" him (C, 6:220/3:250) until he was well over twenty; no wonder he had a feeling of never having had a mother.[12] Note further, just briefly here, that those primitive passions remain relatively inaccessible or untransparent to Cartesian consciousness. That is because, the adult Descartes says, they are linked to a childhood that is partly forgotten, partly floating around, in the form of developmental traces or lack of nutrition and bodily functions, since "the soul was *so* attached to matter" (C, 4:605/3:309, emphasis added), so made, so marred . . .

If "childhood is always the question, and the logical answer is adulthood,"[13] the adult becomes the child by asking the already answered question, as if the old man would have to become that child at the end of the day. Such is the embryonic genius of Descartes' philosophical rediscovery of the world of *cogitare*, which would, likewise, anchor our point of departure here, our "post-Cartesian" adventure or regress. To confirm: We are looking at not just a "methodologically" regimented act of self-reflection or the reflexive closure of the mind but a sprawling reach of consciousness broadly conceived, its subtle phenomenological dynamism which, as hinted earlier, made it possible for the thinker to go on to reflect, later, on the passivity of the soul as well. Evidently, mind-boggling modalities and material specificities of consciousness, especially corporeal correlates such as those six "passions," have not yet been fully articulated in the *Meditations*. There, one can and does think feelingly, as in feeling distant when doubting. However, feeling there, considered as an instance of thinking, is still just feeling *X*, not feeling lovely or hateful or, more simply, loving or hating, the verbally direct kind that will appear centrally only later, in the *Passions of the Soul*, for instance. Then again, in the *Meditations*, such a sweeping designation if not characterization of the "thinking thing" as one and the same thing seems natural, almost developmental as well. For there, Descartes, the filtered and filtering adult setting out to restage the child's question, had only begun to rediscover the soul, the nameless heat and heart of it that thinks not only tautologically but also temporally, procedurally, figuratively, openly surgically.

Again, such a spiral, striated movement of Cartesian consciousness is what I want to trace in what follows, focusing first on Descartes *thinking* feelingly, while leaving the feeling part folded in for a moment (maybe for another book). Again, that is why, at this stage of unpacking my kind of Descartes, I have chosen this embryonic text, the *Meditations*, the First and the Second in particular. Thinking, for Descartes, at least at that midpoint of his philosophical development, is whatever a thinking thing is or appears to be, including its shadows, actual or potential, which entails the problem of not only the world outside but also other minds or the will of the other, including that of God. The trouble here, in brief, is twofold. (1) There are many more and other "I"s than any particular I, examples being I the optically challenged, I the mad, I the dreamer, I the plaything of the evil genius, and so on, all of which are enfolded in the theatrically performative *logos*—logic, language, law—of the *cogito*. (2) Such "I"s, multiple and diverse, are beyond "me," the reflexive/reflexed I, serially beyond my capacity to think here and now. Jumping ahead, I suppose that the inaugural slippages and contacts between those "I"s would function as an interstitial bridge between the *Meditations* and *The Passions*, allowing the I of the former to be pushed farther toward, and affectively channeled into, that of latter, meditative acts being not only discursively regulated but narratively charged.

To reread, along those lines, the undercurrents of Cartesian subjectivity more dynamically is to start reimagining the Cartesian "ego" otherwise, which is what I have set out to do. For I still sense that subterranean odysseys of Cartesian selfhood are not over yet, despite the reductive account of the Cartesian I prevalent in this era of "postmodernism" or "anti-Cartesianism." Inspired by Wendy Lesser on Hume, who showed to her the importance of experiencing infirmity or the supple specificities of thoughts, I did consider titling this book, *On Not Writing about Descartes*. I, too, "even read [Descartes] to discover what I was not writing about."[14] With these serial mini-determinations to charge ahead regardless, I might be now, in fact, in the middle of writing *On Writing about Me*, but I shall continue to try to insert, each time anew, a slightly altered image of Descartes into the book of "Cartesian" idioms yet to be re-excavated.

With the Foreign Idiot?

WITH THE "CONCEPTUAL PERSONAE"

Why the Cartesian *I?* Whence this stress on the subjective embodiment of Cartesian alterity?

Who is not I, to begin with? (1) Every person is—and can say, write, think of, and even try to forget, if possible—an "I." (2) Everyone is one person in and among many, through and by whom many "I"s "pass," in whom alternate figures of the I, dead or alive, ancient or modern, here or there, intersect; sometimes with, and sometimes without, self-awareness or self-knowledge. I am, and am thinking of, the Shakespearean fool on stage, who "struts and frets his hour" (*MacBeth*, 5:5:25) at various stages of his life.

In *What is philosophy?*, Gilles Deleuze and Félix Guattari call this elusive thinker a "conceptual personae" (*les personnages conceptuels*).[15] This doer, one who meditates with that manifold Cartesian mask on and through it, is a "strange type of personae" (*un type très étrange de personage*),[16] "a personality the philosopher has not chosen, a third person,"[17] "the Idiot."[18] This capital figure of the idiosyncratic "private thinker" nearly deaf or indifferent to "the teacher" (the schoolman, *le scolastique*) is not unlike the revolutionary idiot of Russia who, instead of wanting old truths to duplicate, "wills the absurd, . . . turning the absurd into the highest power of thoughts,"[19] that is, to the point where the distinction itself, thinking and not thinking, or ascendency and absurdity, does not quite hold or becomes meaningless, like breathing and smoking. Viewed that way, this persona(e), who thinks by natural right and with natural light, is again immediately, intimately, linkable to Descartes the strange schoolboy, someone in everyone who could become in some ways "very inconvenient to church or state authorities who seek to control individual minds."[20]

> Is there something else, in Descartes' case, other than the created *cogito* and the presupposed image of thought? Actually there is something else, somewhat mysterious, that appears from time to time or that shows through and seems to have a hazy existence halfway between concept and preconceptual plane, *passing* from one to the other. In the present case it is the Idiot: it is the Idiot who says "I" and sets up the cogito.[21]

The philosophical Idiot or the Idiot philosopher is first and foremost (auto-)creative rather than (self-)reflective; rather than setting himself or herself into some same old scenario of the *cogito*, this Idiot sets himself or herself up anew, no matter what, not just wanting truths but, as Deleuze and Guattari rightly stress it, wanting to "create"[22] truths or *the* truth. He or she or "it" enters into, passes between, series and zones of thinking, hardly noticed or supervised even by its other selves.

> The question "Are there precursors of the *cogito?*" can be made more precise. Where does the persona of the idiot come from, and how does it appear? Is it in a Christian atmosphere, but in reaction against the "scholastic" organization of Christianity and the authoritarian organization of the church? Can traces of this persona already be found in St. Augustine? . . . In any case, the history of philosophy must *pass through* [*passer*] these personae, through their chances according to planes and through their variety according to concepts. Philosophy constantly brings conceptual personae to life; it gives life to them.[23]

This idiotic third person that is and *passes* as "everyone," whose perspectival self-distance is concept-creative rather than retro-reflective, thinks for, by, and of himself or herself—or again "itself," insofar as at issue is not "a person" per se, restrictively or typologically personified as such. In other words, the philosopher is not exactly or just a figure of thinking as in Descartes sitting at a table or Plato in a cave; rather, it is an act of thinking figuring itself out in and through such worldly settings.

That Idiot, therefore, as "the concept's friend, . . . potentiality of the concept"[24] in its minimal vital phase, dies hard and travels far across time and space. This figure is cuttingly connective, compositionally otherworldly. This is how such a persona becomes the subject of philosophy. To be more precise, "Le personnage conceptuel est devenir ou le sujet d'une philosophie"—"this personae *is* the becoming or the subject of a philosophy".[25] The insurmountable strength of the philosophical idiot as the virtual you in me and me in you "who perhaps did not exist before us, [but] thinks in us . . . shows [*manifester*] thought's territories."[26] This zonal strength of Cartesian cogitation is not exactly in the dialecticity of its alter ego(s) that generates and propels speculative philosophy. Nor is it locatable in the Kierkegaardian multiplicity of pseudonymity existentially housed in some origins or destinations, or the transcendentality of philosophical subjectivity promoted by Husserlian phenomenology in perpetual crisis or climax. More to the point, the intense and intensely impersonal, transhistorical singularity of the thinking ego's theatrical distance from and to itself interferes with any scholastic or speculative individuation and historic-institutional organization of its psychodiscursive forces. That kind and level of Descartes as the inexhaustible source of intellection par excellence, specifically its philosophical modernity, is what I find most interesting: its resilience. Again, as I will try to restage in each "scene" of Cartesian reflection that follows, what Descartes the critical persona uncovers, savors, and repeats is the crisis of the naked, nascent moment temporarily diverted if not disconnected from a historical line of thinking. What happened to that spirit of a radical break? Why cannot the *cogito*, this same old cliché, be rethought?

Yet, as I have been saying so far, "it" or "*id*" is something that passes by *le scolastique*, while bypassing all kinds of closures, analytic, nominal, or epochal. Consider this literal example of "passing" in the Descartes-Deleuze-Guattarian style: passing philosophically or for a philosopher as if, again, masked (*Larvatus prodeo*). Descartes in a dream (AT 10:181–185)[27] is still, as far as Descartes is concerned, connected to Descartes through memories; Descartes is passing by and through Descartes. Here, "it/*id*" is embodied in the brooding, solitary schoolboy also found in the famous "melon" episode of Dream II. Re-stored in these two inaugural sequences of dreams, to be unpacked in Scene 3, is a figure to whom anyone potentially sleepy or dreamy can relate—good or bad, female or male, young or old, happy or broody. Swept off his feet by a whirlwind in Dream I, this pupil-figure, "left-leaning" and "rightly-aspiring," manages to arrive at the open gate of a college campus leading to the inner chapel, where he is to park himself and pray. The location must have been, so goes the standard interpretation, the chapel in the College of Henri IV in *La Flèche*, the Jesuit School Descartes entered at the age of ten. En route, in the middle of the college court, the schoolboy in the dream passes by a schoolmaster. Realizing that he might have inadvertently snubbed his teacher, the boy tries in vain to go back to greet the teacher while struggling against the wind again (a *malo spiritu*), at which point the pupil is interrupted, his sight obscured, by another passerby who tips him off that if he is looking for "Monsieur N . . . he had something to give him" (AT 10:181), probably a melon. The child in the dream (or upon waking?) then envisages it to be the fruit from the Tree of Knowledge, which Monsieur N has brought him from some "foreign" (*étranger*, AT 10:181) country. *Foreign?*

"WHILE BUILDING IS IN PROGRESS"

A weird creepy feeling came over me that you might know about all this, not wanted to tell me but just know. It's amazing how the past shrinks to the size of your palm, forced to hold all that now[28]—for now, while at least I seem half-awake, still.

An attentive reader of this poem by John Ashbery might be disorientingly reminded here of that mysterious material eruption in the previous passage: the "melon" in Descartes' dream, especially "*this* lemon . . . Italian"[29] (as in Italian cosmology during the Renaissance period). The origin of the melon there is also traceable, more canonically, to a phrase in Ausonius's third Idyll, "the globe of the world," in which case, then, we are "leav[ing] out of account the force of its being 'from a foreign country.' "[30] So is the melon foreign or global, or is it a false binary? Whether globalization is a process of familiarization or its opposite—that is, a de-familiarization of the oneness of "one" as in one country—its disorganizing impact is universal, through which space-time gets recoordinated, almost reborn: Indeed, "what country" or world "is more foreign than the future?"[31] The very experience of the passage of time that comes in the form of an interruptive emergence of matter, of especially a self-contained spherical matter, is neither familiar nor unfamiliar, but globally foreign or strangely global. Such seems the portable modernity and passage of the "melon" passed onto Descartes the modern.

Here, readers of the *Discourse on Method* might recall the sensible point Descartes makes at the start of part three about a temporary shelter, even a rented shoebox, one would need as a provisional lodging "while building is in progress" (D, 6:22/1:122; cf. 6:14/1:117)—that is, during the actual destruction of the grand "old" house of possible falsities and protective illusions. The issue is not simply the logical necessity but the very viability of philosophical, specifically modern, subjectivity emerging anew in a wandering and wondrous form, which needs constant fixing, *sum*, albeit provisionally.[32] This again is a question of "stop," "pause," "point," the philosophic moment that seems to escape the time of life one would try to build into some sort of a narrative whole in order to make sense of it: How does one live *on*, *in between*, physically, psychically, or morally? How does provisionality become almost an eternal condition of human life itself, provided that, to stay in the metaphor, the daily "provisions" one relies on to live become available only for a while? This does not have to be cast as a grand humanistic inquiry into the essence of transient life. Raised here is quite a mundane question, mortality as an existential issue, as Descartes himself wonders:

> I have never taken greater care in looking after myself than I am doing at the moment. Whereas I used to think that death could deprive me of only thirty or forty years at the most, I would not now be surprised if it were to deprive me of the prospect of a hundred years or more. I think I see with certainty that if only we guard ourselves against certain errors which we are in the habit of making in the way we live, we shall be able to reach without further inventions a much longer and happier old age than we otherwise would. But since I need more time and more observational data if I am to investigate everything relevant to this topic, I am now working on a compendium of medicine, basing it partly on my reading and partly on my own reasoning. I hope to be able to use this as a provisional means of obtaining from nature a stay of execution, and of being better able from now on to carry out my plan. (C, 1:649/3:76)

How do I sustain myself between and within sleeps that recur? "To be alive means to live in a world that preceded one's own arrival and will survive one's own departure,"[33] as Hannah Arendt put it, who had not only an intimate self-understanding of political homelessness but also an insight, thereon, into the radical alterity, transitoriness, foreignness of human life, private or private. The point, however, is to embrace just that, to make oneself at home no matter what. The very Cartesian metaphor of interiority as building and living is further inwardly motivated by motifs of migratory transmission, transgression, or transformation, a perpetually provisional move toward and from "the foreign" found at the heart of thinking. Such a precarious life thus processually, reflexively, cherished is a life of Cartesian deconstruction. Rather than monumentalizing life, Descartes is serializing it. In those passages of thinking in transit, in such passing moments linked by the *cogito* setting itself up wherever it goes, something is occurring, happening. Leaving or being left, one is and is passing time somewhere, is marked, surviving, outlived.

Such an autobiographic trail of the life of the embodied mind and ensouled body, which the "post-Hegelian" Merleau-Ponty, too, sees as the Cartesian "watermark"[34] of modern dialectical consciousness, is not nothing, although "foreign," that is, unfamiliar or unfamilial. "The identity of this Genius" that Jacques Maritain urges "the historians of rationalism to settle for once and for all"[35] seems almost genetically elusive, not unlike Shakespeare, the magical composer of vividly indefinable characters, who not only has the genius but arguably *is* the genius, the "peculiar alchemy of genes and circumstances."[36] The Cartesian genius, also notable through etymological resonances of that word (e.g., general, generous, and generic), is found in the very passing of any images or figures of thoughts in motion: "Could it be by any chance cousin to the *Mischievous Genius of the Meditations?*"[37] Note again that cousin denotes related but not the self-same Descartes; rather, therefore, Descartes is a kind of intimate stranger to himself. Evidently, in philosophy—as early as Socrates, for instance, whose irreducible otherness or queerness was a threat to those claiming to be the philosopher-politicians of ancient Greece—"we always meet over again this otherness, these holes, and interestingly we can even discover the foreign in Descartes—and thus show up his slanderers."[38]

"REDISCOVERING THE FOREIGN IN DESCARTES"

The foreign in Descartes or Descartes the foreign(er): further curious in that regard is the sort of touchingly ironic "solution" of the Cartesian problem offered by "the Mexican writer Carlos Fuentes, who knows France well": "what France needs" especially today might just be "an anti-Cartesian revolution to revive dreams and imagination."[39]

Having managed to traveled this far, although I still have four scenes to write, I too would say that what we need today for "vive la terre" (the globe) is another (anti-)Cartesian revolution to rekindle that "vivid and strong imagination"—a "roman ingénieux" (ingenious novel),[40] which Voltaire attributed if only disparagingly to the writings of Descartes. Descartes might also have been sufficiently wined on the night of his dream of November 10, 1629, as has been speculated. Maritain does not buy that explanation,[41] because Descartes allegedly had not touched any alcoholic beverages during that period. Yet that the night was St. Martin's Eve, on the day the French would or used to reserve for ritual debauchery.

> 1629. Descartes has definitively settled in the Low Countries. He leads a
> solitary existence, *"dans le desert"* [C, 1:14]. He protects this prized solitude,
> repeatedly asking his friends not to reveal his whereabouts. The beginning of
> maturity and the definitive choice of the philosophical vocation mark an act of
> separation from the world. Why?
>   As we have seen, the first sign of this new intellectual experience appears to
> be his commitment to retrace "the history of himself."[42]

In any case, this sort of epochal "turning" to and twisting around conceptual selfhood seems akin to "a creative act"[43] of idiocy or individualized idiom, which attracted Deleuze and his friend Guattari. Such a novel philosophical force coming from elsewhere, "the outside," functions as a passage itself yet to be activated and to (re)appear. "If philosophy exists, it is because it has its own content,"[44] "invents," and "tells stories with concepts."[45] In such a "compositional formation of space-times"[46] by self-inventive concepts, "you know, people are missing"[47] "and at the same time not missing,"[48] just as in cases of idiocy, just as in works of art, as Deleuze and Guattari further note (citing Paul Klee): "The functional affinity between a work of art and a people that does not yet exist is not and will never be clear," and at the same time "there is no work of art that does not call on a people who does not yet exist."[49] Something, someone between those "people," makes its way through these pieces of metal sophistry or mental tapestry that we might call philosophy, legitimately or not, lovingly or not, since the order of such compositional intellection irreducible to geometry also remains "irreducible to any communication,"[50] which itself remains irreducibly provocative.

What we are talking about is that peculiarly necessary paradox that is a philosophical concept, that "almost paradoxical genre, the impersonal autobiography" that Descartes "devised"[51] through his alternatively wild, otherwise clean, philosophical vision. "Even the history of philosophy is completely without interest, if it does not undertake to awaken a dormant concept and to play it again on a new stage, even if this comes at the price of turning it against itself."[52] What I am pointing to is a mode of writing that writes itself out impersonally through conceptual personae to the point where it is turned against itself with creative constancy, which is not the same as mechanical consistency. Likewise, here is the philosophical imperative I keep turning and returning to like some pre-textual alibi, the name of the game being how to get out of Cartesian philosophy as a Cartesian. The question is, in other words, how to still do philosophy in some ways in "a style other than that of interpretation, of logical grammarian analysis, or of polyvalence and language games—that is, to rediscover a foundational style, a decided style, a style in the school of Descartes for example."[53]

Again, we have "a mischievous genius in a philosopher's brain—*the Dream of Descartes*,"[54] who is not simply awake but falls asleep to be awakened, falling into time. It is for this reason that I am turning to the sort of "*angelism* which in general characterizes Cartesian philosophy,"[55] as occasionally witnessed by "the sleeping person" who "closes his eyes so he can open them to night."[56] Such a transient person is the point at which foundational sleep and foundational awakening intersect. For this reason, I keep returning to those vibrant interstices of hyperbolic thinking that Descartes' inaugural *Meditations* creates contrapuntally, as his text stages itself, survives itself, by keeping the immediately collapsible geometry of the *cogito-dubito* sustained by the very recurrence, persistence, of its own gray spaces.

How?

"TOWARD A STYLE IN THE SCHOOL OF DESCARTES"

What connects the following four scenic chapters is that *turn* to the liminal subject embodied and embedded in the figures of the thought outside or outside thought, the cast of characters riding along the Cartesian train of thought without somehow being on it.

That self-reflexively progressive gesture of Descartes' philosophy, building itself toward and from its outside, is temporally oriented rather than spatially organized, unyielding to any attempts at simple thematic mapping. It is an act, a performance of and by the thinking subject that writes itself into and out of the texture of time. Again, at issue here is a "style" of thinking, as Alain Badiou stressed, a need to move "towards a new style of philosophy, a style in the school of Descartes for example."[57] In what way does the Cartesian subject become present? Such is the question that insists itself here as a stylized legacy of speculative Cartesianism. As Badiou goes on to formulate the puzzle: "*how can a modern doctrine of the subject be reconciled with an ontology?*"[58]

In my view, those elusive-decisive dual gestures of thoughts in motion, traceable only after the fact, hold a key to the Cartesian reconciliation of the world and the subject that Badiou similarly seeks. Specifically, what I have in mind is the nano-Cartesian moment of differential repetition, the infinitesimally stylized momentum in a rediscovered Descartes, a turning and tuning of time in which the cogitational signatures of "Descartes" are carried and multiplied in kaleidoscopic disguises. Still alive in Cartesianism seem just those border spaces or borderline cases of liminal time embodied—charged, dynamized, and suspended—in and by the "odyssey of alterity"[59] that archivally agitates the cogitating subject. The key idea stitching the following pages is that the topographic obscurity of the human subject, "a necessary opacity in our understanding of ourselves"[60] narratively sustained as such, as Judith Butler puts it, is also oddly vivid and "sticky" (M, 7:24/2:16, "*hoereo*"), and to that extent is irreducibly real or surreal. Surely, Descartes' "methodological" skepticism serves the purpose of the rational(ized) will of modern philosophy; but the accompanying will of the intrigue does and is more than what it claims it to do or be, especially at its fugitively hyperbolical moments. Modern philosophy's self-identity and self-mastery, that self-defining obsession of modern philosophy, remains infinitely incomplete, and we do not need to travel all the way to Hegel & Company to finally see that. Descartes, the founding father, is already a living proof, as we will see.

As Emmanuel Levinas observed rightly, "skepticism is refutable, but it returns":

> Philosophy is not separable from skepticism, which follows it like a shadow it
> drives off by refuting it again at once on its footsteps. Does not the last word
> belong to philosophy? Yes, in a certain sense, since for Western philosophy the
> saying is exhausted in things said. But skepticism in fact makes a difference,
> and puts an interval between saying and the said. Skepticism is refutable, but it
> returns.[61]

Such an "interval" enables border crossing as well, a border-retaining
thought at work toward and with the other. The other as the open source of
self-doubt in particular, as I will show, is what *is* in the *Meditations*, particularly well (dis)covered in the *First Meditation* (M, 7:17–23/2:12–15) and the
first five paragraphs of the *Second Meditation* (M, 7:24–5/2:16–7), where all
the key recurring characters of the Cartesian drama of flighty thoughts
first appear in rapid, compressed succession, or more precisely, in between
the successive moments of paragraphed thinking.

"LIKE A SIEVE STRETCHED OVER THE CHAOS"

What we are seeing there, passing through, is the tension-filled narrative
field of and for the blind (Scene 1), the mad (Scene 2), the sleeper/dreamer
(Scene 3), and a victim figure cornered by this all-around, moral, and epistemological attack by the monstrous other, the evil genius (*malin génie, malus
genius*, Scene 4), all succeeded and "rescued" by God in the third paragraph
of the *Second Meditation*, in the *Deus ex machina* style that, reflexively, supports the very idea of perfection: the tautological, theological, and teleological good.

So what happens "before" God? "Who stands" before God? Here, the
focus shifts from the spatiotemporality of the presence of divinity to the interactive coextensivity of it. Yet "standing" would be misleading, for none of
those four figures of disorienting alterity could, as prefigured by the dream
episodes we have previewed, "stand" up properly. So the question to ask is
rather: who "is stretched" before, and even over, God? Who are these idiots?

> [The philosophers who] institute a plane of immanence like a sieve stretched
> over the chaos . . . contrast[ing] with sages, who are religious personae, priests,
> because they conceive of the institution of an always transcendent order
> imposed from outside by a great despot or by one god higher than the

others . . . pursuing wars that go beyond any agon and hatred that object in advance to the trials of rivalry.[62]

Such a strangely captivating, strangely flighty, subject of philosophy is what this book aims to discover in and with Descartes.

We will follow those logical tactics and narrative threads leading up to the Cartesian stand-in for God, while rendering visible that tricky "sieve" that seems, however, neither immanent nor transcendent but rather quasi transcendental; in passing, I must note that this is where my path of thinking markedly diverges from Deleuze and Guattari's. Of particular interest to me is not the Cartesian God per se, the phenomenology of the "eternal and unchangeable" (C, 1:146/3:23) nature of It/Him, which Descartes formulates into an intellectual function or origin, the source of the "natural light of reason" that enables his metaphysical meditations in the first place. Instead, my reading zooms in on a way in which such a topos of "majestic" (C, 1:145/3:23) creative agency, of the absolute truth, is appropriated as a figure of the savoir, survivor, or guarantor. How and why is it brought into the hyperbolically circular construction or the elliptical inscription of the metaphysical origin, foundation, and destination of indubitable truths, as the impossible but necessary excesses at the core of Cartesian reflection?

With this focus on Descartes the baroque rationalist, with this move toward a metaphysical miniaturization or compression of the textual Descartes, an important contention I am advancing implicitly is that the rest of the *Meditations* (II–VI) is a repeat, a performative reinscription, a review, of the initial philosophical impulses. For instance, what is declared in the last paragraph of the *First Meditation* is structurally stronger than, although not unlike, a new year's resolution: it is a will to meditate, a will to persist in this meditation, to repeat the particular if necessary:

> I shall stubbornly and firmly persist in this meditation; and, even if it is not
> in my power to know any truth, I shall at least do what is in my power, that is,
> resolutely guard against assenting to any falsehoods, so that the deceiver,
> however powerful and cunning he may be, will be unable to impose on me
> in the slightest degree. (M, 7:23/2:15)

Why does Descartes stubbornly persist in all this? Is it because he constantly fails to do so? Descartes is fading in, Descartes is fading out, and

Descartes the philosopher is flickering somewhere in between, which is where he is, and which signals the haunting presence of Cartesianism that I am trying to capture through a certain cinematic simulation of the Cartesian scope and strategy of thinking: to "shade the others so as to make the principal ones to stand out" (D, 6:41/1:132), so as to remain passingly "isolated" (C, 4:330/3:276) with no or little controversies among "the learned and the distinguished with whom I do not wish to quarrel" (C, 4:217/3:249; D, 6:40/1:131; M, 7:1/2:3). There is Descartes in limelight; there is Descartes in the dark; and here we are, the readers who witness both.

MOVING BETWEEN THE LINES AFTER SOME REFUTATIONS
AND RECONSIDERATIONS

Structurally most intriguing, further in that regard, is the (t)issue of (dis) connection between the *Meditation* I and the rest, II–VI: whether and how the desire for the skeptical argument in the *First Meditation* is linked, or transferred, to the "decision"[63] in the *Second* to pursue that line of hyperbolic reasoning; to what extent will is a manifestation of motivated reason. For instance, does the opening line, "Some years ago I was struck by the large number of falsehoods that I had accepted as true in my childhood. . . ." (M, 7:17/2:12), relate, or travel, to this second paragraph of the *Second Meditation*, "I will suppose then that everything I see is spurious. I will believe that my memory tells me lies and that none of the things that it reports ever happened" (M, 7:24/2:16)? Then, how? In the face of this duality of a surprise attack and a fortified supposition, the deeper question I am getting at is this: Here, does time cease to matter? Then, when?

Harry Frankfurt, unlike Descartes, considers the two phases separate or separable and so correctively contends that the first, just a foreground in his view, does not "*precede*"[64] the second:

> Descartes regards his skeptical arguments as *preceding* the general overthrow of his beliefs that is accomplished by his decision to empty his mind, and not as serving only to reinforce or to confirm their overthrow. But this is a mistake on his part. He tends to confuse the first and second phases of his program, and at times he speaks incorrectly as though the skeptical arguments precede the overthrow of his beliefs.[65]

Again, however, my interest lies in that "confusion," precisely that (anti-)"programmatic" problem, its seemingly disordered or displaced temporality: How can such an oddly marked, or marred, (dis)connection between the two, whether affective or discursive, or topological or logical, be "corrected"? What about the very idea or act of linear ordering, "first, skepticism, and second, solution"? Could this methodological response be incorrect? To press on, what if what the ego of *ego cogito* experiences, passes through, is the very knot, the dual presence, of the vulnerability and systematicity of reason(ing) at work? Again, my small intervention is just in that gray(ing) area of Cartesian cogitation, where, to use Frankfurt's illuminating analogy of smoking and skeptical thinking, the thinker lingers, shuttles, lives, between a desire to quit smoking and a decision to do so:

> Overthrowing one's beliefs is, in one respect at least, like giving up smoking. Suppose that at noon on a given day a man puts out a cigarette and announces in all sincerity that he will never smoke again. Has he given up smoking? It would be something of a joke to pretend that he had done so if, as things turn out, he takes another cigarette a few minutes later. . . . And making the decision may be tantamount to giving up smoking, but *only if the decision is subsequently adhered to.*[66]

Again, it is that "joke," precisely; besides, one could still smoke inside his or her head regardless.

Why does that confusion matter in the first place? Why, for instance, in the *Second Meditation* and onward (M, 7:25/2:17) is there this obsessive compulsive reconfirmation or focalization of the cogitational object under deconstruction? Whence and whither this positive reinforcement of the aim of the mental exercise, that is, "to demonstrate the existence of God and the distinction between the human soul and the body" (M, 7:17/2:12), which "I must make an effort to remember" as "it is not enough merely to have noticed this" (M, 7:22/2:15)? What the thinker has already "noticed" in the preceding paragraphs, in the first place, functions as an allegorical condensation of the book: a preview of the kinetic life of the mind, the irreducible presence or presentness of confusion itself.

For a better view, let us look closer this time at the very temporal span of the first paragraph of the *First Meditation* through the first four paragraphs of the *Second Meditation*, which, let me repeat, is the scope of my reading that follows. Note how the narrative moves swiftly from the past ("some years ago I was struck") to the present, on which it dwells and in which it unfolds through an autoinscriptive pursuit of will: "I will then subtract anything capable of being weakened, even minimally, by the arguments now introduced, so that what is left at the end maybe exactly and only what is certain and unshakable" (M, 7:25/2:17). Now, here is how the fifth paragraph of the *Second Meditation* starts, "exactly," with a sudden reflective turn to the past, with timing returning to itself: "What then *did* I formerly think I was? A man. But what is a man?" (M, 7:25/2:17, emphasis added).

Setting aside the issue of the autographical repetition of Cartesian cogitation that structures the narrative logic of this book, let us zoom back in for a while to its inaugural stage, featuring those four characters of elusive alterity, the main characters of my alternative story of the Cartesian "I": the blind (seer, as in "I didn't see it coming," the other world or the world being otherwise), the mad (scientist), the dazed (dreamer), and the cornered (believer). Again, note that, upon "proving" that "I exist" by defeating once and for all global skepticism that the universal demon causes (M, 7:25/2:17) in the third paragraph of the *Second Meditation*, the "I" turns to say:

> But I do not *yet* have a *sufficient* understanding of what this "I" is, that now
> necessarily exists. So I must be on *guard* against careless taking something
> else to be this "I," and so making a mistake in the very item of knowledge
> that I *maintain* is the most certain and evident of all. (M, 7:25/2:17, emphases
> added)

The God-protected house of "I," once it has been instituted in passing, now needs to be constituted, guarded, and maintained constantly in its tripartite pattern, as if it were a path to follow, as if I were still in disbelief, as if beliefs were deferred, although it is "likely that from the beginning God made our world just as it had to be" (D, 6:45/1:133); likely—precisely.

Such is how and why I will track down some of the "I" of the inaugural *Meditations*, just up to the segment featuring the evil genius in the *Second Meditation*, where God is wheeled onto the stage as one who reportedly cleans up all that psycho-physico-narratological mess (M, 7:17–25/2:12–17) with his irrefutable, irreducible goodness. Each chapter, following some of the key compositional clues and order of the *First Meditation*, touches on that strangely speakerly, temporally layered, perpetually disoriented, kaleidoscopic "I" in passing—the "I" in and of the impersonal, recedingly recurring Descartes, the "I" resonant with those willing to listen and to think on with "e-motion . . . the e-moted stuttering."[67] Doublingly blind, mad, dazed, cornered . . . sticky, stuck, "sticking" in a twilight zone of "the co-agitation of the ego,"[68] "this person who may be me"[69] or in me, however loosely or obscurely, is populated with paraheliocentric thoughts of modern or self-modernizing reason that survive, at every turn, on the *logos* of originary ambiguities and interstitial peculiarities in and outside the theater of modern consciousness:

> But why do I think this, since I myself may perhaps be the author of these thoughts? *Now, then what [Nunquid ergo]*? Am I not, at least to some extent, something? *But*, I have just said that I have no senses and no body. *This is the sticking point [Hoereo tamen]*: what follows from this? Am I not so bound up with a body and with senses that I cannot exist without them? But I have convinced myself that there is absolutely nothing in the world, no sky, no earth, no minds, no bodies. Does it now follow that I too do not exist? No: if I convinced myself of something (or thought anything at all) then I certainly existed. . . . I must finally conclude that this proposition, *I am, I exist*, is necessarily true whenever it is put forward by me or conceived in my mind. (M, 7:24–25/2:16–17, trans. modified, emphases added)

Nunquid ergo: Since or if this is the case, in light of what has been said, then what now (*Quidnunc*)? *Quidnunc* voices a thought that is irritatingly disorienting, if not necessarily incorrect, in the face of the very thing that has just been said as if in closing; note, in addition, the self-referentially ironic usage of that word, as mirrored later in *Hoereo tamen*, which suggests that we have reached the sticky, double-sided point of argumentation; having followed the line of argument, we can now see that these two problems would recur alternately in succession.

Quidnunc? The text I have started weaving departs—partly deviates—from Harry Frankfurt's 1970 classic, *Demons, Dreamers, and Madmen*,[70] as partly indicated earlier. As my title suggests, what I will be doing is not exactly *The Defense of Reason in Descartes' Meditations* (the subtitle of Frankfurt's book) but rather a deconstructive reading of figures of alterity there, "the other reading of Descartes," as it were. My concern, again—limited to the *First Meditation* and the first few paragraphs of the *Second Meditation*, not the whole of the *Meditations*[71]—is not about Descartes and others but the images of the other in Descartes, the other that alters something in and of and for me. My focus is then on Cartesian intrasubjectivity rather than intersubjectivity, which has already been explored, for instance, by James Marsh's work on post-Cartesian "critical modernism," where the socially mediated Cartesian self is reconstructed through "dialectical phenomenology."[72] In contrast, my hermeneutical attention is to elements of alterity within Cartesian selfhood, as illuminated by Richard Kearney's *Strangers, Gods, and Monsters: Interpreting Otherness* (2003),[73] a more immediate inspiration where I learned how one could read/reach *X* the other way around:

> Without some sense of self there can be no sense of the *other*-than-self, though this very notion of selfhood is one that can only be reached (*pace* Descartes and the Idealists) through the odyssey of alterity. No account of selfhood dispenses with what the old Irish migrant monks called *circumnavigatio:* the path home through the detour of the world. And even Hamlet, as we saw above, needed Horatio to tell his story. The shortest route from self to self is always through the other.[74]

Likewise, Descartes' thinking thing needed other "thinking things" to see where "it" itself is, has come from, and is heading. That mental substance, severed and isolated as such, is in fact sustained by other stuff, as already shown by the supporting, surrealized cast of characters in the Cartesian drama, those not entirely repressed but irrepressibly, fugitively, staged. Not just Odysseus but Jesus too has (had) to face that identity question, almost every day, up to this day: Who am I? "Who do they say I am?" Who could I (not not) *be*, if neither the son of God nor a rational animal?

"Only a thing that thinks; . . . but what kind of a thing? As I have said—a thinking thing. . . . But then what am I? A thing that thinks" (M, 7:27/2:18; cf. 7:28/2:19; 7:34/2:24; 7:45/2:31; 7:49/2:34).

> After considering everything very thoroughly, I must finally conclude that this proposition, *I am, I exist*, is necessarily true whenever it is put forward by me or conceived in my mind. But I do not yet have a sufficient understanding of what this "I" is, that now necessarily exists. (M, 7:25/2:17)

Such is the universally recognized climax of the *Meditations*, the point at which the Cartesian "I" finally finds its putative anchor, constructively locating it, itself. But still, let us not forget, this conclusion itself had been expressed four years earlier in the *Discourse*, where Descartes said:

> Considering that the very thoughts we have while awake may also occur while we sleep without any of them being at the same time true, I resolved to pretend that all the things that had ever entered my mind were no more true than the illusions of my dreams. But immediately I noticed that while I was trying thus to think everything false, it was necessary that I, who was thinking this, was something. And observing that this truth, *"I am thinking, therefore I exist"* was *so firm and sure* that all the most extravagant suppositions of the skeptics were incapable of shaking it, I decided that I could accept it without scruple as the first principle of philosophy I was seeking. (D, 6:32/1:127, emphases added)

This usual, now standard, Cartesian response, along with its repetition compulsion, despite the seeming self-sameness is, each time, time sensitive, resulting in a series of intricately systematized, differentially recursive self-reflections, rather richly open to its own metamorphic possibilities.

Curiously enough, however, the world (of organized intellection) has been rather unkind, even insensitive, to this Cartesian ego, a philosophical face of "Descartes." Often, it has been historicized—iconized or defaced—into all things universally pernicious as well as serially promising about modernity. Turned into a dead or deadly metaphor for instrumentalized rationality and rationalized technicality, Descartes "has been attacked, reviled and condemned like no other thinkers for most of the last 350 years. Even Pope John Paul II has recently felt the need to criticize him. Refutations continue to pile up. European philosophy is haunted by Descartes and his ideas."[75] Haunted by what, or whom, exactly? "The specter of the Cartesian subject"?[76] But how, why?

Why Now?

"THE SPECTER OF THE CARTESIAN SUBJECT IS HAUNTING
WESTERN ACADEMIA"

Let us look again, a little more closely this time, at the "demonic intellectual force"[77] of modernity threatening the Emperor's sartorial self-image:

Descartes spent much of his adult life among Protestant thinkers, but he always claimed to be a Catholic. Descartes apparently hoped that his philosophy and science would provide the foundations for a new theology, just as Aquinas had sought to bring medieval theology into harmony with the Aristotelian science of his day. For his efforts, Descartes was rewarded by having his works placed on Rome's Index of prohibited books, and he has remained on the "enemies list" for many Catholic philosophers right down to the present. In 1994, Pope John Paul II claimed that it was Descartes who, albeit perhaps unintentionally, set the stage for the destruction of the medieval Christian worldview and replaced it with a framework that facilitated the rise of rationalism, the corruption generated by modernity, and the "death of God."[78]

Again, quite clearly, good old Monsieur Descartes, this antiauthoritarian, antiacademic, amateur scholar-soldier with some groundbreaking, mind-bending thoughts, has somehow turned into a paper tiger, a massive snippet of idée fixe.

Themselves situated in those fields of tension between metaphysical religiosity and scientific modernity, as mirrored in the perennial issues of "mind-body" dualism or "reason-unreason" duality, many Descartes scholars, especially those working in the Anglo-American tradition, have been seeking to resolve such oppositional(ized) dissonances between the idealist grammar and the material imaginations; roughly, one could draw a line from Gilbert Ryle of *The Concept of Mind* (1949)[79] to Daniel Garber of *Descartes Embodied* (2001),[80] Tom Sorell of *Descartes Reinvented* (2005),[81] or Ronald Rubin of *Silencing the Demon's Advocate: The Strategy of Descartes' Meditations* (2008),[82] to name a few, all remarkable for their heroic efforts at analytic reduction or psycho-material harmonization. A self-identified anti-Cartesian such as Rorty, introduced earlier, who recasts that very dichotomized interpretative category as a pseudoproblem, remains distant from, although still tied to, such post-Cartesian philosophical collectives. As Sorell puts it eloquently,

> Except for those who applaud the Cartesian spirit of innatism in linguistics, philosophers in the English-speaking world are nowadays mostly agreed on the need to lay Descartes' ghost. It says a lot for the power of Cartesian philosophy that the activity of interring it still goes on. . . . Still captivated by Descartes' task, they still are inclined to argue about the types of subject

matter it is possible to have an increasingly objective understanding of. What lends sense to these arguments is the clear picture we now have of what it is like to understand the *material* world better and better. An early version of this picture is due to Descartes. It is what makes it so difficult to lay his ghost.[83]

How to make sense of "the *material* world" à la Descartes, what to make of this material or corporal ideation in Cartesian contexts, is a question marked by the ghostly persistence of the philosophical gaze, which asks how an idea comes to matter, not only affecting but actually supporting the world, including the world of the pure mind that supposedly thinks only of itself. Broadly, Ryle and Rubin represent the reductionist or exorcist strand within the dominant "rationalist" tradition of standard Cartesianism, which highlights the reflexive behaviors or directions of the Cartesian mind, that is, how the mind acts upon the body. As Frederick Copleston noted in 1951, in reference to the "telling way" in which "the Cartesian ghost [*in the machine*] is disposed of"[84] in Ryle's butcher shop, this champion of "ordinary language . . . constantly analyzes concepts (a very proper procedure, of course)" but rather "misleadingly" by "using phrases like "category-mistake," "allocation of concepts to logical types," and "the logic of the problem," as if "the problem of the mind were a logical problem" when it is "obviously more" than simply mental.[85] As Ryle takes something substantial out of Descartes' concept of the mind with a view to reintegrating it into his more empiricist, synthetically flattened picture of the active mind, Copleston reminds us of something residually persistent, something spiritual. Ryle's own urge to purge does seem to need some categorical checking, insofar as the baby in the bathwater about to be thrown out, whatever it is or whoever it is, is not just nothing. So nowadays, when looking for ways of correlate what we still loosely call the mind with all the other stuff, scholars such as Garber and Sorell, for instance, who are much subtler than Ryle, follow the path of more nuanced realism by either turning to the "Romantic"[86] Descartes who relies on God as the ultimate buttress for the world order (Garber) or by exploring the "unreconstructed," secularized Descartes alternatively and dynamically (Sorell).

Either way, however, Descartes remains, as captured in Sorrell's sensitive summary of his philosophical legacy, a haunting figure of promises and problems through which the fear of and over the human mind speaks for itself and writes itself out. One direction, as previously indicated, is the Rylean reduction of the intricately inconclusive Cartesian meditation to "the official doctrine" of "the double-life theory,"[87] which needs to be "destroyed and disposed of." The other is an analytic investment in the line of reading Descartes as a theological naturalist or occasionalist if not strictly a dualist, which in turn would allow the interpreter to privilege elements of mind-body interaction over those of interference. In that regard, interactive independence, too, of mental events and physical states is what renders Descartes' "mind-body dualism" hardly clear in itself,[88] and hence haunting, "naturally"[89] or "brutely."[90] If ancient philosophy in the Greco-Latin tradition can be said to be activated and haunted by the dialogical *logos* of Socrates, the master ironist in the open closet, we would find sharper and more specific modern resonances in Descartes, another Eleatic figure who, as the seventeenth century progenitor of universal subjectivism and scientific logic, wears and carries the proper name that has become almost indistinguishable from "Cartesian rationalism."

RE-HAUNT-OLOGIZING THE OTHER SIDE OF "DESCARTES"

My way, then, is to reactivate, to re-haunt-ologize, the other kind, side, figure of Descartes, a sort of flighty yet "primordially dialogic"[91] Descartes who comes across as a softly splintered, "intercessorily"[92] "heteronymic"[93] conceptual personae—obscure, quirky, tricky, ironic, slightly poetic even. What still engages me is not some solipsistic white bread Descartes who only means what he seems to say, but rather all the confused, multigrained, cogitational subjectivities within and beyond the facial "envelopes"[94] of historical, doctrinal, or professionalized Cartesianism: I just want that childlike "idiot" Descartes, who although neither innocent nor romanticizable also remains recalcitrant or almost indifferent to the Heideggerian dismissal and epochal demarcation of the Cartesian modernity of the West. Without psychobiographizing, sensationalizing, or fetishizing the evergreen philosopher's (alter) egos, we can still, I believe, dwell philosophically on *Descartes' Loneliness* (2007) and *Descartes' Nightmare* (2008), the peaceful persistence and its rhythm:

Toward evening, the natural light becomes
Intelligent and answers, without demur:
"*Be assured! You are not alone . . .*"
But in fact, toward evening, I am not
Convinced there *is* any other except myself
to whom existence *necessarily* pertains.
I also interrogate myself to discover
whether I *myself* possess any power
by which I can bring it about that I
who now am shall exist another moment.[95]

Falling asleep over poesy, X reads like a silkworm,
making up the carpet as he goes along. The windows balloon
out to grasses where the women stroll.

III.
I would say that X lives sometime late in the long 18th century,
He also lives in the body of someone (Y) in the miniature 20th.

The centuries sigh like some false catalogue.[96]

Will "I who now am shall exist another moment"? Did "I who now am" exist at a certain moment? I am trying to hear that poetic sigh in and from a thing that thinks such a thing, passing time.

Again if, indeed, "the villified Descartes of twentieth- and twenty-first-century philosophy is not the same as the canonical Descartes,"[97] if the caricatured Descartes is different from the Descartes who gets carried over nevertheless, should it not itself become a compelling reason for anyone to reread the Cartesian canon itself as if from the outside? In addition to being a curious person who thought himself to death almost against his own wish not to think too much, Descartes comes to me as a kind of temporal alter ego that unprograms itself at every point not simply to disappear into self-consuming irony but rather to give itself time for its life, for afterlife in its most secularized and literal sense. What would be the irreducible genius, gene, generativity of Cartesian thinking, thinking taken not only as an act, a textured performance by *res cogitans*, but more significantly as an event in itself that happens between, across, before, after, or beyond thoughts identified—itemized, represented, and objectified—as such (such as the *cogito* or the *sum*)? Whence and whither that ghost thinker in and of Descartes?

In fact, this question of Descartes as the figurehead of the modern philosophical subject, as an international man of modern mysteries and foundational contradictions, is central to the tradition(s) and idiom(s) of Continental philosophy, to the extent that such an image forms an implicit basis of and provides discursive resources for its intellectual sustainability and institutional evolution. Consider what Caroline Williams says, noting its proto-Cartesian temporality in particular:

> Derrida has noted that, so long as questions regarding the constitution of the subject are tied to the ontological question which deals with the *subjectum*, they must remain post-Cartesian. Althusser, Lacan and Foucault are all considered to be post-Cartesians, according to this observation. Of course, the status of this view must remain . . . open to debate. Even when this movement of questioning appears to be overshadowed negatively as a *crisis* of thought or a *doubting* of subjectivity (as it is for Descartes), the *openness* of a mode of questioning, the calling to accounts of the subject, may still produce new figures of thought, and create new forms of subjectivity, *before* any egological containment of the subject takes place.[98]

So what do we do with the Cartesian precedents *and* remains? That, too, is my question pursued here and in some further detail. If, as Jacques Derrida and Jean-Luc Nancy observe, the temporalized subjectivity of the *cogito* is the "sharpest point of the instant"[99] and irreducibly nonsubstantial to that extent, what stands out, what should keep our attention, is that nonsubstantiality, that very (non)sense.

In that regard, Dalia Judovitz's reading of Descartes as a repressed Montaigne, for instance, remains highly illuminating. In it we see a historically contextualized, rich articulation of something-else-or-more-or-less-ness within what Descartes calls "pure mental scrutiny" (M, 7:31/2:21). According to Judovitz, this irreducibly Cartesian moment in thinking taken primarily as active perceiving (M, 7:31–4/2:20–3) arises vitally from the almost eternalized, field-forming tension between philosophy and poetry, which also returns us to Alain Badiou's call, heard earlier, for a new "Cartesian" "style" of doing philosophy today. As Stéphane Mallarmé put it, when such a (strange) thought of something (else) thinking itself out and away occurs, "the feelings—transports, veneration—grow complicated toward this foreigner, also uneasiness that everything has been done, and it hasn't illuminated, through some direct path, the literary principle itself."[100] The problem is with "the haunted, hidden, stamped, inscribed" style, way, or topos of Descartes' writing, "Descartes' reinscription of Platonic allegory,"[101] where modern, and often public acts of architectural system-building, as in "following his own ideas"[102] step by step, constantly intercut with more private, esoteric, hidden, hyperbolic, projects such as cave dwelling, thread making, and illusion creating (or another seventeenth-century obsession): How to refabricate the fabric of the thought of Descartes, the fabulous thinker of the now, in-between? The Cartesian subject as "the fragile absolute,"[103] as Slavoj Žižek characterizes it, remains in the baroque imaginary of Cartesianism as such a trickster figure, leaving philosophy in a sense "truly" philosophical—not so much "Olympian"[104] as constantly chiasmic, interstitially surreal, absolutely "ticklish," always in motion, moving itself and through itself. For "true philosophy laughs at philosophy, . . . [for it is] a-philosophy"[105] under deconstruction, in between building and destroying, between philosophy and "philosophy" covered as such, between I and "I," that real, foolish, undying difference.

THE CHIASM

November 1, 1959

—the cleavage, in what regards the essential, is not *for Itself for the Other*, (subject-ob-ject) it is more exactly that between someone who goes unto the world and who, from the exterior, seems to remain in his own "dream." *Chiasm* by which what announces itself to me as being appears in the eyes of the others to be only "states of consciousness"—But, like the chiasm of the eyes, this one is also what makes us belong to the same world. . . . Chiasm, instead of the For the Other: that means that there is not only a me-other rivalry, but a co-functioning . . . only through a sort of folly—[106]

BRAVELY TOWARD A NEW CARTESIAN WORLD

Inching farther into the text of Descartes, I hope to be able to hold that thought—what thought?—myself.

I shall try to hold the absolutely large and absolutely small at the same time, as much and long as possible, as Descartes sought to do in his attempts at cosmic cogitation. The version of Descartes channeled here is a musical sort of scientist: the minder of the relational gap, the observer of tactile connectivity, the thinker of interstitial mobility, the manifold mind of invisible, intricate, muscles constantly attending, "as if" perpetually "bewitched by relations of mere proportion,"[107] to "the very subtle matter," matter of indefinite largeness or smallness, as illustrated by his scientific demystification of a wine casket's "fear of a vacuum" (C, 11:20/1:87), which is oddly coupled or coextensive with a certain scientific fear of a vacuum. What aroused my interest in this thinker in the first place is such irreducibly complex impulses toward and against the refabrication or refabulation of the world, since the brave new world of Descartes becomes phenomenologically or materially reconstructed, in part, by such elements; rereading through his discovery of "a successful way to weigh air" (C, 3:480–4/3:204–5), I was struck yet again, as if for the first time, by not only its hilarious ingenuity but also the very textual impulse of the Cartesian mind, its obsessive-compulsiveness, which in turn prompted me to pursue this mini-odyssey of my own, yet to be narrated:

> *There are three elements of this visible world.* We have . . . two very different kinds of matter which can be said to be the first two elements of this visible universe. The first element is made up of matter which is so violently agitated that when it meets other bodies it is divided into particles of indefinite smallness. . . . The second is . . . (P, 8A:105/1:258, Article 52)

> Concerning the material which passes into the heart, it should be noted that the violent agitation of the heat which makes it expand not only causes some of the particles to move away and become separated, but also causes others to gather; these press and bump against one another and divide into many extremely small strands which stay so close to one another that only the very subtle matter (which I called "the first element" in my *Principles*) can occupy the spaces left around them. (Dh, 11:254–5/1:322)

> We must concentrate our mind's eye totally upon the most insignificant and easiest of matters, and dwell on them long enough to acquire the habit of intuiting the truth distinctly and clearly. . . . Craftsmen who engage in delicate operations, and are used to fixing their eyes on a single point, acquire through practice the ability to make perfect distinctions between things, however minute and delicate. The same is true of those who never let their thinking be distracted by many different objects at the same time, but always devote their

whole attention to the simplest and easiest of matters: they become perspicacious. (R, 10:400/1:33)

On that encouraging note on the importance of focusing on small matters, the "minute and delicate," let us, without further ado, turn to the stage I of this alternative mini-Cartesian reflection.

Blind Vision: A Photographic Touch

> Some years ago I was struck by the large number of falsehoods that I had
> accepted as true in my childhood. . . . It is possible that I do not even
> have eyes with which to see anything. But when I see, or think I see (I
> am not here distinguishing the two), it is simply not possible that I who
> am now thinking am not something. By the same token, if I judge that
> the wax exists from the fact that I touch it, the same result follows,
> namely that I exist. (M, 7:17, 33/2:12, 22)
>
> *What corrects the error? The intellect? Not at all; it is the sense of touch.*
> *And the same sort of thing must be taken to occur in other cases.*
> *(Or, 7:418/2:281–2)*

The Enigma of Vision Revisited: By Deviancy

Indeed, "how easy it is to be mistaken" (*s'y tromper*) (O, 6:147/113), how easy
it is to see *that* truth: "How crystal clear everything would be in our philosophy if only we would exorcise these specters, make illusions or object-
less perceptions out of them, brush them to one side of an unequivocal
world!"[1] That is, Merleau-Ponty and I fantasize with Descartes, whose
"*Dioptrics* is an attempt to do just that."[2]

I SEE TOUCHINGLY—WITH MY HANDS

To have "clear and distinct" perceptions or ideas—to guard ourselves
against falsities or fantasies as Descartes recommends—seems relatively
easy. Tricky is the attempt itself.

For some evidence, we just need reopen the very *First Meditation*, where the narrating "I" sets out to tell the story of a life-changing awakening: how, "some years ago," he realized that he had been blindly accepting a constructed "reality" as true and yet how "enormous" this task of overcoming such epistemological blindness seems to have been to him. So he ended up putting off the project until he really could and should no longer just keep thinking of it, since so much of his lifetime had already gone into undocumented "pondering" (M, 7:17/2:12). He waits while and until there is "time still left for carrying it out" (M, 7:17/2:12), procrastination being part of the project. Somehow, just like writer Virginia Woolf, Descartes seemed to have been "inclined to wait for a clearer head" while "wanting indeed to consider" his "next book."[3] What happens during that time, that in-between period when the project is brewing, somehow formed, deformed, and transformed? How do we understand that arresting glimmer, that awareness of one's own blindness or blockedness, that nagging thought that keeps our modern mind inactively active?

During that transitory period, just as everyone needs some sort of housing, even when practically living on the street or crashing in a friend's conference hotel room, a thinker needs to be anchored somewhere, somehow. It is a temporary third space, as Descartes envisaged, between the old building that is being destroyed and a new one that is being constructed (D, 6:22/1:122). An example of such a "third" that I suggest we dwell on in this chapter is a transitory moment of blind vision in Cartesian thought, as obliquely indexicalized at the very start of the *First Meditation*, together with the first few pages of the *Treatise on Light* (drafted in 1633) and the *Optics* (1637), both written during that formative period as a companion piece for the *Discourse* (1637), all of which, put together this way, show deconstructive tensions in the Cartesian theatre of the mind and the body quite vividly. After all, it is such a quasi-vision of something yet to be clarified and distinguished that enables "reading Descartes otherwise" in the first place. In that regard, this chapter functions as a kind of further stage setup for the following three other "scenes."

To begin with, we seem able to see readily "how it [vision] happens."[4] But how? How do we understand how we see things? By analogy: Descartes is using an indirect means to see how he sees:

Descartes' blind man provides a good vehicle by which to approach the neglected matter. His appearance, I have said, is unobtrusive. It threatens no great moment. The sheer weight of avoidance makes an indirect approach mandatory. Otherwise, a monumental resistance to self-examination rears its head, takes precedence, and the stop is secreted away. Besides, the blind man's character—like the gravedigger's in *Hamlet*—exemplifies the very experience sought for examination.[5]

Here, self-understanding is theatrically mediated. From the beginning (the First Discourse), in the absence of an alternative medium, the *Optic* relies on figural devices such as a ball and a blind man's stick for the "facilitation" (O, 6:83/1:152) of the reader's understanding of "the action of light" or its "movements" (O, 6:88/1:155). Perceptual beings' access to refraction and transmission, so goes the argument, is tactile first and foremost rather than visual. More vividly, the Sixth Discourse, titled "Of Vision," mobilizes a series of figures such as a blind traveler and his cane (O, 6:135–6/105, Fig. 18); a hand and its groping fingers that feelingly extend, touch, and contract (O, 6:142/108, Fig. 19); the dreaming sleepers as well as delusional maniacs (*les frenetique*) who "often see, or think they see, various objects which . . . are not actually before their eyes" (O, 6:141/108, trans. revised); those otherwise normal people "whose eyes are infected by jaundice or those who are looking through yellow glass or enclosed in a room where there is no light other than that which enters through such glass" (O, 6:142/110). These pieces of evidence of and from the otherwise merely deviant or abnormal, assembled this way, all point to the Cartesian thesis of universal double vision that is still famous and still frightening: "first of all, it is the soul [*l'âme*] which sees, not the eye" (O, 6:141/108, trans. revised), just as it is the hand that sees, not the eye, in the case of the blind.

How does a blind person see? By the hand, by its skin, by "the sense of touch," "the stimulation . . . , the nerves terminating in the skin all over the body" (P, 8A:318/1:281). In Descartes' text, broadly speaking at this point, the very machinic or quasi-neurological materialism, devoid of intentional subjectivity, comes to generate, through the extensive "assimilation of vision to touch,"[6] an "incarnational"[7] account of the "close interweaving of the body and soul."[8] That given, it seems not accidental that, of the five senses, touch, "the least deceptive and most certain" (TL, 11:5–6/1:82), receives the first and longest explanation from him (P, 8A:318–9/281–2) with sight treated at the end (P, 8A:319/1:283). Why is touch more important than sight for this thinker of "clear and distinct ideas," of reason and the intellect? And what kind, sense, of touch does he highlight? He highlights the foundational touch. What is this skinny but sure ground of perception?

Follow this exchange of thoughts for a moment. Turn to the "ninth and most worrying" point of concern raised in the *Sixth Set of Objections*: "Owing to refraction, a stick which is in fact straight appears bent in water. What corrects the error? The intellect? Not at all; it is the sense of touch" (Or, 7:418/2:281–282). In other words, is it not touch that corrects the visual error, the trompe-l'œil? To this query, Descartes responds by saying:

> When people say that a stick in water "appears bent because of refraction," this is the same as saying that it appears to us in a way which would lead a child to judge that it was bent—and which may even lead us to make the same judgment, following the preconceived opinions which we have become accustomed to accept from our earliest years. But I cannot grant my critics' further comment that this error is corrected "not by the intellect but by the sense of touch." As a result of touching it, we may judge that the stick is straight, and the kind of judgment involved maybe the kind we have been accustomed to make since childhood, and which is therefore referred to as the "sense" of touch. But the sense alone does not suffice to correct the visual error: in addition we need to have some degree of reason which tells us that *in this case we should believe the judgment based on touch* rather than that elicited by vision. . . . Thus even *in the very example* my critics produce, it is *the intellect alone* which *corrects the error of the sense.* (Or, 7:438–9/2:296, emphases added)

Note the double flip, or dip, there in the argument. Bear in mind that Descartes' turn or return to the intellect does not bypass the sense of touch but is mediated and stabilized by it, his point being that (1) if and when "seeing is not believing," touching should be the basis of the belief instead and (2) such is a natural function of the intellect—something in reason "tells us" that we should, in this case, rely on touch. The raw, inaugural "sense" of touch, "infantile/childish" (Or, 7:438–9/296) as described in the *Sixth Set of Replies*, is correctively filtered by the discriminating intellect *and* yet the first is also selectively recovered by the second. To that extent, touch is still present in and even formative of Descartes' sense of vision, including and especially the inner vision shared by the sighted and the blind, as Descartes' example of the blind man's stick points to. On a somewhat hastily generalized reading, many tend to think that Descartes simply intellectualizes perception at the cost of ignoring or distrusting the physical senses, and this is the misperception I am aiming to correct here or at least question; it remains clear and true that, as shown previously, Descartes ultimately resorts to intellectual judgment, not the senses themselves, for determining what to rest on, which makes him irreducibly and ultimately a rationalist. But that is not the focal point of illustration at this point, although it is closely relevant to the discussion that follows, especially the next section. Here, suffice to note that the heliocentric "ocularcentrism"[9] of Descartes, the hallmark of his rationalism and by extension of the Enlightenment tradition is actually, textually, grounded or mediated that way—in tactility.

For Celia Wolf-Devine,[10] for instance, the passage cited exemplifies how the *Meditations* and Descartes' subsequent views on vision begin to erase the sense of touch decisively in favor of intellectual judgment. I cannot disagree entirely; again, the residual point that interests me further and that I am trying to recuperate after Descartes is that the Cartesian judgment, the reflective consciousness of the Cartesian ego, *is* still based on a sense of touch, which prosthetically animates—activates, filters, and shelters—it. Such a foundational in-built-ness, interactivity, and extensivity of tactility, all its life seems intrinsic to and even generative of his theory of vision that suffers from "some serious unclarities and inner tensions."[11] What are the ambiguities, and why? Wolf-Devine locates the issue this way: "Unfortunately, his zeal to provide a unified cerebral image of the object led Descartes into unfounded and erroneous physiological speculations as well as on a more subtle level, leading him to see the eye as functioning like a camera"[12] and "the senses as yielding simple snapshots."[13] I almost fully agree, as I will explain more fully in the section where I discuss that "camera" notion, but why is it an "unfortunate" analogy? I must address that issue first. For I am inclined to see it rather as a magical link, almost prophetic. In fact, those internal ambiguities captured by Descartes' inner camera seem telling, more precise than mere metaphors or mess, something other than an avoidable misfortune.

MY VISION DOUBLES IN THE INSTANTANEITY OF THE *COGITO*

What sense, more specific sense, should we make of this tactile elsewhere-ness of Cartesian vision? The seemingly strange thesis, to repeat, is that it is not the eye that sees but the soul; in the case of the blind man, what sees is his hand that holds the stick, with which the soul is somehow networked, as Descartes was trying to prove. If we follow Descartes at least that far, it does appear that not only do we see, but we also, more precisely, perform an act of seeing, seeing ourselves see, which itself is an irreducible act of the muscled mind. What I am trying to discern in turn, in and with Descartes, is not exactly or only the second-order awareness or a transcendental perspective in infinite regress or in its manifold drifting or unfolding. Descartes, the proto-phenomenologist, has yet to meet Kant, Hegel, Husserl, or Heidegger (none of whom will appear in this chapter, which has little room for such important extras). More simply, what I am seeking to bring to the surface is a sense, yet to be made more legible, of multiple, materially horizontal intertwinements of perceptual apparatuses and events, which Merleau-Ponty also stresses when describing the mechanism of Cartesian reflection, namely, how the Cartesian "vision doubles" in the instant(aneity) of the *cogito:*

> The body is both the soul's native space and the matrix of every other existing space. Thus vision doubles. There is the vision upon which I reflect; I cannot think it except *as* thought, the mind's inspection, judgment, a *reading* of signs. And then there is the vision that actually occurs, an honorary or established thought, collapsed into a body—its own body, of which we can have no idea except in the exercise of it, and which introduces, between space and thought, the autonomous order of the composite of soul and body. The enigma of vision is not done away with it; it is shifted from the "thought of seeing" to vision in act.
>
> Still, *this de facto vision* and the "there is" which it contains do not upset Descartes' philosophy. Since it is thought united with a body. . . .[14]

Vision in act: The occurrence of vision and the exercise of it are inseparably simultaneous. More intriguingly in my view, as Merleau-Ponty also points out, the exercise falls/folds back into the body, "the soul's native space," almost wrapping the body back instantly, vibratingly weaving it with its background to the effect of creating a multilayered context and interplay of seeing, perceiving, and knowing. I reflect upon the vision that occurs in, nay, "into," a body, as it were. Mutually folded in, seeing and the seer, thus incorporated, become each time a "chiasmic"[15] envelope of beings:

> What there is then are not things first identical with themselves, which would then offer themselves to the seer, nor is there a seer who is first empty and who, afterward, would open himself to them—but something to which we could not be closer than by palpating it with our look, things we could not dream of seeing "all naked" because the gaze itself envelops them, clothes them with its own flesh. . . .
>
> The classical impasses . . . the difficulties that they may present when confronted with a *cogito*, which itself has to be re-examined. Yes or no: do we have a body—that is, not a permanent object of thought, but a flesh that suffers when its wounded, hands that touch? We know: hands do not suffice for touch—but to decide for this reason alone that our hands do not touch, and to relegate them to the world of objects or of instruments, would be, in acquiescing to the bifurcation of subject and object, to forgo in advance the understanding of the sensible and to deprive ourselves of its lights. We propose on the contrary to take it literally to begin with.[16]

Observe a triple fold in the "double vision"—quite "literally" allegorized, fleshly clothed, in the hands that touch in the blind—as freely lodged in all of perceptual beings. That is how "this *de facto* vision" and a hermeneutical reflection get double-stitched, as if lights instantly inhabited, or were absorbed into, the hands. This is the mysteriously internal, seemingly seamless "shift," back and forth, from the "thought of seeing" to "vision in act." Again, it is the luminous body that enables, animates, and stabilizes such a manifold self-reflexivity of vision. "The eye lives in this texture as a man in his house,"[17] as it is both a space and a matrix as described previously and here:

HUMAN BODY DESCARTES

February 1, 1960

> The Cartesian idea of the human body as human *non-closed*, open in as much as governed by thought—is perhaps the most profound idea of the union of the soul and the body. It is the soul intervening in a body that is *not of the in itself* (if it were, it would be closed like an animal body), that can be a body and a living—human only by reaching completion in a "view of itself" which is thought—

Husserl: the *Erwirken* of thought and Historicity
"Vertical" conception of Thought[18]

Again, such is the phenomenological openness and self-fragmenting, self-extending, ongoingness of the Cartesian body. Moving/living on, this sort of visionary matrix senses "something" opening up and opened up at once, with an impersonal yet dynamic intimacy with itself and its zonal outside. That is what Merleau-Ponty seeks to keep alive when proceeding to highlight the "incarnate" or "tacit" *cogito*: "a preflective contact of self with self (the non-thetic consciousness [of] self . . (being close by oneself)."[19] Further, when he reaches this thesis that "the Cartesian model of vision is modeled after the sense of touch,"[20] he seems spot-on.[21]

However, indeed, "Descartes would not have been Descartes if he had thought to *eliminate* the enigma of vision."[22] How is the "imprint on the back of the eye/on the soul" (*Optics*) related to the "homunculus, the little observer/judge" (*Meditations*)? Or which of them really, ultimately, grounds perceptions, including and especially vision? Although shifting his attention gradually from "seeing" to "judging," if still ambiguously as we will see soon, Descartes "apparently remained satisfied with his account of vision in *Optics*,"[23] vision as tactile, materially dependent, as "he continues to refer his readers to it throughout his life without any indication that he envisioned any major revisions to it" (cf. O, 6:331). The problem, as Wolf-Devine puts it, is "whether both the mechanical and the homunculus models are operative in all perception and whether homunculus model is eliminable in principle."[24] Quite simply, if it were that easy for Descartes to have "clear and distinct" ideas, he would not have tried that hard to cling onto them.

Let us then continue, with Merleau-Ponty, to explore how seeing happens in and through the body, the body taken as a sort of textually necessary, vital prosthesis for thoughts or more loosely the soul. *Res cogitans*, in Descartes, remains astute, a tortured soul:

> For him, there is no vision without thought: but it is not enough to think in order to see. Vision is a conditioned thought; it is born "as occasioned" by what happens in the body; it is "incited" to think by the body. It does not *choose* either to be or not to be or to think this thing or that. It must carry in its heart that heaviness, that dependence which cannot come to it by some intrusion

from outside. Such bodily events are "instituted by nature" in order to bring us to see this thing or that. The thinking that belongs to vision functions according to *a program and a law which it has not given itself.* It does not possess its own premises; it is not a thought altogether present and actual; there is *in its center a mystery of passivity.*[25]

This way, the enigma of vision turns into a question of visual passivity but not inertia: the receptive passivity of "a conditioned thought." "Programmatically," as if by some kind of law of genre and generation unknown to thinking, thinking is sparked and sustained by its own tactile passivity. That is, the focus of the puzzle above is not some optically informative or charged intrusion of and by the other but, more subtly and even more strongly, an "incitatory" impact of the other instituted and responded to "by nature." It is the direct "impressions which come *from the outside* [*de dehors*], passing toward the common sense [*passent vers le sens commun*] by way of the nerves" (O, 6:141/108, emphasis added, trans. revised), which appears to cause "a picture" to appear in the perceiver's mind as an inner vision, in response or correspondence to the picture on the outside that is being looked at in a seemingly mimetico-causal relationship. To repeat: the author of the *Optics* speculates that impressions come directly "from the outside and pass toward" or around the common sense by way of the nerves while bypassing or outspeeding the collaborative intervention of the intellect that judges. A proof or rationale immediately offered for this theory of a direct material transmission of vision is that "if the position of these nerves is constrained by some extraordinary cause, it can make us see objects in places other than where they are [*l'autres lieux*]" (O, 6:141/108).

In short, the experience of touch highlighted here is that of location, neural or spatial:

> The object pressing on us: when we touch something metal or something wood, the object presses in on us; this pressing-in results in a change, even if very slight, in body position, a change detected through the sense of balance. . . . If we try to attend to the sense of touch alone for a moment, putting aside what we experience of the object through the other senses, we sense only the body meeting with a resistance. The object presses my skin inward, and I discover the border between my body and the world. . . . The experience of boundaries . . . the exact area of sensation is experienced. When

we take a step, the pressure of the shoe meets the ground in a particular place. Often, the experience of touch is the experience of location. If I am lying on a warm, sandy beach with my eyes closed, and an ant crawls up my arm, touch locates the exact position of the ant. In all cases, the sensation of touch gives us the sense of our body, not as an object but as a living being.[26]

The ant crawls up my arm, which I get to know because it starts tickling me, and I—or rather, I should say my body—instantly becomes the unfolding map of the ant's journey yet to happen, yet be known. The parallel link between the ant's movement and the neurological path in my body thus created, locatable through this corporeal event called itching, is, on closer inspection, is more inscriptive than mimetic in that the sensation itself does not mirror, resemble, or show any aspect of the ant, its ontological features or specificities:

> There is nothing outside our thought which is similar to the ideas we conceive of tickling and pain. . . . (Tl, 11:10/1:84)

> If I show you that even touch makes us conceive many ideas which bear no resemblance to the objects which produce them, I do not think you should find it strange if I say that sight can do likewise. Now, everyone knows that the ideas of tickling and of pain, which are formed in our mind on the occasion of our being touched by external bodies, bear no resemblance to these bodies. Suppose we pass a feather gently over the lips of a child who is falling asleep, and he feels himself be tickled. Do you think that the idea of tickling which he conceives resembles anything present in the feather? . . . The actions of a feather and a strap . . . a tickling sensation and pain. . . . The light in the objects is something different from what it is in our eyes. I merely wanted you to suspect that there might be a difference, so as to keep you from assuming the opposite. . . . (Tl, 11:5–6/1:82)

The effect of the brushing actions of a feather on a sentient body carries that tactile immediacy, although the feather and the body in question are, obviously, different and separate; that is how Descartes analogizes the mechanism of vision. Joe the plumber might readily accept the proposition that ordinary vision is often mistaken, but he may not, even upon reflection, accept the view that ordinary vision is, in fact, not mimetic. Such a pedestrian idea of mimetic vision, habitually held or even spiritually guarded among folks, is exactly what Descartes tries to demystify more systematically in the *Optics* from the beginning and especially at the end of Sixth Discourse (O, 6:130–147/101–113). Descartes' alternative vision revises such common(ly held) vision by replacing it with the (uncommonly) good vision of the blind: Seeing is (more clearly and distinctly) elsewhere. Such an otherworldly experience of defamiliarization, dislocation, and disorientation makes sense, good sense, in "the world Descartes reserved for a blind but irreducible experience."[27]

Surely that is not all there is to see/be seen in the world of Cartesian vision that seems neatly reconstructed and rigorously delimited by the controlled variable for its proof. His strategy of indirection continues and is continuously intriguing. Recall, for instance, the temporary dysfunction of the eyes, which Descartes famously simulates in the *Meditations* by "willingly shutting my eyes" (M, 7:34/2:24), a case that we will scrutinize shortly. At this point, from that repetition of subtractive reasoning, we only need to extract this next question: How then does a blind person see? How does a Helen Keller see not only this triangle, that tree, or the tune flowing from behind or above but, say, the color of a tulip here or the melting of an ice cube not in my mouth but on the table over there? All of these events do seem to offer "irreducible" perceptual experiences in various ways, but are they also, and equally, intense or intensive? That is, how do the blind see, or sense, non-Platonic, nonextensive, nonideal objects? Where and when does the scale of analysis, of double vision, have to give up or alter itself? What of the intensity or intensivity of perception? Now Descartes is more deeply challenged by the (need to explain the) super-visual power of those born blind who "see" "red" nonetheless through "some sixth sense," as if through speed.

> You *have only to* consider that the differences a blind man notes between trees, rocks, water and similar things by means of his stick do not seem any less to him than the differences between red, yellow, green and all the other colors seem to us. And yet in all those bodies the differences are nothing other than the various ways of moving the stick or of resisting its movements. Hence you will *have reason to conclude* that there is no need to suppose that something material passes from objects to our eyes to make us see colors and light, or even that there is something in the objects which resembles the ideas or sensations that we have of them. (O, 6:85/153, emphases added)

Here is a curious allegory then. The other side of Descartes' example shows only that: the generic limitations of the blind, the constitutive limits of

Cartesian rationalism. It is as if Descartes the thinker remained or wished to be "colorblind" here, the plain truth being that, as he himself shows, the blind remain colorblind, even when aided by the sticks or fingers, no matter how many, how far.

So far, by following Descartes' analogy of a blind man's stick to its hyper-logical end, we have traced the process by which the eye, instrumentally displaced and functionally replaced as such, not only becomes an integral part of vibrantly orchestrated fields of "seeing," but ends up pointing to the ineradicable existence of the "inner eye," which also chimes with Descartes' (somewhat idealistic if not exactly romantic) privileging of an inner world of vision and mental representations over physical sight. Although materially grounded and foundationally inscriptive, Cartesian vision is prosthetically mediated, and the ultimate prosthesis here is geometry. The blind man's perceptions, according to Descartes' model, are kind of intellectually filtered or paralleled, for being geometrically correlated and algorithmically composed; they are locationally translated rather than intensively transferred, even when "incited." What exactly happens on a raw material level, when a set of impressions "from the *outside passes toward*" or around the common sense? That, for Descartes, remains an obscure zone of transmission, a theoretical black box, occupied by perceptual matter itself; to access such a site, he needs (to draw on) another explanatory device such as camera obscura, where the instantaneous imprinting and archiving of simple natures or clear and distinct ideas takes place.

Before turning to the photographic prosthesis as our next scopic concern, we still first need to see how far this tactile enigma, or allegory, of double vision travels through or applies to the perceptual subject: how and how far Descartes' reflective and reflexive "I" follows its own geometricized intuition or responds to its automobilized calls. What lies, shuttles, even surges between the skin and the flesh thus stirred or shaken? Where exactly and how are they vibratingly "interwoven," to use Merleau-Ponty's signature image? How poignant, how pervasive, how porous is this world of de facto blind vision? For even when there is no immediate literal contact between the object and the subject, even where there is a safe distance that prevents tickling from taking place, the same inaugural, organizational principle of tactile vision applies to perceptions in general—to a certain extent. In fact, it rules at the heart of Cartesian self-reflection as staged in the *Meditations*.

TOUCHED, I FOLLOW, THINKINGLY

Take the wax scene from the concluding part of the *Second Meditation*, starting with the reflective *I*'s parasitic dependence, "that dependence,"[28] on that wax at and from the start. See how the wax becomes a mirror for the "I" that infers self-knowledge from that inaugural and lasting encounter of visual tactility, a peculiar kind of mirror that instantly turns into a photographic lens that is somehow coextensive with, although dissimilar to, the natural light of reason in me. My look at the wax turns into a look into myself. Touched, I *follow* and follow *thinkingly:*

> But what am I to say about this mind, or about myself? (So far, remember, I am not admitting that there is anything else *in* me except a mind.) What, I ask, is this "I" which seems to perceive the wax so distinctly? Surely my awareness of my own self is not merely much truer and more certain than my awareness of the wax, but also much more distinct and evident. For if I judge that the wax exists from the fact that I see it, clearly this same fact entails much more evidently that I myself also exist. It is possible that what I see is not really the wax; *it is possible that I do not even have eyes with which to see anything. But* when I see, or think I see (I am not here distinguishing the two), it is simply not possible that I who am now thinking am not something. By the same token, if I judge that the wax exists from the fact that I *touch* it, the same result *follows*, namely that I exist. If I judge that it exists from the fact that I imagine it, or any other reason, exactly the same thing *follows*. And the result that I have grasped in the case of the wax may be applied to everything else located outside me. Moreover, if my perception of the wax seemed more distinct after it was established not just by *sight or touch* but by many other considerations, it must be admitted that I now know myself even more distinctly. (M, 7:33/2:22, emphases added)

I am where I am touched, wherever I am.

The foundational primacy of not only tactility but tactile vision, as illustrated in this chain of prosthetic self-reflections, remains a Cartesian truth, however possibly startling. What fascinates the Descartes of the *Optics*, the (early) modern scientist, is the inchoate point of contact or interaction between rays of light and brain tissues that then becomes conditional, habitual, and autonomous to the point of forming a set of patterns and neurological events. Such material, momentous "*movements* of which the picture is *composed,* acting immediately on our mind inasmuch as it is united to our body" (O, 6:130/101, emphases added), make us perceive things, while almost tricking (or tickling?) us into believing, imagining, or judging that it is *we,* the perceptual agents, the grammatical or philosophical subjects, that compose the picture. The key point Descartes is driving home repeatedly is that, first, such "we" are being bypassed by, if not rendered irrelevant to, the law of vision, and second, what we still "see in our mind," which concerns the author of the *Meditations,* is only that passage, thick and obscure, which Merleau-Ponty calls, as noted earlier, the "there-is"[29] or "depository"[30] where the form of objects is "preserved"[31] as "model-in-thought"[32] or "thought-in-contact."[33]

Although tied to the dualist logic of "seen" versus "hidden"[34] and post-Aristotelian materialist tradition, the originary fertility and foundational intricacy of Descartes' double-view on vision, crystallized in the Sixth Discourse of the *Optics* and dramatized in the *Meditations,* is powerfully transformative, especially in its connective drive and openness, in its epochal dream of alternatively true and truly alternative vision. For instance, the bifocalized vision of Cartesian philosophy extrapolated as such constantly looks for and zeroes in on that non-site/sight, that gluey slippage, between the physical-scientific look at vision pointedly "flat,"[35] horizontal, on the one hand, and the psycho-metaphysical look that is residually "deep,"[36] vertical, on the other. That search is still going on, as seen in contemporary techno-allegories of it such as the GPS[37] (global positioning system) technology or Google Earth in which the mock-cosmic self-reflexivity probes and produces its own algorithmically reproduced surfaces, seemingly "touching" itself. As Merleau-Ponty puts it:

> We must accustom ourselves to understand that "thought" (*cogitation*) is not an invisible contact of self with self, that it lives outside of its intimacy with oneself, *in front of* us, not in us, always eccentric. Just as we rediscover the field of the sensible world as interior-exterior (cf. at the start: as global adhesion to the infinity of motor indexes and motivations . . .), so also it is necessary to rediscover as the reality of the inter-human world and of history a surface of separation between me and the other which is also the place of our union. . . . [38]

The interfaciality of "me" and "the other" is not just superficial, but, if it is superficial, it is in the rather literal sense: of the surface, where*in* is opened up a possibility of intersubjective union, of perceptual mingling and messaging. The utterly simplex, zero-degree code of analysis that Descartes, the modern father of the "secret science,"[39] has conceived out of the pool of consciousness is indeed what Merleau-Ponty aptly calls "the breviary of a thought"[40] in his essay "Eye and Mind."

In his essay, Merleau-Ponty also said, in a less celebratory tone, "Our fleshy eyes . . . , they are *computers of the world*, which have the gift of the visible, as we say of the inspired man that he has the gift of tongue,"[41] and "the secret has been lost, and lost for good, it seems. If we are ever again to find a balance between science and philosophy, between our models and obscurity of the 'there is,' it must be of a new kind. Our science has rejected the justifications as well as the restrictions which Descartes assigned to its domain."[42] What would it mean for one to "reject the justifications *and* the restrictions" from Descartes or anyone else for that matter? Does it not mean to accept it "anew," the ambivalence itself? I still wonder about this extraordinarily nuanced, equivocated passage, seemingly produced in passing, which is also mildly (un)surprising since the text of "Eye and Mind" was cast in part as a critique of modern techno-scientism and cybernetic culture. That very image of inscriptive secretion, the "computers of the world," touches on the question of how we should progressively evaluate and translate, as well as actively use and understand, this finer, more pressing, point regarding the prosthetic passivity of Cartesian vision, with which we now seem to "see" "conveniently *more*, [if] not better" (O, 6:163/125).

Prompted by Merleau-Ponty's "computational" concerns, I am now back to the starting point, splintered again: how the blind see—if "see" is still the right word, "with their *hands*." By now, we should be able to see that even better, since the blind occasionally seem to see better than the sighted do, which is a curious truth also attested by the foundational allegory of *Justitia*, the blindfolded goddess of justice who is not, but becomes, blind while working, like Descartes who hypothetically blinds himself while meditating. That is, neither can be blind entirely or forever; or at least that remains the ideal. So here is the question that Merleau-Ponty must and does try to tackle next, not unlike Descartes who, as seen earlier, should go on and think of *and* against the "extraordinary constraining of the nerves" (O, 6:141/108): What to do with this "*manipulandum*"[43] that "the human being thinks he is and has now truly become, . . . from which there is no awakening"? To wit, as Catherine Malabou more recently asked, *What Should We Do with Our Brain?*[44]

Cogito ex manipulandum: *Photographic "Resistance Is What We Want"*

Recall that in the first Cartesian proposition on the textual tactility of vision we have been focusing on—"first of all, it is the soul [*l'âme*] which sees, not the eye"—deviant or simulated cases functioned as indirect proofs. What comes after or before that, if not who? Let us dwell on that matter, the "what," and leave aside the "who" question, which a later section will address more directly.

"THE SOUL CAN SEE IMMEDIATELY ONLY THROUGH
THE INTERVENTION OF THE BRAIN"

Descartes goes on to write: "it [the soul] can see immediately *only* through the intervention of the brain" (O, 6:141/108, emphasis added). That is what I want to promote as our second Cartesian proposition on vision, which Merleau-Ponty, as seen earlier, suppresses or downplays ambivalently although not entirely disregarding it. To be clear, Descartes' contention is not that the brain alone participates or gets activated when we see something. Rather, the point is that the "internal organs, which are the nerves and the brain" (O, 6:148/114), are the minimal and primary engine behind the production of vision, where seeing "takes place," as though they are the hard drive and the motherboard where computational information "is" or is created, processed, and stored, but not the monitor or the keyboard. Again, the vision is produced and "processed" elsewhere.

As Malabou, the thinker of plasticity, puts it, demands it:

"You are your synapses": I have nothing against this sentence. I simply want to understand the meaning of "being" here,[45] (where) "*life*" (is), which is to say: *resistance.*[46]

What kind of resistance? Punctuational resistance? That punctuational split on contact is synaptically, irresistibly, "haunting"[47] and strangely, materially clear—hauntingly clear—for the thinker in the body, whether it is

Descartes, Merleau-Ponty, Malabou, or whoever or whatever. It is a photographic contact that is prereflectively, reverberatingly, collaboratively sensed as such, within the body and between *"associated bodies."*[48] Such a resonant bilocality of perceptual and material events structures most cognitive activities and affective communications in this world of countless, bottomless movements, switches, lapses. What is that tactile "thing" or this movement of vision that seems to keep falling apart *and* composing itself back with such prosthetic precariousness and precarious persistence? I, too, remain riveted by that question which seems to *be* writing this piece out. In that regard, I am, again, following Merleau-Ponty, who follows Descartes to a certain extent and more immediately than the post-Cartesian thinkers such as Martin Heidegger:

> Scientific thinking, a thinking which looks on from above, and thinks of the object-in-general, must return to the "there is" which precedes it; to the site, to the soil of the sensible and humanly modified world such as it is in our lives and for our bodies—not that possible body which we may legitimately think of as an information machine but this actual body I call mine, this sentinel standing quietly at the command of my words and my acts.[49]

The body of the "there is" is where the ghostly spirit of Cartesian vision gathers into an image, quietly snapping into a figure that I see, a figure that the soul sees through the synaptic network of what I would and should believe and refer to as my brain, wherever it actually is. The "there is" is not the same as the brain or may not be in the brain, although it seems to manifest itself through manifold and unfolding activities of the brain often uncontrollably.

If all that begins to sound unduly info-technological, I do have some technical issues with what Merleau-Ponty goes on to say:

> Only the painter is entitled to look at everything without being obliged to appraise what he sees. For the painter, we might say, the watchwords of knowledge and action lose their meaning and force. Political regimes which denounce "degenerate" painting rarely destroy paintings. They hid them, and one senses here an element of "one never knows" amounting almost to an acknowledgment.[50]

Why only the painter? Why not a photographer? Should not this privilege of "looking at everything but never knowing the thing" apply, actually more readily, to the photographer at least in the classical sense? The photographer is an instant archivist of time as, evidently, when it comes to "looking at everything" within a frame, photographic records are materially more reliable and less judgmental, except when doctored. Think of those most unflattering ID photos or police mugshots, that is, the brutality of facts or "facts" that are rhetorically constructed as closely as possible to facts. To extrapolate that point, "in modernity, the idea of seeing farther, better, and beyond the human eye *had* tremendous currency; photography as the quintessential modern medium aided in this quest. The camera was imagined by some as an all-seeing instrument."[51] Note that the authors already use the past tense for this view. So again why, in Merleau-Ponty, is there this somewhat anachronistic omission or analogue resistance? Is not his despair over the post-Cartesian "loss" of "a balance between science and philosophy" premature or presumptuous, however nuanced?

THROUGH "THE HOLE OF A SPECIALLY MADE SHUTTER . . . COMMON
TO BEAST AND MEN"

As we saw earlier, Descartes himself, the adopted father or brainchild of "representational" thinking, upsets precisely such an "inner worldly self-dialogue" model of vision, especially the young(er) Descartes that penned the prophetic *Optics*. In it, the early Cartesian eye, a sort of "transfer station,"[52] turns the eye socket into the windowpane or the viewfinder: "Natural light is seen in the action of [or as a movement in] a camera obscura."[53] The camera obscura allegorizes "the eye of a newly dead person" or a non-human animal as the lens of the camera, "the hole of a specially made shutter" (O, 6:115/166) through which light passes; Descartes tells Mersenne in 1637 that the diagram used in the *Optics* is drawn from the brain of a freshly slaughtered sheep, adding that the physiology of the visual system is "common to beasts and men" (C, 1:378). It is the Cartesian eyeball, pure and simple, which by extension, as seen in the *Meditations*, is God's retina (his CCTV, as it were) that could just *be* him, recording all the movements in the world, scanning and tracking every molecular detail and nano-movement of all things without and before judging, morally or otherwise. Not only does He archive all of them in the book of lives *and* deaths, but, more significantly, He causes them. Descartes' God, figured here as the invisible panopticon of the universe, "the all-seeing instrument" made visible in this world, is not only the blind archives of motions but also the clairvoyant agency[54] behind them.

As widely recognized, perspectival painting is paradigmatically modern, for it exemplifies mental representationalism, the "picture in the mind" model employed, for example, in the *Meditations* (e.g., M, 7:20/2:18), which turns the thinking "I" into an ideal observer situated at the immovable zero point anchoring all acts of observation. Yet the modernity of photography that externalizes such "an inner world" by turning it inside out has already been prefigured by mechanical materialism in the *Optics*, the work of an amateur scientist inspired by optical inventions such as "those wonderful telescopes" (O, 6:81/152). That is, the double-storied dimension of Cartesian temporality overshadowed by the painterly, or analogue, world of Merleau-Ponty's fleshy phenomenology is that of camera-obscured, photographic time. It is the time of instant becoming, which includes the elastic—telescopic or microscopic—space of hyperbolic fabulation, the "fabrication of giants out of dwarfs,"[55] for instance, which is entirely and almost instantly open to dimensional manipulation, distortion, and reconstruction. For now, "it will be possible to turn a flea into an elephant . . . , and on this alone is founded the entire invention of these small flea glasses made of a single lens, whose use is now quite common everywhere, although we have not yet discovered the true shape that they should have" (O, 6:155/119). And such seemingly technophobic bypassing, on the part of Merleau-Ponty, of the photographic "eye and mind" becomes more problematic when we register the fact that the whole of the Seventh Discourse of *Optics* has been focused on fantastical thoughts about correcting or perfecting vision by such "artificial organs,"[56] as Merleau-Ponty himself notes although only in passing. The sort of Descartes I still find curiously fertile is such an untimely, earlier, generically childlike, "ingenious" genius, who is still developing rather than overdeveloped, potentially pulled in multiple "directions" (*R*). Again, it is such a relatively preprogrammed, nonmimetic, playful, self-directed, open-ended thinker, freshly materialistic rather than wearily idealistic, even when entering into *Meditations*, whom I am suggesting we read again.

Having sought to demonstrate optical mechanism by analogy, the Descartes of the *Optics* is now entertaining the possibility of reinforcing and indeed manipulating it by technical or "artistically or artfully" (O, 6:147,

150, 163/114, 116, 125) supplementary means. So at either stages, "natural" vision as in "natural organs" or "interior organs" (O, 6:147–165/114–126) remains relatively untouched, yet to be identified as a separate reservoir for pure cogitation or theoretical manipulation. Descartes' language at this early stage of published thinking is modestly ambitious, more aesthetic than technical, and his orientation is practical and scientific rather than speculative or metaphysical. For his primary interest was in, at least then, "remedying (optical) deficiencies" or "the faults of the eye," "through art" (through "artificial organs" or "exterior organs") or "practice" (O, 6:147, 150, 163, 164/114, 116, 125, 126), as do "Indians who are said to be able to gaze fixedly at the sun without their sight being obscured, [who] must have doubtless beforehand, by often looking at very brilliant objects, trained their pupils little by little to contract more than ours" (O, 6:164/126)—an example Descartes treats as a piece of fitness advice rather than an optico-metaphysical curiosity.

Descartes today, more theoretically and technically developed, as one might imagine, would still rely on a photography analogy instead of painting (M, 7:19–20/2:13) as the vehicle of such a train of thoughts when thematizing "objective reality" (M, 7:40–3/2:27–9), the source of ideas that lies outside the perceptual subject. Descartes later advances this hypothesis that the idea, of a heat or a stone, for example, must have been "put there" in my head "by some cause which *contains* at least as much reality as I conceive to be in the heat or in the stone" (C, 4:41/3:28, emphasis added). As Gary Hatfield explains, also by using a painting metaphor:

> The formal reality of the idea is like the reality of canvas and paint. The objective reality is like the organization of the paint so that it represents a house, or a tree, or whatever. Assume for the moment . . . that all Cartesian ideas could be represented on canvas using paint. In this comparison, assume that just as all one's ideas are in the same mind, all images are painted on one kind of canvas, using the same oils. They would then all have the same formal reality, since they are all made of the same stuff. But depending on whether the image is of a house or a tree, the paint is organized differently on the canvas. These different patterns are like the differing objective realities of ideas.[57]

Objective reality, enfolded with varying degrees of clarity and distinctness, causes images to unfold in the mind with the corresponding degrees of clarity and distinctness. Its ontology is, at its most reductive stage and level, inscriptively tautological; the painter draws and draws on what she has already seen even when she, like Hieronymus Bosch or Salvador Dali, fabricates something radically weird that does not seem to exist in this world and remains surreal. The basis of that composition would be, then, more strictly speaking, photographic: What Hatfield is discerning, I am suggesting further along this line, is a photoinscriptive moment in a painting.

"I AM = I AM PHOTOGRAPHED"

Installed this way, "the Other is metaphysical."[58] "The *cogito* in Descartes rests on the other who is God and who has *put* the idea of infinity in the soul, who had taught it, and has not, like the Platonic master, simply aroused the reminiscence of former visions."[59] As the *Second Meditation* asks pointedly, "Is there not a God . . . who puts into me the thoughts I am now having?" (M, 7:24/2:16). "The knowing whose essence is critique," as Levinas says, "cannot be reduced to objective cognition"; rather, it comes from and "leads to the Other."[60] What is the modality of that originarily foreign link between one who sees and the Other, which is or is not seen? The *Meditations* says it is "innateness," the divine given-ness of natural reason (C, 4:51/3:35), as the author clarifies later. The existence of God is inferred, extracted, from the idea of perfection touched by, containing, the essence of God; this, again, is an idealist deduction that ultimately discounts sensorial data as proof. Let us go just one step farther down the road, however: How do we "receive" (C, 4:51/3:35) such a gift, "this idea from God"? How, in other words, does the installation of knowledge take place? This occurs by inscription: The answer Descartes provides earlier in the *Optics* (and later in the *Passions of the Soul*), is that object reality "stamps" its image on the back of the brain. This again illustrates the materialist direction, or origin, of Cartesian scientism, which remains extremely contemporary.

If the modernity of painting is wedded to Cartesianism, so is that of photography, even more firmly. Would not Descartes today prefer the photographic model of seeing as an analogy of "clear and distinct" ideas? What is Cartesian about any given photographic image is not exactly its ontoeconomically evidentiary—use and exchange—value as a neuromechanically reproducible object of mediated perceptions. What is Cartesian about a photograph is not only its existential resistance, as discussed earlier, but also its innate impulse autoarchived as such, its " 'ontological" desire, as characterized by Roland Barthes, whose "Cartesian drive"[61] leads him to declare that

> I wanted to learn at all costs what Photography was "in itself," by what essential feature it was to be distinguished from the community of images. Such a desire really meant that beyond the evidence provided by technology and usage, and despite its tremendous contemporary expansion, I wasn't sure that Photography existed, that it had a "genius" of its own.[62]

Shot through both the idealism of painting and the materialism of photography is the ontologized rhetoric of the "real, objective, genuine," rhetoric taken as a narrative orientation of the mind. It is the mind's urge to relate justice to truth by relying on the justifiability of truth. "I will suppose then, that everything I see is spurious. I will believe that my memory tells me lies, and that none of the things that it reports ever happened. I have no sense. Body, shape, extension, movement and place are chimeras. So what remains true? Perhaps just the one fact that nothing is certain" (M, 7:24/2:16)—just the fact that there is something photographically precise and indelible, even in those chimeras.

So, again, how does a blind person see?

> No doubt you have had the experience of walking at night over rough ground without a light, and finding it necessary to use a stick in order to guide yourself. You may have then have been able to notice that by means of this stick you could feel the various objects situated around you, and that you could even tell whether they were trees or stones or sands or water or grass or mud or any other such thing. It is true that this kind of sensation is somewhat confused and obscure in those who do not have long practice with it. But consider it in those born blind, who have made use of it all their lives: with them, you will find, it is *so perfect and so exact* that one might almost say that they see with their hands, or that their stick is the organ of some sixth sense given to them in place of sight. In order to draw a comparison from this, I would have you consider the light in bodies we call "luminous" to be nothing other than a certain movement, or a very rapid and lively action, which passes to our eyes through the medium of the air and other transparent bodies, just as the movement or resistance of the bodies encountered by a blind man passes to his hand by means of his stick. In the first place this will prevent you from finding

it strange that this light can extend its rays *instantaneously* from the sun to us. (O, 6:83–84/153, emphases added)

Light is light: The lightness of light "in bodies" is supernatural as much as it is intrusive. Instantaneously sensed, it is hardly locatable or measurable in any theoretical manner or vocabulary. It is that precise. The touch of light, the photographic "textuality"[63] of "luminous perception," is neither mimetic nor hermeneutical but cryptogrammatological. It is antecedent and superior to the recognition of light, for "the contact with light, the act of opening one's eyes, this lighting up of bare sensation, are apparently outside any relationship, and do not take form like answers to question. Light illuminates and is naturally understood; it is comprehension itself."[64]

Painting sees, but photography shows, including what painting does not and cannot see. The complacency of the elaborate self-portrait (e.g., immortalized beauty) and the cruelty of an ID photo taken by another (e.g., frozen ugliness) are familiar cases in point. Common to both is the rhetorical intent or power of the images to turn the true into the evident via "light"; the justificatory value of photography is, however, higher than that of painting, by virtue of its claimed access not only to evidence but to self-evidence of Being, which also explains the coincidental relation between the decline of realist painting and the rise of photographic reproduction of the real. The feat of materialist culture in the late 1900s onwards entails the defeat of the idealist spirit, at least on that level of hermeneutic persuasiveness. This in part explains why the modernist grammar of photography, in this age of postmodernity that survives on manipulative appropriation, "*manipulandum,*" is still accepted as a more reliable, if still imperfect, form of containing and processing the real—the real that is otherwise fugitive. Here, I'm also recalling Estelle Jussim's remark on the self-reflexive camera as "the postmodern condition of the photograph":

> Photographers who have abandoned the photographic modernists' insistence on "straight photography" (the unmanipulated print), combining words with pictures, painting on prints, or fabricating situations and objects to be photographed, are not necessarily postmodernists. To certify as a postmodernist, a photographer must also challenge the photograph as a reliable, or even rational, system of representation, and deny its aesthetic intent.[65]

In the photographically captured or mediated world where the rhetoric of the real is heightened one step above, the alterity of "the real world out there" ceases to be the secrets of the evil genius, which discriminating reason must summarily demystify through a complete objectification of them. Rather, the radical alterity of the real turns into the externally infinitized measure of truth by which alienated reason gauges its distance, or difference, from what is demonstratively true.

So, again, what does a photograph do better than a painting? It claims a tighter coextensivity between Being and a being it claims to disclose. It is an externalized intensification of the ontological desire of "I see." Photography does not then destroy or disqualify the inner vision of the *cogito* but completes it, prosthetically, correctively, and retrospectively as a mnemonic device that captures the (otherwise invisible) moment. It supplements pure vision by inscription. A photographic click—it is an allegory of the blink of an eye.

My Cartesian thinking seeks to reach the level of clarity and distinctness that the photographical rhetoric of perfect representation seeks to achieve; my very aspiration replaces the ideal observer in me with the photographic Meister, the pure form of "there is" and "there is what used to be there." I, the photographer, must die perfectly; the perfect machine, the eye of impersonal God, stands in for me. The spectrally materialized "I" thinks nevertheless and thinks photographically. Jacques Lacan calls it the "gaze" of the *cogito:* "The gaze is the instrument through which light is embodied and through which I am photo-graphed".[66] "*Je suis = Je suis photographie.*" In the painterly field of cogitation, I am the (hidden, double) gaze; in the photographic field, I am the gaze outside, of the lens.

Res Cogitans: *The Blind Photographer of the Mind*

So far, we have highlighted the tactile intimacy, the material coextensivity, between the "light-writing" of the world and the "natural light of reason" in the Cartesian soul, while using "blind vision" as the foundational concept and photographic precision as regulative, where the built-in metaphor of light disconnects but also, more significantly, connects the blind and the sighted as perceptual agents. Insofar as both are endowed with the Cartesian vision, the "common sense" is pointedly ironized and ironically refortified by a corrective re-visioning of the world, a new world. The guiding proposition so far set against this facile notion of "seeing is believing," namely, that "the soul sees, or the photograph, through the brain," leaves one obvious question unanswered or deferred, with at least one questioner unsatisfied: Now who photographs?

The blind return—in full force.

"I WILL NOW SHUT MY EYES"

Again, how does a blind person see? It is blindness envy, the flip side of fear, or "epistemological insecurity"[67] talking, asking. It is, again, "some blind impulse" (M, 7:40/2:27) that constitutes and complicates the common sense at once. Indeed, "so blind is the curiosity with which mortals are possessed that they often direct their minds down untrodden paths, in the groundless hope that they will chance upon what they are seeking, ... [they roam] the streets ... [or] have spent all their time in the Schools" (R, 10:371/15), just as the life of a blind person remains more precarious than that of a sighted individual, vulnerable, that is, to manipulations by others as well as the usual vicissitudes of daily life. But in the world of Descartes, blindness is not being simply pitied or ridiculed; it is also being privileged, radically reevaluated. What we see amounts to blindness envy. For the analogy also suggests that we need a method just as a blind person does: There is a need for navigational control. Most of us, the sighted, must unlearn our ways of doing things as completely as possible, deschooling ourselves if necessary in order to do things better and learn things more clearly and truthfully in this more firmly grounded and newly constructed world. It is as if Descartes had a fear of as well as for the blind; it is as if a supersensitive eyeball were attached to those fingertips that see more and better. How do the blind do it? Here, the sighted are reduced to eager voyeur-learners. If the fear of blindness is for losing reliable evidence or directions, of falling into the "dark age" all over again, the desire for it comes from a need to secure more reliable evidence, to start all over again.

Unclear? Recall: Is not the *Optics* written from the viewpoint of a blind man with a stick "wandering onto a stage"?[68] Accidental? Precisely. It is the accident pure and simple: The *Meditations*, a temporary suspension of the sense of the world, begin just with such a remembered panic. When in doubt, en/insure?

The text opens with a staged self-deprivation of the senses, notably the physical vision, by the once-eclipsed subject. The author starts to act "as if" (M, 7:19/2:13) he did not receive any visual information; he aborts it as soon as it arrives, as if wishing to protect something (else) from the flow of such empirical data. He "stops."[69] Willfully, he "turns a blind eye" to what he sees, or more precisely, seems to see. Similarly, and more explicitly at the start of the *Third Meditation*,

> I will now shut my eyes, stop my ears and withdraw all my senses. I will eliminate from my thoughts all images of bodily things, or rather, since this is hardly possible, I will regard all such images as vacuous, false and worthless. I will converse with myself and scrutinize myself more deeply, and in this way I will attempt to achieve, little by little, a more intimate knowledge of myself. I am a thing that thinks. (M, 7:34/2:24)

Beware, here: The dissociation of thinking from seeing does not necessarily amount to the separation of the mental from the physical. Nor does the metaphoricization of vision, paralleling the withdrawal of the senses, necessarily lead to the virtualization of ego's sensorial encounter with being. Good old "Cartesian dualists," whom I have been questioning, tend to jump too quickly here, more quickly than the older man in question. For "the fact remains," with Descartes we see here again "that at the moment I think, I think something, and that any other truth, in the name of which I might wish to discount this one, must, if it is to be called a truth for me, square with the 'true' thought of which I have experience."[70]

"I SHALL NEVERTHELESS NOT CEASE TO SEE, IF IT IS ONLY THE BLACKNESS BEFORE MY EYES"

The "tacit" or tactile quality of Cartesian cogitation, "the pure *feeling* of the self, the presence of oneself to oneself"[71]—as Merleau-Ponty says, perhaps himself "wanting to finish [the *Phenomenology of Perception*], . . . struggling blindly on"[72]—is such that "certain ideas are presented to me as irresistibly self-evident *de facto*," although "this fact is never valid *de jure*."[73] In other words, *cogito, sum:* It may not have to be but is the case. For, "a feeling, considered in itself, is always true *once* it is felt,"[74] and "I touch myself *only* by escaping from myself."[75] This is a moment of pure empiricism in pure rationalism: pure contamination. Such is embodied by the blind, most strikingly. This inscriptive tautology of what Derrida calls "auto-affection," this voice that keeps silent, "this silent *cogito* was the one Descartes sought when writing his *Meditations*."[76] For "behind the spoken *cogito* . . . converted into discourse and into essential truth, there lies a tacit *cogito*, myself experienced by myself."[77]

> Operation on signification, a statement of relations between them (and the significations themselves sedimented in acts of expression). . . . Mythology of a self-consciousness to which the word "consciousness" would refer—there are only *differences* between significations. Yet there is a world of silence, the perceived world, at least is an order where there are non-language significations—yes, non-language significations, but they are not accordingly *positive*. . . . The sensorial agent = the body—the ideal agent = speech. . . . [78]

I am with him; or them; or it—that which, in any case, survives the extremely disabling conditions, unuttered, compressed memories.

This way, Merleau-Ponty's post-Cartesian-Husserlian phenomenology—his philosophy of "the tacit *cogito*" in particular—opens up an exciting horizon for philosophy continuing to do justice to deep, or thick, experiences especially, all that temporal jazz. He rightly spotlights those "sedimented" dimensions of our human existence, a small concept (sedimentation, *Fundierung*) borrowed from Husserl, by analyzing how "a past which has never been a present . . . is realized"[79] in the present through such processes of sedimentation, those rhythmical ways in which archived perceptions reiterate themselves through habitual acts including routinized anticipations. With Merleau-Ponty, we get to rediscover what the philosophical vision of Descartes discovers and recovers via " 'contact with truth" at the end of his quest for "evidence, the experience of truth."[80]

> I may well close my eyes, and stops up my ears, I shall nevertheless not cease to see, if it is only the blackness before my eyes, or to hear, if only silence, and in the same way I can "bracket" my opinions or the beliefs I have acquired, but, whatever I think or decide, it is always against the background of what I have previously believed or done. *Habemus ideam veram*, we possess a truth, but this experience of truth would be absolute knowledge only if we could thematize every motive, that is, if we ceased to be in a situation.[81]

Such a topographic and chronogrammatological sense of touch "here is," on which the blind rely prosthetically for the mobilization of their intellect, is generative of Cartesian reflection, a dialectical exercise in seeing and not-seeing conducted in an embodied, and embedded, situation. Every move, every step, thus blended in with its phenomenological neighbors, immediately counts, and count itself. Levinas, too, offers a similar remark on the "localized consciousness of the *cogito*" (not a hyperrational meta-consciousness or transcendental consciousness), which directs me back to Descartes' envy of the blind's near-photographic perception, "so exact and perfect":

> Thought, which idealism has accustomed us to locate outside of space is . . . here. The body excluded by the Cartesian doubt is the body object. The *cogito* does not lead to the impersonal position: "there is thought," but to the first person in the present: "I am something that thinks." The word thing is here admirably exact. For the most profound teaching of the Cartesian *cogito* consists in discovering thought as a substance, that is, as something posited. Thought as a point of departure. There is not only a consciousness of localization, but a localization of consciousness, which is not in turn reabsorbed into consciousness, into knowing. There is here something that stands out against knowing, that is a condition for knowing. The knowing of knowing is also here: it somehow emerges from a material density, a protuberance, from a head. Thought, which instantaneously spreads into the world, retains the possibility of collecting itself into the here, from which it never detached itself.[82]

"A material density" of knowing, mirrored in this parallel image of a simple protruding "head"—not a cranium or a face but a head—testifies to the de facto universality of modern reflexive reason that I, too, would qualify minimally as the pure vigilance of an insomniac. The blind, the mute, and the deaf, too, observes Descartes, possess the autodialogic soul, naturally given to and as reason that *there is.*

But is that all? No, again, a more poignant point to be demonstrated is that *especially* they do. For "the tacit *cogito* . . . is anterior to any philosophy, and knows itself only in those extreme situations in which it is under threat,"[83] in which it experiences—feels—the pure accident that is time, of things that time gives. In that sense, then, the sighted are blinder than the blind to the field of visual experience, of which we all find ourselves as part. How clouded is the vision of the sighted, those who, for example, "watch" television to the naturalized exclusion of the dust on the screen? What is it the sighted see when they see? Do they see at all? The allegory of blindness, described earlier in terms of the memories/memoirs of the blind, runs deeper than what the common sense accepts. Ironically, it is the blind who not only really savor but also most tightly safeguard—bear witness to—the luminosity of photological reason, generically installed in all human beings in the form of "universal wisdom" (R 10:360/1:9) or "intuition" (R, 10:368/1:14), "the indubitable conception of a clear and attentive mind which proceeds solely from the light of reason." It is in that light that Descartes "wishes to present a mechanistic view appealing enough to topple tradition. The view must supplant the former elitist presuppositions with ones thoroughly democratic. Mechanism, in counterdistinction to consciousness, supports the impulse to democracy."[84]

Reached or touched, the Cartesian mind remains photologically oriented and receptive. This case does seem to exemplify the ocularcentrism, "white mythology," of Western metaphysics, whether restaged in the manner of revisionary Platonic idealism or reworked into "mechanised Aristotelianism"[85] that disconnects and reconnects the soul-body link by binarizing the very relationship. For Descartes, the *lumen naturale*, the master trope of perception (or ultimate hypothesis) that demands evidence, is the very and only reliable medium that enables skeptical doubts, namely, questioning: "I have no criterion for mine except the natural light" (C, 2:59/3:78). As Derrida[86] points out during his debate with Michel Foucault on Cartesian madness, on the extent to which Cartesian rationality exercises its political violence (some part of which we will discuss in the next chapter), what is never and cannot be put in question in the Cartesian scene of systematic doubts is that perceptual level, act, of pure differentiation in which even the mad, not to mention the blind, do and must participate.

How else can we reconfigure the Cartesian thinker? This holder of clear and distinct modern vision is equally distributed among all thinkers, minor or major, through whom the natural light repeatedly appears, that is, reappears. Does it not then personify the obscure intersection—blind, fumbling, boundary negotiation—between idealism and materialism? The *res cogitans* remains blind and bound to the very ambivalence of the dual-point of origin of itself, that is, speculative modernity. In this age of technological innovation and hyperengineered capitalism, which constantly converts traditionally transfixed "soul" knowledge into mobile units of stored information, the externalized, manipulated, and prosthetically accessed and processed records of time underwrite and parallel, but not entirely supplant, the internal gaze of the Archimedean knower. And the modern idealist and the modern materialist both, I have been trying to show, carry the Cartesian origin.

While some part of Merleau-Ponty of the twentieth century clingingly reverts to the classical "representational" model of seeing, Descartes of the seventeenth century, whom I am seeking to rediscover along with Merleau-Ponty, inaugurates an inventive discourse of the technoaesthetic incorporation of prosthetic vision, a site for the human animal sight possibly perfecting itself. The contrast between the two thinkers, along with the com-possibility, is still compelling; such is how the spirit of Descartes' philosophy seems to outpace and survive itself. Its revolutionary ethicopolitical implications for freedom as well as control vis-à-vis regimes of truth are promisingly linkable to its material potential, the kind that Walter Benjamin[87] envisages, for instance, through the eye and voice of the movie-going, aura-destroying, and reproducing Proletariat. To be fair, Merleau-Ponty, too, is attuned to such an epochal, paradigmatic shift in modes of the production and reproduction of images of the real, if only in a more straightforwardly despairing tone. His postwar humanism itself, as an antidote to aestheticized ontological nihilism, also seems almost refreshing, at least to this reader who finds herself a little fashionably weary of postmodern antihumanism. The only issue I am raising is with Merleau-Ponty's anthropocentric resistance to technothinking, which appears to function as a paradigmatic block in his otherwise revolutionary phenomenology. Again, simply, why not cameras and computers, which are, after all, time machines? At the heart of our blind man's navigational trust of and negotiation with the world is such a technology of perception and repetition that is already inseparable from the rhythm of pulsations, of life, whether the thinker of tacit cogitation fully registers it or not. So *"while he is painting"*[88] rather than pressing a button or typing a letter, with or without his "secret"[89] technoassistant, I would keep alive the political ethos behind Merleau-Ponty's intellectual plea itself. How? I will replace the painter with the photographer and see what happens. I will see how I can write the photographer into the Merleau-Pontian painter.

Before that, I want to introduce, first, briefly, Henri Cartier-Bresson, a photographer's photographer, from whom I learned to see that world of operational doubleness, of phenomenological intertextuality, of live "seeing." More beautifully than anyone else I can now recall, he describes that compressed moment of time documenting itself by and through the body:

> If, in making a portrait, you hope to capture the inner silence of a willing victim, it is very difficult to *insert a camera between* his shirt and his skin. With a pencil portrait, it is the draughtsman who must possess an inner silence.[90]

The point of it all is: *insert* he must, no matter what, as a draughtsman or as a cameraman, or as both. The point of this quiet exercise in timing is, in other words, to exit *manipulandum.* How? By the *cogito.*

> The act of photography is that of "phenomenological doubt," to the extent that it attempts to approach phenomena from any number of viewpoints. . . . The structure of the act of photography is a quantum one: a doubt made up of points of hesitation and points of decision-making.[91]

The zero point of Cartesian reflection is not fixed in the mind of some homunculus figure somehow fastened to the cogitative "I." As the nimble, springy anchor for the tacit *cogito,* it is mobile itself. As an "operation on signification," to recall with Merleau-Ponty, it sets off the *res cogitan*'s act of "leaping" to catch images or "it," whatever it is; it becomes, and creates, its own significatory fields. The Cartesian zero is, then, not positional but vectorial, and it is temporal rather than spatial. Again,

> Is there not a God, or whatever I may call him, who puts into me the thoughts I am now having? But why do I think this, since I myself may perhaps be the author of these thoughts? In that case am I not, at least, something? . . . Whenever it is put forward by me that I doubt something, I am, I am that thing that doubts; *I am, I exist,* is necessarily true whenever it is put forward by me or conceived in my mind. (M, 7:24–25/2:16–17)

The photographic repeatability of this act of self-doubt, materially saved and temporally footprinted this way through an autobiographical narration, secures, albeit silently, the thinking thing's access to its self-image, its moments of self-objectification. I am photographed inwardly, therein I am.

The nonidentity between the mind and the body, of which photographic images become automatic evidence, is that of proximity rather than primacy. Once the body is posed often before poised, something inserts itself between the inside and the outside of that figure, between a "pure substance" (self-awareness) and a "pure extension" (bodily occupation). The relation between the two is not neatly symmetrical, and its power structure is hardly even. This truth of self-dissonance disclosed by the photographic event of self-observation can become fairly self-evident: The otherwise inaccessible *event* of self-observation on the one hand and the self-observed space located as the specific *situation* of self-observation on the other hand are what photographic time demarcates, dually. All that halt, wait, gap, and suspension of time, all that intertextualized drama of time, seemingly swallowed by the machine only to be released later, is rendered visible only later, through a retroactive "development" or reading of the material framed thereof, citationally arrested as such. The *cogito*'s desire to see "*cogito*" at work is traceable in such petrified images of the archival fever of the present, of which writing is also an example, an unavoidable one at that.

So the "author" of the "sticking" thoughts (M, 7:25/2:17), as previously mentioned, the photographic thinker who records each turn, or shot, *punctum*, of reflection does not and cannot exactly privilege the mind over the body. He only distinguishes one from the other, while trying to clarify and arrange the spatiotemporal relations between them geometrically and sequentially. That is what writing does, among other things: linearize such photographic moments within landscapes of thinking. What, upon reflection, becomes clear to the modern subject is not the difference between the mind and the body per se, which is never consistently maintained in the *Meditations* or anywhere else, but the very borderlined idea of the inside/outside, which photographic images temporally digitalize via the performative rhetoric of punctuality. The ensuing acts of measuring or gridlocking— mirrored in the engineer's vocabulary of "the very exact demonstration" (M, 7:6/6) that mobilizes the *Meditations*, such as "equally, clearer, more precise, more perfect," "more . . . than, as," or "as possible, not as . . . as"— generate and direct every move toward the linear individuation of thoughts, constantly constellating themselves into images, mental pictures. Yet there is something that escapes every thought, shot, which only reinforces the ontological impulse of Cartesian reflection that thereby remains "hauntological" (with the "h" remaining silent in French), as Derrida put it; something immediately "sticks" to someone who thinks . . . who tries to think even a nonthought, as "the referent adheres"[92] repeatedly. Why is there, and what becomes of, this ontological persistence of the referent? Descartes inhabits, while circling around just like the blind on the move, that intersection between egology and ontology left intercut, "un-reconciled," as we described it earlier while borrowing Badiou's Lacanian formulation of the Cartesian problematic, the aporetic legacy and energy of Cartesian modernity. What Descartes the photographer of clarified ambiguity does, I am saying here, is to sharpen that edge.

Again, "resistance is what we want"[93]—photographic resistance. What I am searching for through a post-Cartesian exercise of the *cogito* is a series of invisible envelopes of being, disclosed by the blind, the otherwise sighted: "the hollow in bed that had been prepared . . . by the mere idea of lying down";[94] "a cameraman with its shutter open, quite passive, recording, not thinking, recording the man shaving at the window opposite and the woman in the kimono washing her hair;"[95] a person who, the windows failing, "could not see to see;"[96] the one who, about to die, "hears a Fly buzz."[97] What we sense, and continue to see somehow, is that phototextuality of time "between the light and me"[98] that is neither bright nor dark, neither white nor black, but rather is dazzlingly blue. "Some day, all this will have to be developed, carefully printed, fixed."[99] "But since the habit of holding on to old opinions cannot be set aside so quickly, I should like to stop here and meditate for some time on this new knowledge I have gained, so as to fix it more deeply in my memory" (M, 7:34/2:23).

Surface Revolutions in Descartes' Optical Materialism: Still to Come?

The "new knowledge I have gained," in my case, is that the internal vision that becomes the focal point of Descartes' realist or materialist idealism, whether in the *Optics* or the *Meditations*, is a translation (transmission/transcription) of tactile codes, which itself stabilizes and spiritualizes the Cartesian impulse toward the mechanization of perceptions. Again, the engineering or more ostensibly scientific discourses that predate the *Meditations*, such as *The World*, the *Treatise on Man*, and the *Optics*, are more obvious if not only examples, where something akin to the photographic independence of sensations is explored with some systematic precision, as we have seen.

"SINCE ENGRAVINGS REPRESENT TO US BODIES OF VARYING RELIEF AND DEPTH ON A SURFACE"

Let us look, more closely and conclusively, into the Cartesian tactile code that begins to surface here:

> Our mind can be stimulated by many things other than images—by signs and words, for example, which in no way resemble the things they signify. And if, in order to depart as little as possible from accepted views, we prefer to maintain that the objects which we perceive by our senses really send images of themselves to the inside of our brain, we must at least observe that in no case does an image have to resemble the object it represents in all respects. . . . Indeed the perfection of an image often depends on its not resembling its object as much as it might. You can see this in the case of engravings: consisting simply of a little ink placed here and there on a piece of paper, they represent to us forest, towns, people and even battles and storms. . . . Even this resemblance is very imperfect, since engravings represent to us bodies of varying relief and depth on a *surface* which is entirely flat. (O, 6:112–3/165, emphasis added)

Misperception is caused by misreading or overreading. That is part of the "sedimented" act, schooled habit, of the mind, as discussed earlier. Descartes' passing optical—photographic—shot at the "men crossing the square," which he, upon reflection, tries to truly "re-see," is nothing other than "hats and coats [on the move] which could conceal automaton" (M, 7:32/2:21); "I *judge* that they are men. And so something which I thought I was seeing with my eyes is in fact grasped solely by the faculty of judgment which is in my mind." "It is obvious too that we judge shape by the knowledge or opinion that we have of the position of the various parts of an object, and not by the resemblance of the pictures in our eyes" (O, 6:140/172). That is how and why:

Sense perception sometimes deceives us. First, it is the soul which sees, not the eye; and it does not see directly, but only by means of the brain. That is why madmen and those who are asleep often see, or think they see, various objects which are nevertheless not before their eyes: namely, certain vapors disturb their brain and arrange those of its parts normally engaged in vision exactly as they would be if these objects were present. (O, 6:141/172)

In order for Descartes to conduct a nonjudgmental, almost literal, reflection on those things he has just seen or thinks he has seen, he must revisit the scene that is photographically "engraved," retained, and formed "on the back of his eye" (O, 6:115–28/166–7). Recalling, an act of retrieving information, is equivalent to developing the negative. This also significantly helps us see why Franz Fanon, for instance, focuses on the "eye" rather than the "eyes," when trying to touch (on) sociopolitical realities and mechanisms of significations correctively, not just physically or metaphysically:

It is after all the eye that "corrects cultural errors" happening in the eyes of the beholder: "It is just that over a series of long days and long nights the image of the biological-sexual-sensual-genital-nigger has imposed itself on you and you do not know how to get free of it. The *eye* is not merely a mirror, but a correcting mirror. The eye should make it possible for us to correct cultural errors. I do not say the *eyes*, I say the *eye*, and there is no mystery about what that eye refers to; not the crevice in the skull but to that very uniform light that wells out of the reds of Van Gogh. . . ."[100]

PHOTOGRAPHIC "IMAGES ARE SIGNIFICANT SURFACES" THAT SEE THEMSELVES

If "images are significant *surfaces*,"[101] photographic images are the significant surfaces that see themselves. They present—see—themselves instead of, on behalf of, and for the sake of the photographic viewer often attracted to and misguided by the illusion of depth, who is literally in that sense inferior to and metaphorically blinder than the camera. The camera is a machine "because it appears to simulate the eye and in the process reaches back to a theory of optics. A 'seeing machine' "?[102]

Apparatuses were invented to simulate specific thought processes. . . . All apparatuses (not just computers) are calculating machines and in this sense "artificial intelligences," the camera included. . . . In all apparatuses (including the camera), thinking in numbers overrides linear, historical thinking. This tendency to subordinate thinking in letters to thinking in numbers has been the norm in scientific discourse since Descartes; it has been a question of bringing thought into line with "extended matter" constructed out of punctuated elements. . . . Since Descartes at least . . . scientific discourse has tended towards the re-encoding of thought into numbers, but only since the camera has this tendency become materially possible. . . .[103]

Here, the nonmimetic encoding of Cartesian perception finds a photographic expression: Photomaterialism is an ironic perfection of idealism—a modernist photograph, for instance. The ambiguity of speculative modernity is in the double knot of materialism and idealism.

DESCARTES RESURFACING, WITH "THIS SUBTILIZED VISION THAT
WE CALL THOUGHT"

Descartes begins his philosophical journey as a materialist focusing on the typography of perception (*Optics*, 1637); while searching for the topography of the thinking "I," he undergoes a theatrico-speculative mentalist phase (*Meditations*, 1641), which leads him back to materialism, a more "natural" (Ps, 11:326/1:327), more mature psychosomatism (*Passions of the Soul*, 1649) that eventually seeks to locate an isomorphic, instantaneous link between a passion in the soul and an action in the body—that is, the pineal gland, which he failed to discover even after "looking thoroughly" into a dead woman's body (C, 3:49). While traveling, when *dis-coursing*, the modern mind experiences various forms of its material automatism or performative tautology: the mind unfolds with an a-positional autoinscription, a brain-watching; it indulges in a positional autoplay, a mind game; and it discovers its dispositional automobility, which shows itself in shifty sentiments such as hatred and generosity, a passive-aggressive self-analysis. In the *Optics*, something is photographing; in the *Meditations*, I am photographed; in the *Passions*, something photographed is in me.

What is to be seen in this reconstructed trilogy of Cartesian blindness? The photogenetic/graphic survival of the mind. Neither exactly an inert imprint nor merely a static homunculus, the Cartesian man moves somewhere in between: He is a blind cameraman, "someone lying in wait."[104] He is undead. He is a specter—of Descartes, of what we call "Descartes."

Again, how does a blind person see? Or how can I see better, otherwise, like the blind?

September, 1959

Descartes (*Dipotrics*): *who* will see the image painted in the eyes or in the brain? Therefore finally a *thought* of this image is needed—Descartes already sees that we always put a little man in man, that our objectifying view of our own body always obliges us to seek *still further inside* that *seeing man* we thought we had under our eyes.

But what he does not see is that the primordial vision that one must indeed come to cannot be the *thought of seeing*—This thought, this disclosure of being which finally is *for* someone, is still the little man inside man, but this time contracted into a metaphysical point. For finally we know no vision but that by a composite substance, and it is this subtilized vision that we call thought. . . . It will be the engulfed brute being that returns to itself, it will be the *sensible* that hollows itself out—[105]

That in mind, with that brute optical being in us, now let me move onto the next object that is lying in wait—not for me, but for itself, buried somewhere, "sensibly hollow," between lines of thought.

Elastic Madness: An Allegorical Comedy

Yet although the senses occasionally deceive us with respect to objects which are very small or in the distance, there are many other beliefs about which doubt is quite impossible, even though they are derived from the senses—for example, that I am here, sitting by the fire, wearing a winter dressing-gown, holding this piece of paper in my hands, and so on. Again, how could it be denied that these hands or this whole body do not belong to me? Unless perhaps I were to liken myself to madmen [*insani*], whose brains are so damaged by the persistent vapours of melancholia that they firmly maintain they are kings when they are paupers, or say they are dressed in purple when they are naked, or that their heads are made of earthenware, or that they are pumpkins, or made of glass. But such people are insane [*sed amentes sunt isti*], and I would be thought no less extravagant [*demens*], if I took anything from them as a model for myself. (M, 7:19/2:13, trans. modified)

The great benefit of these arguments is not, in my view, that they prove what they establish—namely that there really is a world, and that human beings have bodies and so on—since no sane person has ever seriously doubted these things. The point is that in considering these arguments we come to realize that they are not as solid or as transparent as the arguments which lead us to knowledge of our minds and of God, so that the latter are the most certain and evident of all possible objects of knowledge for the human intellect. (M, 7:15–6/2:11, *Synopsis*)

Save the "Self-Knower": Do We Have . . . or Am I . . . a Case?

I know myself—save that knowledge.

DESCARTES' MADMEN "DISQUALIFIED" OR REHABILITATED

In the four-page opening passage of chapter 2 of the *History of Madness*[1] and later in the essay "My Body, This Paper, This Fire,"[2] Michel Foucault launched a point-by-point self-defense against Derrida. Previously, in his forty-six page essay "The *Cogito* and the History of Madness,"[3] Derrida had pointed to some traces of Cartesianism ironically but unwittingly enacted by Foucault.

In that madness chapter of the *History of Madness*, Foucault advances an insightful point on Descartes' thought-experiment in question, a passage that anyone who has taken Modern Philosophy 101 would readily recognize, perhaps too quickly. Foucault observes that, although Descartes in the *Meditations on First Philosophy* appears to embrace madness by entertaining it almost to the point of risking his own sanity, he in fact rejects it not just ultimately but preemptively; Descartes precludes madness. In Foucault's view, Descartes' trick, his methodological skepticism, is formally strategic and discursively effective: not counting mad persons as valid philosophical subjects while pretending to count them in. While the qualities of madness are at least and visibly considered as a possible explanation for Descartes' seemingly strange act of thinking, just at that point the madman practically is "disqualified"[4] or at least "discredited."[5] Hence, madness is "the absence of an *oeuvre*,"[6] the "inevitable void in the length of history."[7] This calls to mind Foucault's parallel archaeological attempt to unearth "all the words without language that appear to anyone who lends an ear, as a dull sound from beneath history, the obstinate murmur of a language talking to itself—without any speaking subject and without an interlocutor, wrapped up in itself."[8]

Nonetheless, it is this very "murmur" from beneath the void in the history of madness to which Foucault lends a sympathetic ear, this "wellspring of sense, however silent or murmuring"[9] on which Foucault attempted to focus, that Derrida finds structurally questionable, forever aporetic. Is that murmur audible? Derrida asks. My question in this chapter circles around that as well, although my approach to it differs from Foucault's and Derrida's rather paradigmatically. After I have shown where I depart from them, I will offer my own, slightly lighter angle on Descartes' madmen.

So let us return to the madmen. To start with Derrida's question, roughly: If the murmur of Descartes' madmen is audible, it is already reasonable or thinkable; if not, how can anyone write a book about it to begin with? As Michèle Le Doeuff's put it, Foucault embodies "the 'paradoxes' . . . about madness: that reason first excludes unreason and . . . it is again reason which proceeds to speak of unreason."[10] It is in that vein that Derrida is suggesting further that Foucault is after all more Cartesian than Descartes, more ambitiously and thoroughly completing the cycle of the Cartesian violence of reason, of vicious circularity. Yet it is not a simple accusation directed at a thinker. The deeper issue here, as Derrida senses, is the "originary, strange complicity"[11] between madness and historical reason, "madder than madness,"[12] something other than historical instantiations or representations of madness. What Derrida is after is not a nearly inaudible murmur but an unheard-of voice.

The story of Cartesian madness reemerged when Foucault returned to the scene in 1972 via "My Body, This Paper, This Fire," where he trivializes the "unheard-of voice" Derrida speaks of as what keeps his little Cartesian reading exercise going. Foucault reduces it to a little disciple's trembling voice reflecting, amplifying, that of the dehistoricized, decontextualized Master, namely, the voice of Descartes from beyond the grave. According to Foucault, Derrida, following his virtual textual Master, writes as if he knew what *logos* meant. In Foucault's view, Derrida "encloses [*enfermer*] the alienated madness outside [*à l'extérieur du*] philosophical discourse"[13] while "systematically"[14] disregarding some of the crucially different senses—juridical, clinical, metaphysical[15]—of it operating in the text. In this seemingly innocuous passage on madness, Foucault senses a discourse of madness at work. There, what is going on, Foucault points out, is practically a qualifying examination: "I remain qualified to think, and therefore I make my resolution."[16] Such is what Foucault's philosophical imaginary hears the Cartesian subject saying.

It is as if the very last thing that Foucault or Derrida would wish to become is a certified or qualified Cartesian, whether as the examiner or as the examinee, the question being not whether one can pass the Cartesian examination but whether Descartes, metonymized by the whole scene of examination or inquisition, can be surpassed or bypassed and if so, how. The task, in other words, is to go outside (of) Descartes . . . if such a thing is possible. Where does this eternalized curse on Descartes originate, this terror of error, this terror of being (mis)identified, framed, as a Cartesian pedagogue/disciple? (If such a thing exists, that is.)

This complicated dread or fear that we might as well just call the Cartesian complex is far from private or personal or psychological. Consider the highly institutional and adversarial context[17] in which Foucault the French master and Derrida the French-speaking disciple in France of the 1960s, both known for their erudite and sophisticated attacks on modern rationalism, problematize the status of *the* French institution "des Cartes," the "theory (Descartes, not Freud),"[18] whom they ought to know by heart. Derrida's prefatorial dramatization—internal to his deconstructive engine and strategy, already rehearsed at the very beginning of his 1967 "Cogito" article—of the interminable unhappiness of the academic subject acknowledging but not knowing the interminable debt toward the leading master(s), whose mirror(s) he cannot yet "must break,"[19] shows quite realistically, vividly, existentially, the self-empowered struggle of thinking's thinking against, or into, the grain of traditional thinking, which may be after all, as he notes resoundingly, absent.

And then?

Over two decades later, Derrida returns to the scene of examination as if there still were room for examination. At the conference on November 23, 1991, celebrating the thirtieth anniversary of the publication of the *Histoire de la folie à l'âge classique*, Derrida revisits Foucault on Descartes by speaking this time "not of Descartes but of Freud."[20] In this public reflection on the *History of Madness*, incorporated into a broader and deeper meditation on *the book* as in bookkeeping as arboreal acts of tracing and promising, Derrida resumes the dialogue with the late Foucault, now doubly impossible, doubly necessary. It is impossible because, through this necessarily imaginary dialogue, he now also seeks "To Do Justice to Freud" (the title) "in memory of Georges Canguilhem" (the tribute), the man who had been Foucault's mentor, who as "an inspector and president of the *agrégation* examination board, concretely backed Foucault's research"[21] along with Jacques Lacan's, whose work remains genealogically linked to that of Descartes, the father of modern rationality, as well as that of the Oedipal pretext in this debate, namely Freud. So we get the picture: an autogenealogical sort of picture that instantly becomes almost immeasurably large.

"Thought is conditioned by fidelity and fidelity honed by thought,"[22] Derrida says in the opening paragraph of that 1991 talk on Descartes, Freud, Canguilhem, and Foucault among others, while foregrounding his double-structured thesis on those "knots,"[23] the "powerful logic"[24] of psychoanalytic resistance and cogitational justice. Does, or would, Foucault think likewise? For Foucault, also a thinker of the double, thought is shaped by injustice and injustice-fueling fidelity, including fidelity toward resistance. So the double lock he struggles with becomes that of cogitational injustice and psyochoanalytic analysis that is driven by and toward cogitational mastery. It is as if Descartes (re)produced two "Descartes," one of cogitational justice and one of injustice. But just where is Descartes? Who knows? Or is Descartes in the middle?

Who is the real son, the inheritor of the cogitational spirit of Descartes, whether good or evil, sane or mad, just or unjust? Rather, what or where is the objective reality of this philosophical drive toward an origin, an unknowable, unreachable origin? Derrida makes a show of the originary indeterminacy and interminability of philosophic thinking; he drives it home, so to speak, through a spiral performance of philosophical self-inquisitions, perhaps a little madly:

> Is there any witnessing to madness? Who can witness? . . . Is there a possible third that might provide a reason without objectifying, or even identifying, that is to say, without examining [*arraisoner*]?[25]
>
> Is not what Freud was looking for, under the names "death drive" and "repetition compulsion," that which, coming "before" the principle (of pleasure or reality), would remain forever heterogeneous to the principle of principles?
>
> It is *the spirit of this spiral* that keeps one in suspense, holding one's breath—and, thus, keeps one alive.
>
> The question would thus once again be given a new impetus. . . .[26]

"THE EXCESS OF MASTERY RUINS MASTERY"

"The excess of mastery ruins mastery" (*L'excès de maîtrise per de la maîtrise*),[27] as Derrida summates in his last tribute to Foucault.

Each time and every time, this recursive trap of modern reason ruins and is ruined by proto-Cartesian Unreason (*la Non-raison*), capitalized classical unreason such as hyperbolic delusional madness or rhetoricized schizo-paranoia. Such "'Cartesian moments' within a lot of inverted commas"[28] were especially palpable at the dawn of European modernity, as Foucault highlights in the *History of Madness*. Foucault sees its emergence more im-mediately and clearly as a historical event, a point in a historical-political timeline that unfolds itself cuttingly, rather than as a philosophical fable, a quasi-meta-narrative of *logos* semidifferentiating itself in a spiral move-ment. It is the kind of "silhouette" of "cogitational justice" we saw earlier and see later in Derrida's version of a double-knotted history of madness, if possible at all, where one's thought just follows itself, insists itself, demands itself, despite the cogitator, regardless of the cogitator:

> Although I intend to speak today of something else altogether, starting from a very recent rereading of *The History of Madness in the Classical Age*, I am not surprised, and you will probably not be either, to see the silhouette of certain questions reemerge: not their content, of course, to which I will in no way return, but their abstract type, the schema or specter of an analogous problem-atic. If I speak not of Descartes but of Freud, for example, if I thus avoid a figure who seems central to this book and who, because he is decisive as regards its center or centering of perspective, emerges right from the early pages on, right from the first border or approach, . . . evoked only on the edges of the book and is named only right near the end, or ends, on the other border, this will perhaps be once again in order to pose a question that will resemble the one that imposed itself upon me thirty years ago, namely, that of the very possibility of a history of madness. The question will be, in the end, about the same, though it will be posed from another border.[29]

How and when does an edge turn into a silhouette? In this transcriptive move that recasts the duel of "Reason-Unreason" (Descartes-Foucault) into a duet of "Consciousness-Unconsciousness" (Descartes-Foucault-via-Freud), one would indeed see the "typical" power of disorienting "abstrac-tion," the supplementary "specter of an analogous problematic." In a certain deconstructive curvature of excentric thinking emerging from a passage such as Derrida's, one could further discern the edge of differential discur-sivity emerging, with a certain Foucault standing guarded otherwise. For Derrida, unreason—part of impossibly larger reason, so to speak—is the "wellspring of sense,"[30] well-divided by an invisible wall, constantly over-flowing the dual ends of space-time. So "however silent or murmuring,"[31] it appears approachable and inexhaustible. It remains phenomenologically dynamic, philosophically sheltered. For Foucault, such unreason more definitely and simply, especially when mobilized, becomes "a sort of open wound, which in theory constantly posed a threat to the link between subjectivity and truth,"[32] and a specific threat.

Yet as Foucault himself extrapolates in *The Hermeneutics of the Subject*, such discontinuously pluralized moments of discursive differences also lie within the broader Socratic tradition of philosophizing that privileges self-knowledge as a—or even *the*—location or starting point of truth. Such a split or slit within guiding notions of reason and a "history" of reason (as opposed to unreason, as Foucault himself tends to sharply distinguish) produces certain movements of thought recalcitrant to dialectical formulations or colorations. So, as Foucault goes on to observe, the "Cartesian moment . . . functioned in two ways; it came into play in two ways: by philosophically requalifying the *gnōthi seauton* (know yourself), and by discrediting the *epimeleia heautou* (care of the self)."[33] The aspect of the "Cartesian moment" that particularly interests Foucault, and now myself although in a different way as I will show shortly, is just that pivotal point in and of the "*cogito,*" at which the focus of thinking shifts paradigmatically from self-care to self-evidence, from an ethical concern that one has about himself or herself to an epistemological demand that one puts on himself or herself. For example, for Foucault, the *Meditations* and the very *First* in particular function as a fertile index to—and the exemplar of—how the history of madness, hitherto left untold but about to be told by him, parallels that of modern reason, or the modern *exercise* of reason, to be more precise. Such a momentous time, mobilized and memorialized by the discursive subject seeking a piece of evidence and especially ontological self-evidence that would function as a point of access to truth, is "conceptual" rather than "chronological,"[34] which is not to say it is ahistorical. On the contrary, such a conceptual event can be and often is historic to the point of becoming "epochal" at every point of activation, as materializing in modern philosophy taken as a network of political as well as phenomenological movements anticipating Hegel, Husserl, and Heidegger.

Foucault's aim in advancing this claim on Descartes is politically motivated, and the insight there is immeasurably deep. He is not interested in some double-dead old rationalist whose afterlife has long expired. He is after the conceptual culprit, the philosophical Father to be taken seriously and studiously resisted. Indeed, philosophy should see with Foucault the historical correlates of its own epochal "act of force or take-over (*coup de force*)"[35] that not only parallels but produces sociopolitical realities of the times with and from which it seeks to depart. Particularly instructive in that regard is the critical import of the *History of Madness*, which attends to the constitutive margins and "wounds" of the classical reason at work, along with that of the *Hermeneutics of the Subject*, which scrutinizes the hermeneutical temporality of those problems, those surgical remainders. There, Descartes' *Meditations* are framed afresh as a telling allegory of how the madman is excluded summarily from the community and an odyssey of modern subjects to the effect of saving the "self-knower" and, oddly enough, excluding those communal subjects. The epistemological disqualification of one who is incapable of self-knowledge leads to the strategic fabrication and fortification of one who is capable of self-knowledge.

This way, the *Meditations*, this epochal masterpiece of 1641, comes to exemplarily enable, anticipate, and reinforce the institutionalized epistemic violence and specifically the repressive reductionism of classical rationality, from which no one is entirely free, practically or technically. One of the most obvious cases Foucault mentions, in that context, is the opening of General Hospital (*Hôpital Général*) "in Paris in 1656 by royal decree, . . . essentially a pauper's prison constructed to rid the city of idlers and beggars and other socially useless individuals."[36] The *History* and the *Hermeneutics*, read together this way, readily demonstrate why Descartes or the Cartesian legacy is negatively exemplary, especially for Foucault if not that much for Derrida, and why indeed Descartes still matters.

JAZZIER?

Descartes matters otherwise, too, which is what I want to show in the rest of the chapter.

The narrative drive of Foucault's theory is reflexively foundational, even ironically meta-Cartesian, largely in the sense that the argument of the *History of Madness* itself significantly hinges on a successfully demonstrative deployment of "Cartesian reason," specifically an analytic exposition of the limits of the "Cartesian moment." We have already considered some key aspects of this point through the lens Derrida explored: The *History of Madness* as a putative counter-discourse to that of reason is self-referentially impossible or self-defeating in the sense that any such attempts will end up being a narrative construct of its own sense-making. How does a shadow appear without light? The revisionary solution offered by Derrida to this theoretical conundrum of performative self-contradiction was, in summary, to quasi-transcendentalize *logos* by keeping the originary *logos* operative but indeterminate, where madness and reason are yet to become different. Such semi-undifferentiated *logos*, somehow impurely protected but protected nonetheless, would remain irreducible to its historical—in this case, Cartesian—manifestations, performances, or determinations. Thus, Derrida's analytic gaze turns to the level of a narration that "narrates itself,"[37] no matter what; he looks to the level of *cogito* that is madder than the mad, as it were. Is that how and why Descartes matters? Partly yes, but not entirely.

What matters differently, for me, is a liminal Descartes inserted, or flying, or sneaking in between Foucault and Derrida, lingering halfway in between. The other (side of the) issue as I see it, which I will detail in the second half of this chapter after noting some immediately relevant points from Foucault on Descartes, concerns the binarily overdetermined reading of the Cartesian touch of madness, whether historicized or quasi-transcendentalized. As I will try to show by locating my point of departure there, a deeper or more intimate appreciation of Cartesian madness would require a different sort of theoretical reflexivity, closer to reflexological attention. Like Foucault, I will focus on the transitory, conceptual distinction and movement between "self-care" and "self-evidence" drawn as such, but I also want to show that the clear distinction between them, if and when deployed as an inflexible analytic grid, does some injustice to subtler, richer, proto-phenomenological aspects of the Cartesian legacy that remain differentially distant if not distinct from any misguided or oppressive regime of representational self-knowers. As with Derrida, I will seek to do justice to the phenomenological and narrative forces of the cogitational "I" that slips through historical determinations and configurations of it, but I also want to show that the immanent materiality and eventuality of it resists any transcendentalizing or hauntologizing move. Unlike Foucault and Derrida, what interests me most within those disjunctive moments of Cartesian reflection is a more concrete and immanent phenomenological elasticity of cogitation—jazzy turns of thinking. What follows amplifies that gesture.

Restarting with the "New Dividing Line"

As *logos* works by line . . .

CLEAR AND DISTINCT?

The passage at issue—the textual focus of the debate between Foucault and Derrida—is the zone of inaugural thinking marked in and around the first five paragraphs (M, 7:17–19/2:12–13) of the *First Meditation* (M, 7:17–23/2:12–15), the fourth of which, the ultimate key, I cited at the beginning of this chapter. In those opening passages, as we will see later in detail, Descartes sets out to list and discuss "what can be called into doubt" (M, 7:17–23/2:12–15), especially the putative evidence of the epistemic reliability of himself, the author.

For an ironic contrast, Foucault is pointing to what remains beyond doubt for Descartes from the start—or even before that, in some important sense. Foucault is questioning the preestablished discursive economy of Descartes' methodological skepticism, the "path"[38] of self-reflection thus taken, which in Foucault's view is already drawn by the reflexive autoinscription of Cartesian reason. The method of hyperbolic doubt was meant to be simply instrumental, neutrally experimental, and rigorously self-critical, but it is not—such is Foucault's point. By interrogating the built-in teleology or the preinscribed limit of Cartesian reflection that manifests itself in the autoauthentication of the thinking ego, Foucault contends that Descartes, in fact, insidiously excludes the madness hypothesis, if nothing else, before and with a view to reaching the *sum* (I am). The very possibility of the *cogito* (I think) is not only contingent but grounded upon the embodied elimination or invalidation of this particular element or example of unreason, madness. As a result:

> A new dividing line has appeared, rendering that experience so familiar to the Renaissance—unreasonable Reason, or reasoned Unreason—impossible.

Between Montaigne and Descartes an event has taken place, which concerns the advent of a *ratio*. But the advent of a *ratio* in the Western world meant far more than the appearance of a "rationalism." More secretly but in equal measure, it also meant the movement whereby Unreason was driven underground, to disappear, indeed, but also take root.[39]

Is the "dividing line" clear and distinct? Is the autoconstitution of the *ego cogito* necessarily linear and linearly oppositional, automatically leading to the construction of a repressive institution? Why not conceive of the automatic emergence of that line more dynamically and fluidly? Can we not interstitialize it, rather than institutionalize it, by inserting another line through or across it, rather than against? Is not Foucault's line of reading in itself rather rigidly drawn, as if inversely reciprocating the "violence of the alien-insane (*aliénés*) in their moments of frenzy"?[40] When French physician and medical expert François-Emanuel Fodéré "arrived at Strasbourg hospital in 1814," as Foucault relates,

> he found a kind of human stable, which had been set up with great ingenuity. For the mad "who misbehaved or soiled themselves," there were two cages at either end of the room, which had just enough room for an average-sized man. The cages had a floor raised about six inches off the floor, covered with straw, "where the unfortunates lay down, naked or half-naked, to eat their food or relieve themselves."
>
> What is in place here is clearly a safety mechanism to guard against the violence of the insane in their moments of frenzy. Their raving is first seen as presenting a danger to society.[41]

As illustrated, Foucault's compassion toward the insane, the clinically caged, those fellow human beings institutionally individuated and controlled with such a counterhysterical need for collective distance, remains unquestionable. Yet the question remains as to why and how his own analytic apparatus itself seems epochally locked-in, theoretically overdetermined by a touch of its own paranoia and persecution anxiety. Whence and whither this passionate revolt against "the father of modern philosophy," the presumed philosophical big brother behind all such bureaucratic banalities and brutalities? Why does the movement of rationalism—the historical manifestations of it, for instance—have to be top-down, heavy handed, and only powerfully productive and productively exclusive of its perceived

"Other"? Or does it? Is there not something reductive, even vaguely incorrect, about the now almost fixed view of Cartesian rationalism and its methodologicotechnical apparatus as being *"reductive* and *compositional"*?[42] Are we not misreading or missing something important here? Is this a hasty bureaucratization of the Cartesian legacy itself?

The putative, compositional violence of the Cartesian "grid" remains a post-Cartesian fiction or prosthesis to which all the historical, political, technoscientific ills and evils of *"ego conquiro"* are often summarily or centrally attributed. Navigation, computation, and even vegetation or deforestation all seem to depend on it, on the very idea and acts of transposing a fuzzy gluey messy world into neat boxes and objects of field-coordinated representations. Yet have we forgotten that Descartes' divide-and-conquer method, such as the Cartesian coordinates and rules of "step-by-step" (R, 10:379–380/1:20–21, Rule 5) sequencing, is itself an invention, an ingenious directive as in the *Regulae ad Directionem Ingenii* (1633), which is itself a prosthetic mental construct? True, there is no denying, as Enrique Dussel has already shown clearly, that:

> Modern European philosophy, even before the *ego cogito* but certainly from then on, situated all men and cultures—and with them their women and children—within its own boundaries as manipulable tools, instruments. Ontology understood them as interpretable beings, as known ideas, as mediations or internal possibilities within the horizon of the comprehension of Being.
>
> Spatially central, the *ego cogito* constituted the periphery and asked itself, along with Fernández de Ovideo, "Are the Amerindians human beings?" that is, Are they Europeans, and therefore rational animals? The theoretical response was of little importance. We are still suffering from the practical response. The Amerindians were suited to forced labor; if not irrational, then at least they were brutish, wild, underdeveloped, uncultured—because they did not have the culture of the center.
>
> The ontology did not come from nowhere. It arose from a previous experience of domination over other persons, of cultural oppression over other worlds. Before the *ego cogito* there is an *ego conquiro:* "I conquer" is the practical

foundation of "I think." The center has imposed itself on the periphery for more than five centuries. But for how much longer? Will the geopolitical preponderance of the center come to an end?[43]

Rather, the more "practical" question today (and also arguably the more stimulating) seems to be: *how* will the geopolitical preponderance of the center come to an end? True, one must still focus, à la Foucault, on the fact that madness "was driven underground" and why and how that happened; one must still dwell, à la Dussel, on the fact that the Amerindians were located "on the periphery for more than five centuries" and why and how. In addition, however, we should now perhaps venture across, if not "outside," the Cartesian grid to rediscover how unreason, the voice of the mad and the marginalized, could then be dubbed over reason's act of silencing it. How?

RECOMPOSITION, NOT REDUCTION

An act of close rereading. My suggestion, broadly in this context, is that we start recomposing western European modernity, including and especially the clichéd figures such as the ruling elites of the Euro-Anglo center, which has already formed the archaeologico-historical bedrock of the global present. So here, more specifically, the question on which I prefer to confer with my readers is not why we must avoid repeating Cartesian violence and rationalist trappings. If structurally binarized and psychically inverted this way, we are likely to repeat what we intend to avoid. Rather, a better question to transfer seems to be, I am suggesting, how Cartesian meditation itself as a global historical trace of classical modernity and in particular the creatively destructive and destructively reconstructive spirit itself can be renewed, contemporized, and transformed. One way to approach afresh networks of post-Foucauldian, postcolonial issues of rationalist violence such as the critical concerns raised on the old "new dividing line" would be to practice something like an alternative theoretical anachronism, an excentric backtracking: a mad, alien, guerilla reading that disorientates the center through a constant, fertile reconfiguration and remapping of it.

In the remaining space of this chapter, I will trace Foucault's line of thinking on Descartes, "the new dividing line" as well as the primary line that has triggered Foucault's. In pursuing, in turn, a derivatively differential analysis of Descartes' moves, I aim to show not only how Foucault's Descartes and mine are different but also how, in some productively ironic ways, Foucault's Descartes, in its most rigorously coordinated form, helps one relocate and reevaluate the rationalist philosophy of Descartes: its new dimensions, depths, and possibly directions. I want to show that Descartes, read in light of Foucault's shockingly interesting and yet slightly hysterical historicization of him, is not that reductive; nor is his rationalism that violent. This is what a philosopher in me keeps telling me, and I am left wondering what other possible lines of reading this good old boy of modern philosophy or the "I" in him can offer and, in turn, deserve today.

Compelle intrare (iterum): *Foucault (and Descartes)*

The *History of Madness* as a whole analyzes archived evidence in Europe since the mid-seventeenth century of reason's growing and coordinated violence against those considered insane (*les insensés*). In this work of massive doctoral excavation submitted to the *École normale supérieure* and in a sense for the mad (including Foucault's classmate Jacques Martin, who was then suffering from fatally debilitating schizophrenia), Foucault offers, as we glimpsed earlier, a historically sensitive, minisurgical analysis of Descartes' seemingly casual mention in passing of mad people. Foucault saw it as deceptively inclusive and illustrative of the "advent (*l'avènement*) of a *ratio* in the western World"[44] that heralded "the Classical Age," which spanned the post-Renaissance mid-seventeenth century to the pre-Kantian eighteenth century and laid a technological groundwork for the systematically sustained exercise of reason during the subsequent "Age of Reason," the modern period.

That four-page section is subheaded as *"compelle intrare"*:[45] "compel them to come in," or "force heretics to come in." This caption brilliantly captures both the structural and the historical dimensions of Cartesian ambition, part of early modern European aspirations. Originally from Luke 14:23, this biblical slogan, popularized by St. Augustine and later remobilized jointly by the church and the parliament of England in 1662 after the restoration of the monarchy, sought to justify the otherwise coercive, politico-theological Act of Uniformity, also known as "the Great Ejection": All clergymen, including non-Episcopal ministers, who refused or failed to observe all the rites and ceremonies stipulated in the *Book of Common Prayer* (1549), the only book to be used, during their church services were summarily ejected. The state-sponsored religious conformity enforced this way remained effective until 1872 with the implementation of Act of Uniformity Amendment Act.

Zoom in on the elements of what Dussel calls "the practical response," from which "we are still suffering." The point to note is that this religious establishment, thus legally codified, barred all nonconformists from entering into spheres of influence, those intricate networks of academic, administrative, cultural, economic, genealogical, military, political, and theological power. Once "ejected," no clergyman could obtain a degree from the universities of Cambridge or Oxford, the twin gateways to the center of the Anglican universe. *Compelle intrare* therefore functioned at once as a promise and a threat in the game of a political life, as a lure of inclusion for some and a warning of exclusion for some others.

Replace the Church of England with early modern French rationalism often metonymized as "Cartesian"—that seems the analogical framework Foucault employs. With this structural and historical allusion in mind, let us then turn to his opening remark on Cartesian madness:

> After defusing its violence, the Renaissance had liberated the voice of Madness. The age of reason, in a strange takeover [*un étranger coup de force*], was then to reduce it to silence.
>
> On the methodical path of his doubt, Descartes came across madness beside dreams and all the other forms of error. Might the possibility of his own madness rob him of his own body, in the manner in which the outside world occasionally disappears through an error of the sense, or in which consciousness sleeps while we dream? . . .
>
> In the economy of doubt, there is a fundamental disequilibrium between madness on the one hand, and dreams and errors on the other. Their position is quite different where truth and the seeker of truth are concerned. Dreams and illusions are overcome by the very structure of truth, but madness is simply excluded by the doubting subject, in the same manner that it will soon be excluded that he is not thinking or that he does not exist. A specific decision has been taken. . . . [46]

In chapter 1 of the *History of Madness*, Foucault shows how the Renaissance period in some ways allowed those seemingly deranged to roam around or across the territories of regimented significations in the form, for instance, of purificatory exclusion such as "*Stultifera Navis*" (the Ship of Fools).[47] Also recall the fools, clowns, lunatics, village idiots, and queer ghosts in Shakespeare's plays, together with the centrally subversive roles they play in royal courts in intriguing proximity to the throne. In chapter 2, Foucault shows how those "threateningly" marginal, otherwise insignificant figures get imprisoned in turn "in a strange takeover" by a discursive "act of uniformity" during the Classical Age. Here, he is drawing a parallel, both historical and structural, between the theocratic, English "Act" of Uniformity in 1662 and the practical "decision" of Descartes' philosophy in 1641 which, he is suggesting, is more furtive and more forceful. Why?

This historical paradigm shift holds the key: the increasingly reductionist and hysterically intolerant attitudes toward not simply insanity or a lack of faith per se but specifically insane or spiritually deviant persons or behaviors. It is in that context of the formation of modern subjectivity, namely, personification, that Foucault picks out—or on?—Descartes. Foucault shifts the focus of analysis from the richly ambivalent gestures of the Renaissance culture to the more linear Cartesian "act" of incarceratory exclusion that, he is saying, is simultaneously targeted at and generative of the philosophical invalid. Foucault is circling and amplifying the resonances between the theocratic *compelle intrare* during the Restoration period (1660–1789), which calls into question any seemingly deviant forms of professions of faith, and the philosophic *compelle intrare* locatable in the ambivalently skeptical rationalist tradition modernized by the *Meditations on First Philosophy* (1641) and in particular the *First Meditation*, which calls into question what can and cannot be doubted. *Compelle intrare* is duplicitously violent or violently duplicitous. The operational duplicity of *compelle intrare* should be already clear enough and easy to understand: Outsiders are invited to be expelled. But what is violent about this seductive imperative?

Violence, symbolic or literal, occurs when the fold turns into a line, implicit or explicit. To begin with and to be fair: Cartesian rationalism *is* attracted to—although, yes, threatened by—the new, something "surprising" and "novel," for instance, that causes "wonder" (*l'admiration*), "the first of all the passions" (Ps, 11:373/1:350, Article 53: Wonder). Wondrous thoughts bursting, breaking out of the boundaries of the intelligible and yet to be coordinated, yet to be clarified and distinguished would be not unlike the

Platonic "divine madness" at work (which is a topic to be covered in the next chapter on dream). Here, the Foucauldian thread of reading Descartes that we are trying to discern justly is in line with the fact that, indeed, for Descartes anything, any idea, any event, any firework "may happen before we know *whether or not* the object is beneficial [*convenable*] to us" (Ps, 11:373/1:350, emphasis added). We need to set it aside for a while, but we will shortly return to this equally obvious point that such Cartesian wonder "*may happen before* [*peut arriver avant*] we know whether or not the object is beneficial to us" (Ps, 11:373/1:350, emphasis added). For now, as promised, let us focus again on hearing Foucault, a post-Kantian Foucault, who has something equally important to say about the dialectic of the new and the old, itself sustained by its implicit teleological setup, its language of choice and control, inclusion and exclusion, as illustrated by that categorical division and judgment "whether or not beneficial." The point to note is loud and clear: Receptive to the new or not to, reason always wins because it sets the bar, even if it happens to be a new bar.

> Unreason in the sixteenth century was a sort of open risk, the threat of which could always compromise the relation between subjectivity and truth. [*La Non-raison du XVIe siècle formait une sort de péril ouvert dont les menaces pouvaient toujours, en droit au moins, compromettre les rapports de la subjectivité et de la vérité.*] The path taken by Cartesian doubt seems to indicate that by the seventeenth century the danger has been excluded, and that madness is no longer a peril lurking in the domain where the thinking subject holds rights over truth: and for classical thought, that domain is the domain of reason itself. Madness has been banished. While *man* can still go mad, *thought*, as the sovereign exercise carried out by a subject seeking truth, can no longer be devoid of reason. A new dividing line has appeared, rendering that experience so familiar to the Renaissance—unreasonable Reason, or reasoned Unreason—impossible.[48]

The "first" or primary thought in action becomes last and final, when a movement toward infinity turns finite, folding back upon itself constantly, serially, as if in immediate need of reflexive security. There is something dangerously new and something safely new, and reflexive reason sorts them out instantly. This way, the call to *compelle intrare* comes to mimic the "violence of the alien-insane in their moments of frenzy" formally and firmly, as hinted earlier. A *cogito* at work needs to keep its other, the object of its *dubito*, as closely and extensively as possible. Interesting to note in this regard is that indeed Descartes, playing the role of the methodological paranoid, advises us "never to trust completely those whose have deceived even once" (M, 7:18/2:12). If that character ran out of untrustworthy folks, he would have to invent one so that the location of trust could be seen. This way, the transgressive moment and movement of madness become vitally violent: The possibility of violation becomes the virtual foundation of actualized ratios.

Such a transitory shadow of the Cartesian light of reason at work is found in what Foucault calls a "region/zone [*région*] of exclusion."[49] This zone, arising and materializing in various ways, be it the Great Hospital of Paris, the campuses of Oxbridge, Dussel's First World of Colonial Power, or a page from Descartes, is where one could sense if not exactly locate the exceptional forces and counterforces of Cartesian delirium that have been employed and dismissed at once, duplicitously and violently. Delirium, as in *délire, de-lira*, out of or going off the furrow or track—that is, deriving from a path or the right path—was explained by James Robert in *A Medical Dictionary, including Physics, Surgery, Anatomy, Chymstery and Botany, and all their Branches relative to Medicine*, volume 2 (1745) in an entry that was cited by Foucault:

> 3. *Understood in this fashion, discourse covers the entire spectrum of madness.* Madness, in the classical sense, does not designate a certain change in the mind or the body, but the existence of a *delirious discourse* that underlies the alterations of the body and the strangeness in behavior and speech. Thus the simplest and most general definition that can be given for madness is delirium itself: "*Delirium*—from *Deliro*, to rave, to talk idly; which is derived from *Lira*, a ridge or Furrow of Land. Here *Deliro* property imparts, to deviate from the Right, that is, right Reason."[50]

Delirium becomes the prime example of madness during the Classical Age mainly because of its deviational tendencies fearfully circled as such, then almost equivalent to "the necessary and sufficient condition for an illness to be considered as madness."[51]

Let me now summarize the Foucauldian account of the Cartesian delirium before setting out to recast it from a neo-Cartesian viewpoint. It is a quasi-Freudian narrative of the ghostly return of the repressed: The delirious are (1) repressively ruled and ruled out by Descartes, who counts and counts on only those seemingly or allegedly able to tell reality from illusion; yet (2) they return in the form and figure of a nearly total threat, both epistemological and moral, such as the evil genius.[52]

On the one hand, the delirious, as Foucault's story goes, have been summarily evicted from the house or community of thinkers by Descartes' literal and symbolic (i.e., enunciatively strategic) "evasion"[53] of them. They are jettisoned not simply in the course of but by the very voyage of modern reason thus economized. Foucault sees in such a discursive standardization of the subject and the world of the *cogito* not just "an intellectual strategy"[54] but more significantly a modern historical and political event. Descartes' exclusion of the mad from the projected group of rational subjects amounts to "an act of force": "a strange takeover" [*un étranger coup de force*][55] by the *cogito* that pushes outside the field of its activity the mentally invalid, *amens* or *demens* specifically, not simply *insanus*.[56] Such a preemptive "disqualification"[57] of the seemingly deranged and the "*delirious discourse*" itself "that underlies the alterations of the body and the strangeness in behavior and speech"[58] enables that exclusive action of reason that materialized in juridico-medico-political actions such as the Great Confinement. Thus, again, as we saw earlier, "I" alone "remain qualified to think; and so I make my resolution."[59]

On the other hand, in the second phase of the story, the reasonable too, including the figure of ultimate self-authentication, the sovereign of classical reason, becomes subject to control. He remains spatially and temporally circumscribed—by his own discourse of truth, by his own understanding of how to access the truth out there that lies distantly; historically, transcendentally, divinely, and so on. This way, the subject in power becomes controlling and controlled at once. What separates the delirious and the reasonable is wafer thin, almost irrelevant to the intellect itself: If the first is "in" madness, the second is in "the distance" of madness. "It will be said not that we were *distant from* madness, but that we were in *the distance of* madness. In the same way that the Greeks were not distant from hubris because they condemned it, but rather were in the distancing of that excess, in the midst of the distance at which they kept it confined."[60] Likewise, "'This man is mad' is neither a simple nor an immediate act."[61] It, the enunciation in particular, is "tactics of separation," as noted in *Maladie mentale et personnalité* (1954), a skeletal prolegomena to the *History of Madness*. Those "qualified to think," in the Cartesian sense as characterized by Foucault, are those capable of reflective self-distancing like yo-yo players, Freudian or not, mini or mega: self-spacing and self-temporalizing. They are those able to draw "a new line" in relation to themselves.

What haunts the Cartesian subject then, including the post-Cartesian subject such as the reflective theorist in Foucault, is not delirium per se. Or rather that is only half the story. What is haunting is more precisely the very idea of differential exaction, the inviolable already inscribed in *delirum*, in the modern form of the *logos* grid, which becomes in actuality active and elastic like the ancient Greek chiasm (χ, Greek *chi*) on which Merleau-Ponty (scene 2) also relies for a phenomenological figuration of what happens when thinking happens. Here, we see, as we do in the Freudian topography or fort-da of the mind, a double *U*-turn or twin-turn of reason and unreason: the deeper the roots of a tree, the higher its branches. Such, as we will see later in the chapter on God, is also the unnerving proximity between God and the evil genius, sustained only by the tautological line of moral self-evidence.

How else, richly, can we understand this otherwise mobile, narrative law of symmetry or the binary economy of reflection? Note further the link between *lira* as money and *libra* the book. Such elements of accountability, fluctuating economy, and bookkeeping, moral or psychological, motivate Foucault's ethical, aesthetical, and psychopolitical exposition and deployment of figures of delirium. That is, the delirious are for Foucault *the* negative exemplar, highly abnormal with respect to and immediately abjected from the "normal" "rational" world that exploits—produces, uses, and rejects—deviant figures of its own making in order to sustain its economy of representation, materially or ideationally. It rings true. But again, if that cannot be the whole picture and story of Cartesian rationality, as I have been seeking to demonstrate so far, how else could or would the delirious enter or reenter the Cartesian web of being?—if they cannot just be the shadows and underdogs of modern ontology and epistemology, that is.

Let us look again:

[Paragraph 4] Again, how could it be denied that these hands or this whole body do not belong to me? Unless perhaps I were to liken myself to madmen [*insani*], whose brains are so damaged by the persistent vapors of melancholia that they firmly maintain they are kings when they are paupers, or say they are dressed in purple when they are naked, or that their heads are made of earthenware, or that they are pumpkins, or made of glass. But such people are insane [*sed amentes sunt isti*], and I would be thought no less extravagant [*demens*], if I took anything from them as a model for myself. (M, 7:19/2:13, trans. modified)

And then? Descartes breaks off.

[Paragraph 5] Brilliantly reasoned indeed [*praeclare sane*], as if [*tanquam*] I were not a man who sleeps at night and often has all the same experiences while asleep as madmen do when awake—indeed sometimes even more improbable ones. (M, 7:19/2:13, trans. modified)

Indeed, "this" world becoming "unmoored"[62] this way, the "black hole"[63] of Cartesian cogitation begins to affect the skeptic. As a result, as Descartes had to say at the end of that paragraph:

I begin to feel astounded [*obstupescam, tout étonne*], and this very feeling of stupor [*stupor, mon étonnement*] itself only reinforces the notion that I may be asleep. (M, 7:19/2:13, trans. modified)

And then? Descartes breaks off again.

[Paragraph 6] Suppose then that I am dreaming and that these particulars. . . . (M, 7:19/2:13, trans. modified)

Placed this way, the fourth paragraph where the madman makes a brief appearance does become pivotal, although for a series of reasons slightly and significantly different from the set Foucault has articulated, which now seem relatively weak or insufficient, although closely relevant.

To recall, Foucault's reading of Descartes in the *History of Madness* and "My Body, This Paper, This Fire" is ultimately focused on the moment and movement of interiority, of the *cogito*'s normativized, compulsive folding back. He sees repression and exclusion in that seductive imperative "*compelle intrare.*" Yet we now also find those psychical, mental, and narrative breakoffs liberating and open-ended, do we not? Well, I do . . . Do not those points of contingent exteriority, at least two by my count above, deserve some especially temporal attention? Quite literally, the scope of

Foucault's analysis is either extremely immanent or extremely contextual, which perfectly and to a significant extent rightly serves the purpose of his own narrative. He does not consider the neighboring paragraphs in the *First Meditation* at all or closely enough while building his insightful reading of the fourth paragraph into the historicized narrative on why and how reason exercises violence on its other, madness.

Fault finding is not the task I've assigned myself, however. Quite the contrary: Foucault's sharp framework of analysis has enabled me to locate my own framework, and from his scrupulous attention to the unthought, I have learned ways to follow and produce alternative lines and discourses of reading. In fact, Foucault, the philosophical friend of madness par excellence, would and should be the first one readily and richly aware of the enduring "enigma of that Exteriority"[64] of threshold experiences, which is not the same as limit knowledge or boundary consciousness. Here is how the first appendix of the *History of Madness* marks out that sense, that extra sense, which enigmatically, as we recall, Foucault himself reduced to none just when Descartes was at stake:

> One day, perhaps, we will no longer know what madness was. Its form will have closed up on itself, and the traces it will have left will no longer be intelligible. To the ignorant glance, will those traces be anything more than simple black marks? At most, they will be part of those configurations that we are now unable to form, but which will be indispensable grids that will make our culture and ourselves legible to the future.[65]

Grids remain, although remaining transformable culturally and epochally, and I sense at least three lines.

THE FIRST BREAK

The first break is at the gap between the fifth paragraph and the sixth, where Descartes shifts from "feeling asleep" to "suppose then that I am dreaming." This is the very first point in the whole series of the *Meditations* at which the formal-analytical movement of "supposition" occurs. That is, the linear, coordinated "march" of hypothesis is about to take place: Methodological reason per se has not yet been represented in this minitheater of philosophical representation. Up to that point, the Cartesian "I" has been experiencing and risking the very real and empirical possibility of itself becoming or already being mad. What we see is something akin to a gambler in action or an artist at work: playing, free associating, risking, escalating, radicalizing, hyperbolically totalizing.

Such a skeptical sliding or insomniac hankering after the infinite is repeated or repeatable but not in a way that it becomes simply part of controlled experiments, a function of completely precoordinated design, as Foucault insists. *Au contraire*, as Derrida writes:

> Descartes, in his reflections [*la réflexion*] on the *cogito*, becomes aware that the infinity not only cannot be constituted as a (dubitable) object, but has *already* made infinity *possible* as a *cogito* overflowing the object.[66]

The Cartesian infinite as focally embodied and temporally compressed in the act of *cogito* remains beyond control as well as subject to control, to use a Foucauldian idiom; and such a phenomenological force of the infinite, an excessive flow or a flow of the given, has already been rehearsed at the very start of the *Meditations* as we will see later when discussing the third, "big" break.

THE SECOND BREAK

The second break is at the gap between the fourth paragraph and the fifth. There, Descartes moves on quickly, almost jumping off, seemingly abandoning the question that has yet to be resolved by himself: Is the "I" above *self*-identified as mad? Does Descartes at that point think that he himself is or could be mad? The answer is literally unavailable. The madmen—many a mad man in all diversity and multiplicity—have been suspended there: introduced *and* left behind, outside or inside the text. Descartes neither negates nor affirms his own lunacy candidacy, whether he is or sees himself among those seen as sanity deficient. The end of this paragraph says nothing more or else. Nor does the *alter ego* in this self-dialogue say anything, for the madman Descartes talks to or about or with does not talk back. How should we understand that silence, this provocative lacuna, this editorial cut? Indeed, as Foucault notes, "after all Descartes speaks so little, and so quickly, about madness."[67]

Then what about this move, this self-referential comment: "What a brilliant piece of reasoning!" (*praeclare sane*)? How could one read it? Or should it be read? What exactly is "brilliant" about that piece of reasoning on and

with madmen? Who is saying it—to whom, in whose voice, is this procla-
mation addressed? Again, Descartes does not explain the reason where it is
due. This is the other side of the second break, to which, as far as I am aware,
Descartes scholars have not yet paid significant attention, and Foucault is
not an exception.

This passing observation from Carriero on this exalted passage as a
"suggestive sketch" is instructive:

> This is meant to repudiate the thought that there is no way for the meditator
> to do what Descartes wants her to do—question her senses fundamentally—
> without supposing she is mad: for she can suppose that she is dreaming.
> Although doing so gives her another way to suppose that her senses do not
> provide her with any cognitive access to reality, Descartes clearly expects the
> meditator to continue to find what he is asking her to do odd or peculiar
> (e.g., he will soon ask her to seriously suppose that she does not even have a
> body). . . .
>
> There is, then, as was to be expected, a certain amount of drama in the
> run-up to the dreaming doubt. The drama continues through the presentation
> of the doubt itself. . . . Although this passage is usually taken to provide a
> skeptical argument, it must be admitted, I think, that what we get is more in
> the line of a suggestive sketch than a worked-out argument. Faced with the
> absence of an explicitly laid out argument in the text, commentators have
> needed to rely on their own resources (and other of Descartes' texts) in order
> to tease out an argument.[68]

Is this "sketchy" move just "teasing," however? That would be to underesti-
mate the inner force of the skeptical argument or drama. The *cogito* that
spills and leaks, that passingly "overflows" before and after methodological
overthinking takes over, does not show itself in the "composed and reductive" enunciation and contention of the "*cogito, sum.*" It remains interstitially fluid and shaped by its own direction. "*Cogito, sum,*" reached and
confirmed, becomes part of a stacked, multilayered memory, the recyclable
evidence of efforts in the past, but it is glued by a certain enthusiasm that is
not yet or no longer the same as certainty but closer to that "wondrous"
state. That is to say, the overflowing *cogito* does not claim. Rather it ex-
claims, although almost unnoticeably. Touched, slightly pushed, by a
language that is excentric and radically "idiotic" in the sense of being automatically idiomatic, the premature *cogito* that is nonetheless a *cogito*

presents itself through an exclamation that is intransitive, primary, literal, tonal, physical, and mental . . . a touch of madness indeed.

Curiously, the first French translation in 1647 by Due de Luynes, which was closely examined and entirely approved by Descartes himself and is still widely used as the standard edition, skips over that, turning it into a turn of reflection itself: "*toutefois*" (yet). The text starts with that, just that: "*Toutefois j'ai ici à considérer que je suis homme.*" Descartes himself has formalized it, this second time around; perhaps he just forgot what "it" was or felt like initially.

Whatever the case, this gap is telling. Foucault, too, simply bypasses this sudden break, this difference, this minisurge of power, which is, however, subtly powerful, if not straightforwardly forceful as in "the act of force." Still, it is a pause worth looking into:

> Has it never happened, as you were reading a book, that you kept stopping as you read, not because you weren't interested, but because you were: because of a flow of ideas, stimuli, associations? In a word, haven't you ever happened to *read while looking up from your book?*
>
> It is such reading, at once insolent in that it interrupts the text, and smitten in that it keeps returning to it and feeding on it, which I tried to describe.[69]

This phenomenological event of "looking *up*" would be an electrically charged, autocreative pause resonating with the "Aha!" moment, which could be entirely mute, muted, or even forgotten, only to be restaged and remembered in different forms—through syncopated repetitions.

The significance of the *cogito* that overflows its own grid at every turn is inexhaustible. Every time it takes place, it moves the soul. In that sense, it is more and less than "*conquiro.*" As a mental leak or lack, it instantiates itself through a sonic surge, a squeak, rather than syntactical enunciations or formulations. Inaudible to *res cogitans*, the squeak of a *cogito* is temporally archaeological and to that extent environmentally oriented and intersubjectively significant. It is extra meaningful. The squeaky moment of cogitation, in sync with that interrupted, three-dimensional moment of "reading while looking up from the book," springs from "a semiotic space, a three-dimensional (potentially n-dimensional) system in which there is a purely symbolic mode of being between these two interfaces,"[70] between, for instance, the madman and the philosopher, both multidimensionally embodied by Descartes at work. Between the two, there is a perspectival pause that is more connective than reductive, more elastic than eliminative.

The thinker at such transitory stages is not unlike Nigel in the presence of the mother, a five-month-old child who squeaks in the face of the pigeons that start to scatter around, who thereby interfaces with beings around him, including the mother to whom the squeak appears to be addressed. The reporter of this scene is systematic linguist M. A. K. Halliday, whose articulation of intrastratal or interfacial semiosis vividly captures the "elastic space"[71] and seriality of proto-Cartesian reflection as well. Inspired by Nigel's pigeon-induced duh, duh, duh, "v.h.p.s. (very high-pitched squeak),"[72] Halliday writes:

> What is construed in this way, by this total semogenic process, is an elastic space defined by the two dimensions given above: the "inner" dimension of reflective/active, "I think" as against "I want," and the "outer" dimension of intersubjective/objective, "you and me" as against "he, she, it" (Again, there is a naming problem here; we could say that the "out there" dimension is that of person/object, provided we remember that "object" includes those persons "treated as" object, i.e., third persons. Instantially, this means any person other than whoever is the interlocutor at the time; systematically it means any person not forming part of the subject's (the child's) meaning group.)[73]

"Those persons out there," *systematically* outside the "meaning group" and yet *instantially* in the shifting zones of "microfunctional meanings,"[74] are Descartes' madmen whom Descartes marks with a "v.h.p.s." By contrast, Foucault the historian of systems of thought focuses too restrictively on "that system": how those people "out there" are systematically edited out by being rendered meaningless or useless. Aside from the fact that his system of thought on discursive rationalism skipped or smoothed over that squeaky passage in question, as pointed out earlier, the fact remains that he did so despite his intellectual orientation toward precisely such "acute, sharp" (*aigu*) and sharply trembling moments of tension and separation between reason and unreason:

> When the time came to deliver the mad and free them from their shackles, it was not an indicator that the old prejudices had been done away with; it simply meant that eyes were suddenly closed for a "psychological sleep" [*sommeil psychologique*], and that the watch that had long been kept over unreason was

slowly abandoned. Classical rationalism can be thought of as being more sharply [*le plus aigu*] linked to that watch.[75]

What would Foucault do with this line: "brilliantly reasoned indeed [*praeclare sane*], as if I were not a man who sleeps at night"? He might say that Descartes' evocation of a strange man who does not sleep confirms yet again the exclusionary impulse of classical rationalism; there, sleeplessness is being rendered abnormal as an extension of madness, while vigilance, metaphorically again, is glorified. He might conclude again that the gesture of sharper exclusion is finalized through the geometrical incorporation and representation of the insomniac lunatic.

Our hypothetical Foucault would repeat those "old prejudices" against classical rationalism. But note what Descartes says after that passage, after he "began to feel astounded" and to suspect he may be indeed asleep. From there, we see that he has trouble sleeping at night because of this massive anxiety attack that turned into "an arduous task," from which he wishes to escape (M, 7:23/2:15). Why can we not allow Descartes to become more interesting, more organic, more environmentally-friendly? Why can we not read Descartes as a living text and not just as an anthropomorphized symbol of an oppressive cliché, the institutional ghost of "French philosophy," wherever it is now?

The *Meditations* are a theatrical setup indeed, and yet in this supposed six-day diary crafted over six years, a strangely fluid, mysterious incision was made, too, which is more private and less loud than an axiomatic proposition. Is it not about time that we let go of the Nietzschean-Heideggerian prejudices against modern rationalism? The fact that the *Meditations* were tightly composed for effects of narrative immediacy, vivacity, and accuracy does not invalidate the other fact that it enacts and even poeticizes the temporal singularity if not the living presence of the *cogito*, the *cogito* taken as a sustained proto-phenomenological event or even scandal. The force field of Cartesian madness is an elastic site of cogitation that concretizes itself freely with irreducible rhetorical figures and figural forces in place, which needs registering and remembering on the part of the reader, including a rereader. For, again, arguably nowhere else in the *Meditations* does one see such a vital sign of unbridled, if only slightly ironized, enthusiasm. Curb your enthusiasm, says one Cartesian narrator, while the other narrator does the opposite.

THE THIRD BREAK

So the third and "big" break, as hinted earlier, is something like an epistemological big bang. I am exaggerating here a little, but a sense of loss of
control does frame the whole of the *First Meditation*. The loss of a grip on
reality is the communicative frame of this philosophical diary. How that
affects the whole of the *Meditations* as a reactively virile quest for objective
reality transcendentally buttressed by God is a separate and much larger
issue, which I can only touch but not (even begin to try to) contain in this
book. Here, suffice it to illustrate the rather moody, affectively charged
beginning of the proto-Cartesian Cartesian text.

Tear and fear: From the start of the *Meditations*, those two affective elements seem to have gone missing. Something happened before this composition, something sensational that tore apart young René's seemingly fully
formed subjectivity. Recall that setting: a winter's night in the traveler's
lodge, in the stove-heated room (*pole*, oven-room) where the *Meditations*
reportedly took place, "a Dutch stove, . . . a sort of chimerical home, in a
corner of a boat," where a child would suddenly discover that "she is *herself*,
in an explosion toward the outside."[76] Indeed, "Descartes," too, as the story
goes and is told many times, "arrived at the minimal, fundamental truth of
his existence curled up by himself in soliloquy in the corner of a warm
room."[77] What is that threat from which he recoils like a baked prawn?
What is it that caused him to wrap himself up with the trappings of philosophical introspection? No, a shock:

> [Paragraph 1] Some years ago, I was *struck [animadverti, suis aperçu]* by the
> large number of falsehoods that I had accepted as true in my childhood and by
> the highly doubtful nature of the whole edifice that I had subsequently based
> on them. I realize that it was necessary, once in the course of my life, to
> demolish everything completely and start again right from the foundations if
> I wanted to establish anything at all in the sciences that was stable and likely
> to last. But the task looked an enormous one, and I began to wait until . . .
> (M, 7:17/2:12, emphasis added)

"Struck" is an overtranslation but a faithful overreading. What it brings
out most "acutely" as Foucault would have seen is the virginal sense of surprise and danger, of stupefaction, impregnated in the host text yet easily

missed by a mere "notice," a merely correct translation of *"animadverto"* or *"s'aperceivor que."* John Carriero also rightly pays attention to this word *"animadverto"* (turn my soul toward) as it appears later in the text (M, 7:29/2:19), marking it as "especially momentous."[78] What I will add to that is simply this point: The turn has in some significant sense has already taken place *before* the beginning. That is, Descartes begins to "wonder"—he wonders how to get to "know" the world all over again. Such a striking force of "the new that arrives" reappears as if in vengeance: Dumbstruck, Descartes decides to demolish everything for a change. "Through revenge, Descartes engineers a series of startling reversals."[79] Meditation is an affective event first.

Such jazzy turns of thought, which shape the internal structure and rhythm of the *Meditations* as a whole, are vividly anticipated in the very first round of thinking, the five opening paragraphs of the *First Meditation*. To recall those, in summary:

1. The inaugural experience of dislocation
2–3. A recuperative will
4. The first attempt at restoring equilibrium against sensations of becoming mad
5. The sustained/reinforced disequilibrium and suspicion

The first round (paragraphs 1 through 4) of the *First Meditation* is framed by colossal stupidity, beginning with the "I" *made* stupid, ending with the "I" *feeling* stupid. Similarly, the fictional dreamer (paragraph 5 onward) becomes awakened in a twofold manner: If what causes him to *become* alert is the transgressive force of otherworldly thoughts, what makes him *stay* alert is the reflexive recognition of that force. If the first kind is encounter, the second is recognition: "the interruption of mad-becoming,"[80] as Deleuze puts it, noting a curiously discursive, self-stabilizing function of the Platonic moment of recognition, of which one modern example is Cartesian self-reflexivity. In contrast to a mere "encounter" (*rencontre*), "recognition . . . measures and limits the quality (of contrary perceptions) by relating it to something, thereby interrupting the mad-becoming" (*arrête le devenire-fou*). As Deleuze goes onto to observe further, an affinity, both conceptual and psychic, seems to exist between Platonic recognition and Cartesian reflexivity that "interrupts" and thereby secures itself from the

possibility of "becoming," if not being, "mad." Now with the sleep sequence kept at bay, let us focus again, and one last time, on the madness
followed by stupidity.

Look at that originary stupefaction or stupor, the original "*stultitia*"
(foolishness, silliness) of the cognitive subject: the hiccup, syncopated moment, of cogitation. Two missing links put together frame the first round
of thinking: [*Gap$_1$*] the moment of striking remaining invisible, accessed
through rippled memories of the panic attack; then, the silence of madness,
the subtle evasion of "I would be thought no less extravagant if . . . [*Gap$_2$*]
But as if I were not a man who sleeps at night. . . ." The first syncopation:
merely struck, the "I" of "I think" remains oblivious of the stone that first
hit him, the event; he remains "ontically" secured in his own offended consciousness. The whole of the *Meditations*, seen from the stone's point of
view, is a map of affects, drawn by recollection, traced by the textual representation of affected consciousness. But the map remains incomplete, for
the second syncopation follows: the meditator's disjunctive silence about
madness, both literal and allegorical. The virtual departure, in the text, of
the *Stultifera Navis* is strangely elusive. Literally it is forgotten, yet alle-
gorically it is resonant. The first syncopation is a blow to the dormant
mind, and the second is the blow of a whistle.

The terror of error persists throughout, initially softened by memory,
further stultified by irony. "I would be thought no less extravagant than the
madmen" is *not* the same as "I am not mad," but it is, more strangely, open to
the interpretation "so I am mad." Such is Cartesian irony. Such an instantaneous occurrence of or suspension of the third between two incompatible
meanings resists being localized in any systems of sense and nonsense—
except in the very "curved"[81] "swelling"[82] of the *cogito*, of the *cogito* dreamed
up and acted out each time in various "secret movements of our own."[83]
Such forces and implications of Descartes' self-subversive gestures are far
reaching, as Janet Broughton observes in a suitably convoluted manner: "If
I am right in thinking that Descartes' meditator does *not* find it ridiculous to
say these (otherworldly) scenarios are unlikely to be correct, then it is ironic
that Descartes' own work in philosophy should have contributed so significantly—as I am sure it did—to the development of our contemporary con-
victions to the contrary."[84] The self-same intellect not only falsifies but
fortifies, an origin of a certain compulsive-obsessive study disorder:

Studium: it goes back to a st- or sp- root indicating a crash, the shock of impact. Studying and stupefying are in this sense akin: those who study are in the situation of people who have received a shock and are stupefied by what has struck them, unable to grasp it and at the same time powerless to leave hold. The scholar, that is, is always "stupid." But if on the one hand he is astonished and absorbed, if study is thus essentially a suffering and an undergoing, the messianic legacy it contains drives him, on the other hand, incessantly towards closure. This *festina lente*, this shuttling between bewilderment and lucidity, discovery and loss, between agent and patient, is the rhythm of study.[85]

Thus, what is "laughable" after all—after all this philosophical show of schizoparanoia, the very "rhythm of study," the Cartesian style—is exactly that: terrorized reason. So goes the very last paragraph of the *Sixth Meditation:*

> I should not have any further fears about the falsity of what my senses tell me every day; on the contrary, the exaggerated doubts of the last few days should be dismissed as laughable. This applies especially to the principal reason for doubt, namely my inability to distinguish between being asleep and being awake. (M, 7:89/2:61)

Relevantly Untimely: Without Any Doubt

Descartes is joking—or is he?

CAN THE PHILOSOPHER LAUGH?

At the end, the philosopher laughs it all off, the terror of error. The philosopher caught up in some self-referential chuckle does seem close to the madman. Or perhaps the philosopher is just that: the madman becoming less edgy, semi-watchful. Yet to sing and swing once again,[86] (s)he is half carried over, half lost, into the world of dreams, just about to fall into a world where the overstretched, "heightened [*exaspérée*] sensibility is compensated for by zones of insensibility, similar to sleep"[87] . . . as we will see shortly in the next chapter on Cartesian dream, a Cartesian fall, a dormant fall.

THE FUGITIVELY MAD, BRIDGING BETWEEN POSSIBILITIES

The madman, a figurative bridge between the localized possibility of de-lirium and the possibility of globalized delirium, is prominently missing from the last page of this timeless masterpiece of the mid-seventeenth century French philosopher of, as I have been highlighting, intertextual subjectivity. That is because madness is always already something at work in the background, if not something that works, madness being, as Foucault reminds us, "the absence of work." The inchoate touch of madness held in view so far, of "de-lirium" in particular, is a kind of multidisciplinary, mul-tisensorial buffer zone of sentient life where everything actually happens and is already happening. Onto-phenomenological access to the inchoate porosity of *stultitia* seems, however, an ever unthinkable possibility for the reflective subject, for *res cogitans* can only laugh about *it*, as if it existed or did not; as if the being and nonbeing of *res cogitans* were an issue for itself and in itself, to borrow a Heideggerian-Sartrean formula. The "I" who thinks is, in all its phenomenological richness and indeed madness, always already affected by the ticklish fluidity and elasticity of interbeings, with which it is intricately networked. Such a derivative or deviational, and often hilarious, porosity of interfacial experiences and languages seems to be a key feature of a tree of life conceived not so much dialectically or inversely but, à la Deleuze, rhizomatically: Is it not what sustains the embodied mind?

DESCARTES *IS* UNTIMELY

"Philosophy need not be afraid of being out-of-date"[88] or out of place. The case of "mad" Descartes we have reviewed is an embodiment of intellectual freedom sustained by the "*invented*"[89] methods and strategic antiauthori-tarianism, who is still alive and well, whenever and wherever he was or is to be born. Such is my conclusive thought at this point. As Vincent Carraud writes:

> Cartesianism was not born one night in November 1619 out of three founding dreams. Like all the ism-ending words, it is real only from a pedagogical and polemical point of view. As a matter of fact, we must understand the whole movement of the ideas circulating in this complex half of the European

seventeenth century. Relevance of Cartesianism? I do not know. Perhaps Descartes' philosophy is more interesting through the *breakings-up, the contradictions, the aporias* it originated in Cartesian's Cartesianism. But is Descartes' philosophy relevant as the first-rate place for such philosophical work? Without any doubt.[90]

Philosophy, as with Plato on Socrates, chronicles its own untimeliness. Philosophy performs its own belated futurality to which, tragicomically enough, it remains blind. Descartes, with his transformative suspension of time, inseparable from but irreducible to the history of the Euro-American *conquiro*, is a prime example, as Foucault saw with a chilling insight, if only otherwise.

Instead of repressing, let's make use of the connection b/w awake/asleep (handwritten marginalia)

Philopoetic Somnambulism: An Imaginary Freedom

Brilliantly reasoned indeed! As if I were not a man who sleeps at night, and regularly has all the same experiences while asleep as madmen do when awake—indeed sometimes even more improbable ones. How often, asleep at night, am I convinced of just such familiar events—that I am here in my dressing-gown, sitting by the fire—when in fact I am lying undressed in bed! . . . Indeed! As if I did not remember other occasions when I have been tricked by exactly similar thoughts while asleep! As I think about this more carefully, I see plainly that there are never any sure signs by means of which being awake can be distinguished from being asleep. The result is that I begin to feel dazed [*obstupescam*], and this very feeling of stupor [*stupor*] only reinforces the notion that I may be asleep. (M, 7:19/2:13, trans. modified)

I am like a prisoner who is enjoying an imaginary freedom while asleep; as he begins to suspect that he is asleep, he dreads being woken up, and goes along with the pleasant illusion as long as he can. (M, 7:23/2:15)

The Threefold Dream of Descartes: Private, Theoretical, and Theological

An insatiable appetite for life: With this, we might understand, at least in part, why one dreams.

DREAM APLENTY

By "dream," I mean both the projective kind, futural, as in "my dream is to become an American Idol," and the retrospective kind, nocturnal, as in "I was a Kafka in my dream last night." Either way, the dreamer can imagine, think, otherwise. For dream is an excess and a necessary excess that shapes desire. It knows neither bounds nor depths. Fulfilled, it immediately generates a higher level of *telos* from within (e.g., Now I should become a Global

Idol); interpreted, it leads the dreamer into a deeper level of ignorance
(e.g., How come my lovely father is also a patriarchal oppressor?).

A life devoid of dreams is a life deprived of a hunger for Being, in the
same way that dreamless sleep is a temporary death in life. There is indeed
a twin-brotherly resemblance between *Somnos* (aka *Hypnos*), the god of
sleep, and *Thanatos*, the god of death born of *Nyx*, the goddess of the night.
Sleep, as we learn from the ancient Greeks, is a minisimulation of death,
and death is an eternal slumber, "the awareness by each person of a *Destiny*
in which his own personality was not annihilated but *put to sleep—requies,
dormitio.*"[1] One can desire to die, but there is no desire after death. That
also partly explains why *Somnos*, not *Thanatos*, had to be the father of *Mor-
pheus*, the god of dreams. Life, taken as a given excess, as a given trouble, is
a hunger for something, and this hunger remains irreducible as long as there
are things to consume, to live on and for. With Ernst Bloch, let us call this
"taste of something more" dreaming, the "beginning of something other
than the desire to dress up":

> The lack of what we dream about hurts not less, but more. It thus prevents us
> from getting used to deprivation. . . . Just a short breathing-space, this never
> sufficed for long. Above all, dreaming always outlived the brief and private day.
> So this is the beginning of something other than the desire to dress up, to see
> ourselves as our masters wish to see us. . . . It will aim at something more, and
> everything that it attains tastes of this something more. So that it seeks to live
> not merely beyond its own means, but beyond the poorly available means of
> conditions as a whole. Longing holds strong and true, especially when it is
> deceived, even when it is racing aimlessly now in one direction, now in another.
> All the more or so, when the path leads unerringly and caringly forwards.[2]

Dream is an insatiable appetite for life. The Bachelardian proposition, "the
beginning of life is the beginning of a dream"[3] can be understood in this
vein as well. Dream inaugurates one's life, one's thinking life: It is a push, a
life force behind life. Is life, then, a series of chosen dreams? Are we, mortal
dreamers, all eternal sleepwalkers led forward "unerringly and caringly"?

The philosophical life of Descartes is an archetypal example. For him,
the beginning of a new philosophy meant the beginning of a new life, a
new dream. Neither trivialized nor excluded, his dreams are recognized,
reregistered, and reinscribed. As Jean-Luc Marion writes:

Descartes is unique not because he experiences dreams—divinatory or otherwise—but because he *perceived* them, at first, as perfectly insignificant. Yet the dreams are interpreted, and as a result Descartes gains a decisive self-assurance. Why then claim that the dreams were insignificant? In fact, this is not a paradox. The dreams in themselves do not reveal anything. They eventually *become* meaningful through the intervention of Descartes himself, thinking lucidly and soberly, rather than through their own self-evidence or the role of the authoritative hermeneut. The significance is found not in the dreams themselves (nor in the divinatory framework for their eventual interpretation), but in the mastery exercised over them by a "mere man" who, while asleep, stops dreaming and begins to think. Strange moment, outside of dreams although still in sleep, in which the dream becomes the object, thought rather than dreamt, of *a thought that is neither asleep nor awake*. . . . He folds into one the two roles of interpreter and recipient; or rather, since these roles are endowed with contradictory characteristics, he disengages himself from the role of recipient and raises himself up. . . . [4]

That "strange moment, outside of dreams although still in sleep," those blurry perceptions "folded into one." What follows footnotes that "thought that is neither asleep nor awake" as if it were a person. What follows traces that distancing "movement"[5] of Descartes, the perpetual self-interpreter, half awake, half asleep, the philosophical somnambulist.

WITH DESCARTES THE PHILOSOPHICAL SOMNAMBULIST

In chasing around our somnambulist, let us be careful not to harass him out of his meditative repose, his toasty Proustian bed, later literally allegorized by an oven, as we saw earlier:

> Descartes acquired the habit of sleeping long and late, ten to twelve hours a night, and of staying in bed till noon. His philosophy was born in the maternal comfort of a bed's warmth, as if he were seeking the substitute physical solaces for his anxieties that a child seeks. If Socrates' philosophy was conceived in the market-place, Nietzsche's on mountain walks, and Marx's in a journalist's office, Descartes' philosophy was nurtured in a bed.[6]

So let us try to understand the intricate passivity of his passion rather than the virility of his action, about which we have already heard too much, too well; the passions "always *receive* the things that are represented by the acts out of volitions in the soul" (Ps, 10:342/1:335, emphasis added, Article 17: The Functions of the Soul). We shall be ready then, active in remaining passive. After all, that seems just how Descartes the somnambulist is: See how he moves about, shuttling between the bed and the oven.

Let us look closely at the interplay between *mythos* and *logos* in Descartes, between Descartes the dreamer and Descartes the philosopher. Let us look into the symbiotic continuities, topological or tropological, between the formal constraints and poetic strands of his thoughts. If philosophy, as Derrida quips, "is the invention of prose"[7] and thus "speaks prose," the material resources for that logocentric invention of philosophy are to be found in what the invention draws on: the excess of imagination, an excess yet to be enunciated by the grammar of thinking. In this fashionably "anti-Cartesian" era, when the word Cartesianism immediately and misleadingly evokes the fossilized image of dry scientism or reductive theoreticism, the question of how Descartes the rationalist follows his own threefold dream—his logico-poetic vision that is fantastically absurd and private as well as rigorously disciplined and largely sharable—should interest any thinkers, Cartesian or non-Cartesian, insomniacs or sleepyheads. If, as Nietzsche observes, philosophy is the confession of the philosopher, I would say further that philosophy is the dream of the philosopher passingly unfolding itself. "We have," writes Nietzsche, "no dreams at all or interesting ones. We should learn to be awake the same way—not at all or in an interesting manner."[8] What I am following is the latter path of reading, into which we have moved, already.

But why somnambulism? What is so interesting about this "abnormal condition of sleep in which motor acts (such as walking) are performed," as the usual dictionary definition goes? It is the "abnormal" structure of somnambulism, particularly the uncontrollable indeterminacy of its ontological status. Neither asleep nor awake, in neither repose nor action, the somnambulist is both passive and active. This abnormality is a structural challenge to the dichotomous mode of thinking in which inaction (*stasis*) establishes its self-identity by antagonizing its opposite, action (*dynamis*), and vice versa. Sleepwalking as an interplay (or intersection) between the horizontality of sleep and the verticality of walking defies such analytic binarism, the grid itself. It is unsettling. In this way, not only does the binary confusion remain unavoidable in the world of somnambulists but it also becomes almost *the* enabling condition for its viability. That is, sleep-walking exists as a confused state, as an ambiguous event. This is a case of a confusion becoming a twofold condition for the possibility of recognition.

Still uninterested? Yet to be convinced? Well, perhaps I have gotten carried away, too far, far too quickly. I shall pause here and try to make sense of this nonsense. I shall continue my reverie, if only more lucidly.

To clarify the background against which somnambulism has become a philosophical issue, there is an inseparable link, as we will see, between Descartes the dreamer and Descartes the philosopher, between the nocturnal sleeper and the daytime walker. It is this continuity that makes Descartes quite a fascinating case. That continuity makes Descartes not only one who dreams an interesting dream but more specifically a performative dreamer who realizes or enacts his dreams in a certain way, which is threefold: private, theoretical, and theological—all at once. The specification of the meanings of the "dream of Descartes," required at this point, may not resolve the problem of referential complexity, but what the semantic clarification can do is to locate the origin of that (con)fusion, those "folds" of the threefold, "Olympian" dream of Descartes.

First, there is the literal dream Descartes had on the night of November 10, 1619.[9] "As Gustave Cohen has already pointed out, the date of the discovery of the admirable Science, November 10, 1619, was the anniversary of Descartes' first visit to Beeckman,"[10] with whom he "had spent the previous twelve months"[11] debating mathematical issues and to whom Descartes had dedicated his first work, *Compendium Musicae* (1618). So we are talking about the psychophysical event during his sleep that night, which Descartes later carefully recorded in his private diary, "the little notebook bound in parchment" labeled *Olympica*. This book of secrets allegedly accompanied him all the time, wherever and whenever he went off in search of a hideaway. According to Adrien Baillet, who had seen the original manuscript and subsequently lost it, the significance of the Olympian dream is cosmic. For immediately before retiring to bed, Descartes appears to have noted in his diary that he had "discovered the foundations of a marvelous science."[12] This private "full enthusiasm"[13] was transformed, serially, into three consecutive, visionary dreams he had later that night.

• First, Descartes was assailed by phantoms and a whirlwind (Dream 1: The School/Church), and he subsequently underwent a bodily pain he believed to have been caused by an "evil demon."

• Then, he heard an unbearable noise like a thunderclap (Dream 2: The Thunder); terrified, he awoke at once, only to see many sparks of fire scattered around the room. He tried to calm himself down with reasoning; his terrors shortly faded away, and he fell asleep again.

• Subsequently, the dreamer came across a dictionary on the table, next to which was an anthology of poems, which aroused his curiosity (Dream 3: The Books). The dreamer opened the book and chanced upon a verse, later identified as the Seventh Ode of Ausonius: "What road in life shall I follow?" (*Quod vitae sectabor iter?*).

• Next day, upon waking, Descartes wrote, "It was the Spirit of Truth (God) that had wanted to open unto him the treasures of all the sciences by this dream . . . November 11th, 1620. I began to understand the foundation of the wonderful discovery." Having confirmed his philosophical "mission" this way, Descartes promises himself the following: "Before the end of November, I shall head for Loretto. I intend to go there on foot from Venice, if this is feasible and is the custom. I will make the pilgrimage with all the devotion that anyone could normally be expected to show. At all events I will complete my treatise before Easter, and if I can find publishers. . . ."

The story so far: Here is a man who has been devoting all his waking time to "dreaming of" inventing a new philosophy; while asleep, he is dreaming another dream. Note the pivotal centrality of the question with which the dream concludes and also, in a sense, unfolds: "What road in life shall I follow?"

Our question from here: Who is this "I"? Why and how does that matter? The "I" appearing in this sentence enfolds three figures: the modern philosopher, the lucid dreamer, and the Ausonian poet. All three have amalgamated into one obscure individual on the go, the young René. Upon waking, Descartes "walks" to the shrine of Wisdom, literally and metaphorically: "after I had spent some years pursuing these studies in the book of the world and trying to gain some experience, I resolved one day to undertake studies within myself too and to use all the powers of my mind in choosing *the paths I should follow*" (D, 6:10/1:116, emphasis added). When I walk out of "my country and my books" (D, 6:11/1:116), I am bound to walk into something else: a "stove-heated room, where I was completely free to converse with myself about my own thoughts" (D, 6:11/1:116). Again, this is as Descartes recalls it.

The metaphorical and symbolic dimension of this Olympian dream, inseparable from the literal event, is so powerful that not only Sigmund Freud[14] but also Descartes himself saw it as a "dream from above." Indeed, could there be any other way to make sense of the extraordinary force of the event? The difference between Freud and Descartes, however, is that the former demystifies it by offering a psychological explanation, and the latter glorifies it by attaching a theological significance. One wonders how or whether Descartes would have reacted if he had heard Freud saying, rather dismissively, that "they are dreamlike (rather than thoughtlike) formulations of ideas which could have been created just as well in a waking state as during the state of sleep."[15]

he held the supernatural view

AND "WALK WITH THE CONFIDENCE OF A SLEEPWALKER"

After the Olympian dream, Descartes "walks with the confidence of a sleepwalker,"[16] of a butterfly even:

> In a dream, the subject is a butterfly. . . . Our position in the dream is profoundly that of someone who does not see. The subject does not see where it is leading, he *follows* [*il suit*]. He may even on occasion detach himself, tell himself that it is a dream, but in no case will he be able to understand himself in the dream in the way in which, in the Cartesian *cogito*, he grasp himself as thought. . . . After all, I am the consciousness of this dream.[17]

The dream of Descartes that is "abstract, poetic, and symbolic" is indeed a "strange mixture of rationalism, religion, and mysticism!"[18] What the somnambulist "follows," as if in an automatic response to a call, is precisely that: "a map of the universe in the lines that time draws on . . . old walls,"[19] where, over time, the cracks widen, sketching out a new continent of itself. What could have been simply daily nonsense was treated as a visionary truth. Descartes chose *this* dream, *this* nonsense as his guiding light among countless other equally wild or absurd dreams he may have had up to that point in his life. One might make a "conscious" decision, but the decision itself remains beyond or outside the realm of consciousness.

opening himself up

Did I say earlier that life might be a series of chosen dreams? Am I dreaming? If so, let me carry on.

To summarize, the Olympian dream is an event of pivotal importance to Descartes' philosophical life. His literal dream was self-translated into the final justification for a necessity to realize his other, metaphorical "Cartesian dream" of inventing a whole new science that is infallible. This dream, retranslated in theological terms, is that of a reunion with God, the infinite, perfect, and benevolent Being. In Descartes, despite *and* due to his near-fanatical "rationalism," theoretical vision is inseparable from the dreamlike poetic vision he also had; the first is supplemented or even completed by the second.[20] In the dream of Descartes, a desert meets waters, and a philosopher meets a poet:

> It may seem surprising to find weighty judgments in the writings of the poets rather than the philosophers. The reason is that the poets were driven to write by enthusiasm and the force of imagination. We have within us the sparks of knowledge, as in a flint: philosophers extract them through reason, but poets force them through the sharp blows of the imagination, so that they shine more brightly. (Pt, 10:217/1:4)

What a *brilliant* note! But again, who is speaking here? Descartes the poet or Descartes the philosopher? Descartes the imaginative writer or Descartes the judicious thinker? The one who sees "the sparks of fire" (Dream 2: The Thunder) or the one who declares, "I shall head for Loretto"? *All* of them.

Eureka! Thinkers, dreamers, writers do this all the time, do they not? As in the case of Descartes, *mythos* and *logos* are often united in the holy *bathos* of thinking. Such is also the *raison d'être* of bathtub escapism. A retreat to the bathroom in times of cogitational difficulty is a well-known remedy, esoteric yet apparently effective. The threefold dream of Descartes functions just like that mind-hugging bathtub in which a solid thought, a thought "extracted through reason," opens itself up to the world of the fluid. Also worth noting in that regard is the fact that Descartes' desiderata include not only the clock and the eyeglasses but the artificial fountain,[21] the fountain being a perfect example of geometry becoming fluid, and fluidity becoming geometrical. Descartes' Olympian dream, to amplify the analogy, is a threefold womb of cogitation, not unlike Plato's *Khora*, the receptacle.

I Think, Therefore I May Be Dreaming: This Is How I Am

> Brilliantly reasoned indeed [*praeclare sane*]! As if I were not a man who sleeps
> at night, and regularly has all the same experiences while asleep as madmen
> do when awake—indeed sometimes even more improbable ones. How often,
> asleep at night, am I convinced of just such familiar events—that I am here in
> my dressing-gown, sitting by the fire—when in fact I am lying undressed in
> bed! . . . Indeed! As if I did not remember other occasions when I have been
> tricked by exactly similar thoughts while asleep! As I think about this more
> carefully, I see plainly that there are never any sure signs by means of which
> being awake can be distinguished from being asleep. The result is that I begin
> to feel dazed [*obstupescam*], and this very feeling of stupor [*stupor*] only rein-
> forces the notion that I may be asleep. (M, 7:19/2:13, trans. modified)

We are already fairly familiar with this passage, which I still find fascinating and relatable every time.

REDREAM

I *am* interested in rereading the text, but not to find the same thing; also,
I *am* interested in old questions but not in repeating them. I am not concerned with the question of whether the asleep-awake distinction can be
established or maintained in Descartes' system of thinking. This is partly
because my mind is, right now, not clear enough to deal with such a polemical issue head-on. It is also partly because Descartes himself, as we will
see shortly, became weary of that brain teaser, which, when parroted aim-
lessly and excessively, is likely to induce more boredom than enthusiasm.

What I will be following instead is the direction of Descartes' thoughts;
I would like to see where they are heading as well as held. The thematic
question that guides us is not of yes or no, but of *how*. How does the
puzzling—specifically somnambulistic—ambiguity at stake play a formative role both in Descartes' narration of the dream event? How does the
excess of *poesis* supplement the lack of imagination often detected in theoretical philosophies? How does dream become a necessary excess in one's
reflective life?

Why? As illustrated in the *Discourse on Method* as well as the *First Meditation*, Descartes' decision to invent a philosophy "firm" enough to serve as

the foundations of all sciences grew out of a personal need as well: a need to know the "right method of conducting reason" (the subtitle of the *Discourse*), a need to "follow the right path," a need to be right. Such a vital need for stability prompts Descartes to examine his life in the past, and this radical self-reflection leads him to a deeper realization that he might have been leading a life of delusion and deception. The problem of illusion he poses turns rather allegorical: His life might have been nothing but a long, elaborate dream from which he now tries to wake up. This dream-hypothesis is a metaphysical threat to the naïve assurance of an unexamined life. Descartes' philosophical odyssey starts to unfold when he sets out to deal with this crisis, this abyssal problem (the *First* and *Second Meditations*), the metaphysical intensity of which the hypothesis of the evil genius, for being more hyperbolic than the dream hypothesis, reinforces rather than alleviates.

WITH "FORCE AND BLOWS OF IMAGINATION"

Viewed in this light, Descartes the philosopher may come across as an anti-dreamer par excellence who antagonizes nocturnal dream. Such is Catherine Clément's charge:[22] "Sleep is dangerous to thought; this is a constant. One of the first threats from which Descartes protected himself when he shut himself up to arrive at the idea of the *cogito* was sleep, and the illusion of dreams that is its outcome. Philosophy stands watch and stays awake." This is true, yet only partly so, because Descartes' distrust of dream is only epistemological and theoretical in the rather narrow senses of those words. In fact, Descartes' philosophy of the *cogito*, seen more intimately, is dream-friendly or integrated. The passive-aggressivity of a somnambulist with which he incorporates the abyssal trope of dreaming into his system of thinking is quite complex, as we have been seeing so far; well, the Cartesian complex, as we already saw in Scene 2. For our purpose here, more to the point is that the philosophical power of Cartesianism lies not so much in the extent to which reflective consciousness guards itself against the eventual fading-out of consciousness—that is, sleep—as in the extent to which reflective consciousness submits itself to the force of *mise en abîme*, to the force of hyperreflective imagination; the poetic "force and blows of imagination" (Pt, 10:217/1:4).

The philopoetic "force" of Cartesian thinking is well-captured, for instance, by this claustrophobic question Descartes keeps asking himself:

> I am *like a prisoner* [*quam captivus*; Fr. *un esclave*] who is enjoying an imaginary freedom while asleep; as he begins to suspect that he is asleep, he dreads being woken up, and goes along with the pleasant illusion as long as he can. In the same way, I happily slide back into my old opinions and dread being shaken out of them, for fear that my peaceful sleep may be followed by hard labor when I wake, and that I shall have to toil not in the light, but amid the inextricable darkness of the problems I have now raised. (M, 7:23/2:15, emphasis added)

The oxygen for this otherworldly self-reflection is in the compensatory—imaginary—freedom autogenerated by the very pressure, the mere possibility, of thinking, of progressive thoughts. To paraphrase the question of the Cartesian insomniac here, through this recursive self-questioning I am subjecting myself to, what would stick out, what would get stuck not "at the end of the tunnel" but just *in* that tunnel? What would remain true, what would remain objectively real, what would remain free from and of illusions? Armed with the consistent boldness as well as the anxiety of "a rebellious youth,"[23] Descartes explores that edge of thinking: What would remain true, even if I am dreaming? Given that there are no inner "marks by means of which we can with certainty distinguish being asleep from being awake" (cf. D 6:32/1:127; 6:39–40/1:130–1; M, 7:19/2:13–4; 7:77/2:53; Or, 7:529/2:360) apart from some mechanical/external means (Tl, 11:173/104) or memory (M, 7:89–90/2:61–2) to which dream, unlike waking thoughts, is not linked in any self-reflectively controlled manner and which are therefore still unreliable, what would *then* remain true "whether I am awake or asleep" (M, 7:20/2:14, cf. D, 6:38–40/1:130–1; M, 7:70/2:49; Or, 7:509–513/2:347–8)? Derrida also pays attention to this force of Cartesian madness that is auto-generative, structurally excessive, and narratively interminable, partly as a way of saving Descartes some philosophical room, as it were, from Foucault's politicized assertion that Cartesian rationalism is constituted on the basis of the summary exclusion and systematic incarceration of madness,[24] a charge we already considered in the last chapter. One of the key Cartesian questions Derrida stresses is precisely that: "What would remain true, *even if* I am mad?"[25] This is a question that does not preclude but on the contrary opens itself up to the possibility of radical dreaming, just like that radical madness we saw earlier.

Cartesian dreaming, including daydreaming, as a case of Cartesian thinking is not resistant but receptive to touches of hyperbolism insofar as it is bound up with hypothetical imagining. The "imaginative force" of Cartesian reflection is such that the serialized allegories of danger—the hypotheses of madness, of dream, of evil genius—are not exorcized from but embraced within, or shall we say more fluidly "around," the system of thinking. Bordo also got it right, I think, when she writes (albeit in a slightly less approving tone):

> "Maybe all this is a dream?" is not a question that haunts Descartes. Rather, he is troubled by states—like madness, like dreaming—that so completely "occupy" experiential space that there is no room for questions about the correspondence of those states to reality. The dream state is convincing *not* because it is so vivid that it simulates reality . . . but because, for all its murkiness, it *is* "reality" for the dreamer. . . . "dead to the world" sleep is something one is either *in* or *not in*, and while *in*, it is not a state which one has any distance on such that one could question the status of the world as given.[26]

It is that need for "distance" that Bordo finds problematic "*psycho*cultur-ally."[27] For her, this distance, however tiny, psychically necessitated as such, has become a typically masculinized norm, as illustrated in the pre-Oedipal boy's developmental separation from the mother; this in part explains that gendered, theoretico-scientific urge, *The Flight to Objectivity* (1987), partly "the 'artifacts' of an upper-class, white, male culture."[28] I too see it. "Ships at a distance have every man's wish on board," with the man tracing her movements on (and just off) the horizon, with "his dreams mocked to death by Time," as Zora Neale Hurston put it, so summarily, in the opening lines of *Their Eyes Were Watching God* (1937); "now, women forget all those things they don't want to remember, and remember everything they don't want to forget. The dream is the truth. Then they act and do things accordingly."[29] Still, the fact is that thinking around death toward time that hears mockery no more, one moves on, dreams on, lives on, male or female, masculine or feminine, or whatever. That is, the Cartesian dream of transcendence is itself immanent. Is it not interesting that Descartes, acting like that "Watcher"[30] on the lookout, also "acts and does things accordingly," just like those Hurston is describing? When "Watching Time" sometimes, sometimes one becomes just one.

What happens, I mean, *during* that flight or sail, actual or virtual, to death, to that time outside or across time, to the deadline, the line beyond which death embodies the absolute and final certainty? It is here, or the quasi-Heideggerian there, that my question lingers. Is there not something in between that objectivity to which the *cogito* flies and this subjectivity from which the *cogito* departs? Can the *topos* of that "flighty" desire or urge itself—the Cartesian drive, or the Cartesian complex?—be neatly configured or specified? What if the *topos* of this unspecified foreign object-subject has itself become liquid but is still "not nothing" (M, 7:24/2:17; 7:25/2:18)? "In that case am I not, at least, something?" "I am (not) nothing so long as I think I am something." Not yet some thing, but just something in "soul" time, as it were. What would remain true, even if I am dreaming or being mad or duped or blindly gendered or queerly unlocatable *or whatever?* The undeniable truth: As Descartes saw and said, I am, I am that which exists in the form of dreaming, being mad, duped, either-gendered, omni-queered, or whatever. I am that "experiential" space of questioning, that "distance," that irreducible, ineluctable, insanely unstoppable act of spacing itself.

What if, however, as Heinrich Heine once imagined in 1826, God the guardian angel of my radical dream suddenly "awakens from His dreams and rubs his sleepy eyes and smiles"? What if:

> The world is the dream of an intoxicated God who has stolen away à la française from the carousing assembly of the Gods and lain down to sleep on a lonely star and does not know himself that he has also created everything he dreams, and dream images take shape, often madly lurid, but harmoniously sensible—the *Iliad*, Plato, the battle of Marathon, Moses, the Medicean Venus, the Strassburg cathedral, the French Revolution, Hegel, steamships etc. are excellent individual ideas in this creative divine dream. Yet it won't be long before the God will awaken and rub his sleepy eyes and smile!—and our world will have vanished into nothing, indeed, will have never existed.[31]

Well, whatever, none of my business: God's irony is God's business. OK, then, what "if God himself should prove to be our most enduring lie?"[32] Well, again, in which case, God, as the author of all beings—

including Heine's book, *Das Buch Le Grand*, in which both God's possible sleep and his follow-up awakening are archived across and beyond the narrative timeline—is responsible for all that drama, not I, René Descartes, God's fabrication. But here is the catch: The benevolent being, by definition, does not lie and or else that being would have to lie with a good or no intention where deception, although usable, could not be the ultimate aim. Besides, sleeping is not an error but only a weakness, which again is not an attribute of divinity.

> In saying that God does not lie and is not a deceiver, I think I am in agreement with all metaphysicians and theologians past and future. The point you make against this has no more force than if I had said that God is not subject to anger or other emotions, and you were to produce as counter-examples passages from Scripture where human feelings are attributed to God. As everyone knows, there are two quite distinct ways of speaking about God. The first is appropriate for ordinary understanding and does contain some truth, albeit truth which is relative to human beings; and it is this way of speaking that is generally employed in Holy Scripture. The second way of speaking comes closer to expressing the naked truth—truth which is not relative to human beings; it is this way of speaking that everyone ought to use when philosophizing, and that I had a special obligation to use it in my *Meditations*, since my supposition there was that no other human beings were yet known to me, and moreover I was considering myself not as consisting of mind and body but solely as a mind. It is very clear from this that my remarks in the *Meditations* were concerned not with the lies, but only with malice in the formal sense, the internal malice which is involved in deception. (Or, 8A:142/2:101–2, Second Set)

What we are looking at, again, is that strange, autogenerative space of irreducible questioning, philosophical autodistancing, the very ground for thinking other possibilities, "the other," thinly insulated against all other destructive possibilities and yet insulated nonetheless: the *sum*, "mindfully" occupied as such.

DREAM RELENTLESSLY, EVEN IF YOU ARE DREAMING

The inaugural and enduring modernity of Cartesian philosophy lies in the clarity of the force, rather than the outcome, of a series of passingly pressing questions to which Descartes the questioner subjects himself, especially in the *First* and the *Second Meditations,* which were also previewed, or re-hearsed, in the *Discourse.* "Clear and distinct" perceptions and ideas them-selves, including the idea of God, are simply to be followed, all of which God the perfect being has already and allegedly planted in the human mind, as we will see in the next chapter. But briefly here:

> How do we know that the thoughts which come to us in dreams are any more false than the others, seeing that they are often no less lively and distinct? . . . In the first place, what I took just now as a rule, namely that everything we conceive very clearly and very distinctly is true, is assured only for the reasons that God is or exists, that he is a perfect being, and that everything in us comes from him. It follows that our ideas or notions, being real things and coming from God, cannot be anything but true, in every respect in which they are clear and distinct. . . . Once the knowledge of God and the soul has made us certain of this rule. . . . (D, 6:38–9/1:130–1)

Therefore, if Descartes is seen as an anti-dreamer, that is because he is a "relentless"[33] dreamer, the demanding and persistent sort operating not only on a more global scale but also touchingly real, even surreal; "we en-counter an imagination methodically, implacably, and quite ruthlessly up-rooting all the traditional and commonplace props of imagination and cogitation. In the *Second Meditation,* Descartes reduces the self to a placeless (U-topian?), dimensionless point of pure, and dangerously slender, intellec-tion."[34] Dreaming of becoming like his God, Descartes the somnambulist becomes a utopian dreamer anchored and living in *this* world, *in* this world:

> Should we identify a point . . . in Descartes' dream? That moment is already overdetermined, but, no matter: not only irony that the master of reason, of clarity and distinctness, discovers his method by way of a dream touches us, but, the fact that he becomes master *in* the dream. He thus challenges the long-standing subordination of the dreamer to external source: for Joseph and his brothers; for Socrates, appealing on his last morning to a dream, in order to call his disciples beyond the incapacity which a lifetime of teaching has failed to cure. This dream is traditionally a form of commentary, a subordination—but then, in Descartes, we find the dream asserting itself, *asking for* rather than given in deference *a reality* on which the waking experi-ence turns out to be commentary, not the other way around. "I dream, therefore, I am," Descartes could have argued—since, his thinking, too, might have been dreamt.[35]

There is after all a reason why Pierre Bourdin (1595–1653), from whom Descartes was eager to seek intellectual support in vain, was a Jesuit Father: He knew it all, suspected it all, already. He perceived this insoluble—and potentially subversive—dilemma of infinite regress with an exemplary acuity. The incisiveness thoroughness of his inquiry, showcased in the *Seventh Set of Objections and Replies*, resembles that of the Spanish inquisition:

> What if dreaming is a *single* operation which enables you sometimes to dream that you are dreaming, and at other times to dream that you are thinking while awake? What will you do now? Since you are silent, are you prepared to listen to me? (Or, 7:494/3:335, emphasis added)

To this "what if," Descartes replies and does not reply by saying:

> When I said that I was thinking, I did *not* inquire *whether* I was awake or asleep while I was thinking. I am surprised that he dubs my method "the method of dreaming," when it seems, to say the least, to have jolted him out of his slumbers. . . . But it may be that beginners will be led astray here into thinking that if someone doubts whether he is awake or dreaming, then nothing can be certain and evident to him, but things can only seem or appear so. To prevent this, I would like people to remember . . . that if something is clearly perceived, then *no matter who* the perceiver is, it is true, and does not merely seem or appear to be true. (Or, 7:511/2:347–8, emphases added)

In other words, Descartes is avoiding the question:

> "Am I awake or asleep?" How can you be certain that your life is not a continuous dream, and that everything you think you learn through your senses is not false now, just as much as when you are asleep? (S, 10:511/2:408)

It is nobody but Descartes himself who introduced and kept the suspicion this far, let that in this world whatever it is, let that affect this thinking; yet the reflective turn of his mind is such that the skeptical thought itself has already undergone an internal transformation. That is, thinking has already taken place, wherever it has. *Cogito, sum*. Descartes is no longer interested in how this question of possible delusions and delusional life can be answered; he is now interested in how it can be overcome, as if asking how the fear and sorrow of death can be overcome . . . or avoided at once? I remain an undecided voter: Descartes, "I," the voter, seems just that aporia, the space of thinking interwoven by daydreams and nightmares and any-thing stretched in between, seamlessly or eruptively. Am I dreaming? The issue, as Descartes recognizes, is "evidence-transcendent,"[36] "the belief that you are *not* a brain in a vat can never be disproven empirically," and it is unanswerable to that extent. Descartes braves the possibility that he may be dreaming, hence his constant attention or evasive distraction to the other question: "What would remain true, *even if* I am dreaming?"

> This "I am," this *ego sum* that Descartes does not doubt is independent of whether or not I sleep and of whether or not everything I perceive is on the order of dream.[37]

This, I have been trying to highlight, is a brave new set of Q&A, heralding a brave new world, forcing open a newly discovered world of necessary singularity as well as possibilities that all point to that necessity *sum* in whatever modalities or locations. Recall Descartes' affirmation of *this* world, of "clear and distinct ideas"—hence, the possibility on our part of reading him as a lucid sleepwalker.

I Sleep, Therefore I Am Happy: Some Cartesian Thoughts on Why Snooze

> The *First Meditation* describes Renatus entering his place of retreat one cold Monday morning. Once the fire was lit, he set about trying to destroy his natural confidence in various kinds of belief, category by category, ending up terrified at what he was doing to himself and wondering whether bright nocturnal dreams of certainty might not be preferable to the frightening obscurities of wide-awake daylight alertness. Renatus therefore allowed his mind to surrender for a while to the seductive seemings of the senses, fingering a piece of fresh beeswax, carefully melting it at the fireplace, and almost scalding himself when he tried to pick it up again. Meanwhile, he was keeping a constant written record of all the thoughts that went through his mind. Next day . . . the idea of God . . . the transformed Renatus . . .[38]

> I know indeed that it is almost impossible not to give in to the disturbances which new misfortunes initially arouse in us. I know too that ordinarily the best minds are those in which the passions are most violent and act most strongly on their bodies. But *the next day, when sleep has calmed the turbulence*

that affects the blood in such cases, I think one can begin to restore one's mind to a state of tranquility. This is done by striving to consider all the benefits that can be derived from the thing which had been regarded as a great misfortune on the previous day, while turning one's attention away from the evils which this thing had been imagined to contain. (C, 4:236–7/3:253, Letter to Elizabeth, June 1645, emphasis added)

SLEEP FURIOUSLY

The Cartesian dream unfolds during winter, such as the winter of 1619. It is the time when animals hibernate and thinkers stay indoors. Winter is the time for a retreat for all. To recall: "Descartes arrived at the minimal, fundamental truth of his existence curled up by himself in soliloquy in the corner of a warm room."[39] It is cold outside, the wind is strong, and Descartes is alone in his room, staying up until late, playing with the fire and a slab of wax. The famous "stove-heated" room (D, 6:11/1:116) must have provided an ideal condition for him to become an Epimenides, the legendary Greek sleepyhead whose iconic status is a delightful counterexample of "no pain, no gain" or "no pain, no fame": this scandalous philosopher, according to the legend, nodded off for fifty-seven years in cave. This is indeed encouraging, soothing in fact. But is it desirable? Then, in what sense?

This section is an intermission and a necessary one. I should like to offer small Cartesian thoughts on the philosophical significance of sleep, sleep as a form of resignation or withdrawal, which is also an enabling condition for procreative thinking—again, "dreaming." Sleeping and any resultant dreaming are not necessarily a biological flaw or an epistemological threat. On the contrary, they can be something very positive and nourishing all around, physically, intellectually, spiritually.

Plato would have approved of Descartes the lucid dreamer, whose liver is as clear as a mirror:

> The liver . . . God made it smooth and close in texture, sweet and bitter, so that the influence of the mind could project thoughts upon it which it would receive and reflect in the form of visible images, like a mirror. . . . Gentle thoughts from the mind produce images of the opposite kind, which will neither produce nor have connection with anything of a contrary nature to their own, and so bring relief from bitterness, using the organs' innate

sweetness to render it straight and smooth and free, and making the part of the soul that lives in the region of the liver cheerful and gentle, and able to spend the night quietly in divination and dreams, as reason and understanding are beyond it.[40]

Plato's esoteric treatise on the "mirroring" function of the liver is to be understood in a larger context of his poetics in which the weakness of sleep is considered not a threat to intellect but a gift from a god, a receptacle for divine inspirations. The passage shows further that philosophy broadly conceived—inclusive of Plato, that is—sometimes elevates the status of sleep to that of a holy retreat. I restart from where I left off a while ago:

> For our makers remembered that their father had ordered them to make mortal creatures as perfect as possible, and so did their best even with this base part of us and gave it the power of prophecy so that it might have some apprehension of truth. And clear enough evidence that god gave this power to man's irrational part is to be found in our incapacity for inspired and true prophecy when in our right minds; we only achieve it when the power of our understanding is inhibited in sleep, or when we are in an abnormal condition owing to disease or divine inspiration. And it is the function of someone in his right mind to construe what is remembered of utterances made in dream or waking by those who have the gift of prophecy and divine inspiration, and to give a rational interpretation of their visions, saying what good or evil they portend and for whom, whether future, past, or present.[41]

The moral is simple enough but easily forgotten: The "perfection" of human understanding can be achieved not by the definitive exclusion of the irrational but by a dialectical interplay between the irrational and the rational. To go to bed and make oneself ready to dream, taken as a "gentle" and strategic withdrawal of the rational mind, is a philosophically significant act. The profundity of sleep is to be found in its economized inaction.

FALL ASLEEP

The same insight applies to falling asleep that is possibly, naturally, more desirable than being asleep. I can think of at least two reasons. First, the accident precludes the intervention of rational will which can be often counterproductive. For instance, the other day, when this writer seems to have been trying every means possible to avoid writing this book, a book of sleep fell on her lap, and she opened it quite mindlessly to where it says:

> I'm falling asleep. I'm falling into sleep and I'm falling there by the power of sleep. Just as I fall asleep from exhaustion. Just as I drop from boredom. . . .
>
> To these we can add: how I'm fainting from pleasure, or from pain. This fall, in its turn, in one or another of its versions, mingles with the others. When I fall into sleep, when I sink, everything has become indistinct, pleasure and pain, pleasure itself and its own pain, pain itself and its own pleasure. One passing into the other produces exhaustion, lassitude, boredom, lethargy, untying, unmooring. The boat gently leaves its moorings, and drifts.
>
> The pain of pleasure comes when pleasure can no longer bear itself. It's when it gives itself up and stops allowing itself solely to enjoy (*jouir*). Exhausted lovers fall asleep.[42]

When one "passes out," something—something indistinct and yet clearly enjoyable—is passed onto or passing through that already drifty individual. Such is the phenomenological logic, pleasure, and "power" of "the fall of sleep," of losing control, solo or duo, which is something other or else than the neurological event; akin to *jouissance*, obviously? So the second reason for promoting and preserving such dormant thinking is that the will of the accidental often rewards the lack of the rational intent with a gift of inspiration or serendipity.

Take Alice in Wonderland, another one who falls. In that case, the gift is the White Rabbit. Indeed, she could have been falling asleep; even if that had not been the case, she would not have volunteered to sleep.

> So she was considering in her own mind (as well as she *could*, for the hot day made her feel very sleepy and stupid), whether the pleasure of making a daisy-chain would be worth the trouble of getting up and picking the daisies, when suddenly a White Rabbit with pink eyes ran close by her.[43]

At and from the start, Alice was simply "tired of sitting by her sister on the bank, and of having nothing to do," for "what is the use of a book without pictures or conversation?"[44] Here, the bookish Victorian sister wasting a lovely summer day reading a pictureless book is boredom incarnated, from which—if we were to follow Jean-Luc Nancy again, here—Alice had to become distant, almost logically. Boredom felt as such, as Martin Heidegger reminds us kindly, is not indifference or even a mental defect but a disguised desire for "awakening."[45] Without the startling appearance of the White Rabbit, Alice would have been condemned to summertime, yes, "lethargy." But look! What a curious thing! A rabbit who says to itself, "Oh dear! Oh dear! I shall be too late! (when she thought it over afterwards, it occurred to hear that she ought to have wondered at this, but at the time it all seemed quite natural)."[46] With this hidden, vertiginous force of daydreaming, Alice falls into slumber; from here, the addictively delightful mathematical drama of Lewis Carroll, the misfit, unfolds. The "mad tea party" will go on, as long as there remains a dormouse snoozing all the way through. The guardian of the party, seen from here, is nobody but the very dormouse, the dormant silly thing—the hidden surprise. If dreaming is irrational and unfit, interpreting is rational, an attempt to measure. And the point is (1) *both* of them are necessary, in the sense that passive resignation and active reflection are to supplement each other in the actual workings of the (pro)creative mind, and (2) one can say that the former precedes the latter, if the order of origination needs spelling out.

Interestingly, this motif of "intellectual surrender," the loss or loosening of mental control as a virtue, is also found in the preface to G. W. F. Hegel's *Phenomenology of Spirit*, where philosophical modernism specifies what Plato calls the "rational part" of mind as "self-consciousness," the waking consciousness kept alive by the sharp front teeth of a dormouse. "The power of spirit," observes Hegel, "is only as great as its expression, its depth only as deep as it dares to spread out and lose itself in its exposition":

> Such minds, when they give themselves up to the uncontrolled ferment of the divine substance, imagine that, by drawing a veil over self-consciousness and surrendering understanding, they become the beloved of God to whom He gives wisdom in sleep; and hence what they in fact receive, and bring to birth in their sleep, is nothing but dreams. Besides, it is not difficult to see that ours is a birth-time and a period of transition to a new era.[47]

Losing oneself to become larger and deeper, part of "universal" consciousness: Plato's Hellenistic, often self-centered and specific role-playing gods have been uniformly transformed into the Christian God who does everything and loves infinitely, embracing and connecting you and me, individuated human beings. Yet the "receptive" structure of thinking as a gift of affect remains the same. Following this relatively esoteric path of thinking, one might even feel obliged to ask, "Is modern philosophy anything other than the dream of a new century?"[48] Could modern philosophy be part of a god's or God's project? A dream of Hypos, for instance? We will have to return more head-on to this question in the next and final chapter.

At this point, we only need note that for a reflective skeptic sleep means a temporary surrender, a temporary suspension of doubt itself; by contrast, insomnia is "the excess of consciousness, i.e., the consciousness of the possible."[49] Sleep, for a full-time thinker, is a wise resignation, not a defeat or a defect. Sleep welcomes the other, the other of conscious thinking, and this is how it remains receptive of and to wisdom, divine or practical.

The wisdom of Cartesianism is to be found in such counterbalancing pragmatism, which puts any idealistic reveries in perspective. "The preservation of health has always been the principal end to my studies" (C, 4:328/3:275, *A Letter to Marquess of Newcastle*, October, 1645) (cf. P, 9B:2/3:179, Preface). "This doubt, while it continues, should be kept in check and employed solely in connection with the contemplation of the truth" (P, 8A:5/3:193). Worth noting also is that from the start, in the *First Meditation*, Descartes assures himself that he will not indulge too much in the hyperbolic (or hypnotic) thought experiment that he himself has proposed:

> In view of this, I think it will be a good plan to turn my will in completely the opposite direction and deceive myself, by pretending *for a time* that these former opinions are utterly false and imaginary. I shall do this *until* the weight of preconceived opinions is *counter-balanced* and the distorting influence of habit *no longer* prevents my judgment from perceiving things correctly. *In the meantime*, I know that no danger or error will result from my plan, and that I cannot possibly go too far in my distrustful attitude. This is because the task now in hand does not involve action but merely the acquisition of knowledge. (M, 7:22/2:15, emphases added)

For Descartes, as he himself says at the end of the *Sixth Meditation*, meditating as a form of exercise of skeptical reason is "pretending" (M, 7:77/2:53). The challenge Descartes posed himself while "pretending for a while" is: "how far" can I proceed with this pretension? Of course, when he anticipated at the start of the *First Meditation* that "in the meantime, I know that no danger or error will result from my plan, and that I cannot possibly go too far in my distrustful attitude" (M, 7:22/2:53), he knew relatively little of what to expect of that game of hyperbole, which ends up fueling hypercritical rationality. Or was he being disingenuous? Either way, in that regard Descartes might be at least a failed good man who thought that at the end of the day he could just enjoy those "happy summer days" (the phrase with which the story of Alice ends). The *Meditations* conclude, relatively unsensationally:

> But now, when I am beginning to achieve a better knowledge of myself and the author of my being, although I do not think I should heedlessly accept everything I seem to have acquired from the senses, neither do I think that everything should be called into doubt. (M, 7:77–78/2:54)

So with this equilibrium has been restored. Whether we agree with him or not, one thing we need to register very clearly and loudly here is this: Descartes—contrary to our postmodern prejudice that he is a demanding, engineering thinker of 24/7 "vigil" and nonblindness—promotes a peace of mind at the end. Just sleep, if you need to.

The kind of skepticism Descartes pursues, however extreme it may seem, is (as is also well known) methodological, not temperamental; it is practical and goal oriented. He wants and needs to be realistic about the expectation. Is that not why he included in his narrative the fact that he "happily" and "lazily" "slides back into his old opinions" when necessary? Here, the need is psychological rather than logical. Descartes' hyperbolic doubts remain somehow psychologically self-regulated this way, and the psychic economy of equilibrium determines the required extent. When read against this background, the following fragment in Descartes' diary becomes illuminating: "I notice that if am sad or in danger and sadness *occupies* work [*tristia* occupent *negotia*], I sleep deeply and eat voraciously. But if I am *full* of joy, I do not eat or sleep." (Pt, 10:215/1:3, trans. revised, emphases added). Here, the budding philosopher is taking note of his own behavioral pattern vis-à-vis eating and sleeping, which are the most beastly—simply in the sense that they involve no substantial kind or level of brain wattage consumed by intellectual attention, only some brain cells with which all mammals are equipped—actions of all human activities. So the Cartesian idea already sampled here is that if and when sadness occupies me, if and when I find myself otherwise "occupied," *ego sum* through that route, too. In other words, again, I exist in and through a compensatory—imaginary—equilibrium, which is out of reach of any questioning or any representation at the end of the day:

> "I am," however, heard murmured by the unconsciousness of a dreamer, testifies less to an "I" strictly conceived than to a "self" simply withdrawn to itself, out of reach of any questioning and of any representation. Murmured by unconsciousness, "I am" becomes unintelligible; it is a kind of grunt or sigh that escapes from barely parted lips. It is a preverbal stream that deposits on the pillow a barely visible trace, as if a little saliva had leaked out of that sleeping mouth.[50]

What enters my mouth becomes part of me, and I am what comes out of my mouth.

The moral of this salivary scene of the *cogito* at work? What would Descartes say or do about this offshoot? The philosopher, if willing to receive wisdom "from above" or wherever, needs to eat and sleep well, and must not work too hard: "We live from 'good soup,' air, light, spectacles, work, ideas, sleep, etc. . . . We live *from* them. These are not objects of representations . . . they are always in a certain measure—even the hammers, needles and machines are—objects of enjoyment."[51] Likewise, the philosopher must live a relaxed, organic life; a hungry Socrates on a coffee diet and driven only by multiple intersecting deadlines is not a desirable pupil in the Cartesian school of thought. The philosopher must learn, instead, how to absorb the positive energy of laziness and half-thinking: not how to think a thought but how to let a thought take place.

Again, Plato would have approved of Descartes. After lecturing on the necessity of reserving a place in mind for the unconditional reception of a god, Plato goes on to discuss eating and digestion. He draws an analogy between the "ungoverning appetite for drink and food" and the "gluttony of philosophy and culture."[52] His intention is clear and clearly pedagogic: He is warning against extremism by problematizing our "incapacity," our lack of "willingness to listen to the divinest element in ourselves." "The Wisdom [*la Sagesse*], the true food of mind" (P, 9B:3–4/1:180), both these thinkers stress, is to be acquired judiciously and consumed sparingly.

DREAM FROM ABOVE

Having touched upon the comforting supplementarity of the "dream from above" and through the mouth, I cannot leave untouched the more apparent, larger dimension of it, namely, its constitutive religiosity, the topic I seem to keep deferring to the next chapter, as if I could then see a happy ending of it. What I should still mention here as a point of observation is that a "dream from above" as a kind of mental remedy to psychosomatic troubles is an exit gate to Heaven, where the intensity of skeptical limit-consciousness is sublimated, where negative consciousness is "redeemed" or liberated. The uncomplicated straightforwardness of religious redemption, often symbolized by a beam of light shining from a celestial object in a perpendicular line, is a notable contrast to the neuropsychological complexity of human doubts, often figured as an abyssal labyrinth. Think about, for instance, Joseph, the poor fellow whose mortal brain could not work out how on earth his wife had become pregnant. The damaging mystery surrounding the Virgin Mary's conception of Jesus Christ had necessitated one definite solution, and the concluding answer was found in the prophetic dream the disturbed husband had while asleep (Matthew 1:18–24):

> But while he thought on these things, behold, the angel of the Lord appeared unto him in a dream, saying, Joseph, thou son of David, fear not to take unto thee Mary thy wife: for that which is conceived in her is of the Holy Ghost. . . . Behold, a virgin shall be with child, and shall bring forth a son, and they shall call his name Emmanuel, which being interpreted is, God with us. Then Joseph being raised from sleep did as the angel of the Lord had bidden him, and took unto him his wife.[53]

Where then does Jesus come from? From God, says Joseph. Where then do "the clear and distinct ideas" come from? From God, says Descartes.

> If we did not know that everything real and true within us comes from a perfect and infinite being then, however clear and distinct our ideas were, we would have no reason to be sure that they had the perfection of being true. But once the knowledge of God and the soul has made us certain of this rule, it is easy to recognize that the things we imagine in dreams should in no way make us doubt the truth of the thoughts we have when awake. For if one happened even in sleep to have some very distinct idea (if, say, a geometer devised some new proof), one's being asleep would not prevent the idea from being true. (D, 6:39/1:130)

By now, we might be tired of the same point being made over and over again. But that is precisely the point. That is what Descartes does with his dream-sleep argument: He repeatedly forges links between God and "clear and distinct" ideas despite and because of those dreams. Thus, the difference between Joseph and Descartes is vocational rather than generic: The former is a simple carpenter, and the latter is a scheming architect. "The Lord has made three marvels; something out of nothing; free will; and God in Man" (Pt, 10:218/1:5). Descartes is part of a greater scheme of God, the real schemer being, in the Cartesian scheme of things, God the perfect designer of Being, not Descartes the imperfect product. Here is then a further difference between Joseph and Descartes: For Descartes, "God is pure intelligence" (Pt, 10:218/1:5) first and foremost, rather than pure love or intimacy. It is what "sees" him or what he sees, not what/who speaks to him or that to which/whom he prays. The Olympian dream of Descartes is "a forceful divine push"[54] or pull.

I Dream, Therefore I Am Touched: Cartesian Thoughts on Why Dream

PRESS FORWARD

The link, if not bond, between Descartes's *res cogitans* and what he calls God is still affectively reciprocal. Specifically, it is tactile, as I will show in the rest of this chapter. One does seem to push the boundaries of ordinary understanding or more broadly thinking in order to reach this extraordinary realm of mental activity called the "imagination," does it not? In particular, I'm thinking of the Husserl's Cartesian "pressing forward [*durch*]":

> The original Cartesian motif: that of pressing forward through the hell of an unsurpassable [*durch die Hölle einer nicht mehr zu übersteigenden*], quasi-skeptical epochē toward the gates of the heaven of an absolutely rational philosophy, and of constructing the latter systematically.[55]

Saving a more detailed and extensive discussion of the connection between the Cartesian thinker and God, those "gates of the heaven of an absolutely rational philosophy," I will conclude this chapter by showing how something like a "touch of (divine) imagination," however dead or dreadful this metaphor may sound, rhythmically structures the Cartesian philopoetics of somnambulism.

Perhaps still surprisingly to some, including those who probably have skipped or object to the key ideas of Scene 1 of this book, Descartes, to whom the Enlightenment owes much of its innate ocular centrism, relies heavily on the sensation of touch for the construction of a "firm" and "solid" philosophical system. If, by the Cartesian objectification or representation of the world, one understands the visual mapping or control of the matter, this understanding seems to be lacking something substantial, namely, substance. The fixative energy of ideation or idealization becomes gaseous unless it is supported by the matter, unless it originates from the matter that resists such objectification, the Kantian "thing-in-itself." I think of the brain itself as an example. Descartes seems to have firsthand experiential knowledge of that fundamental restlessness of motility, which he supplements by introducing tactility into his text; for example, I think of his quirky explanation of how the brain functions.

HOLD HANDS

In fact, Descartes the thinking writer is curiously bodily tactile as well as visual. Should I draw attention to this character in his "dress-gown, sitting by the fire" (M 7:19/2:13)? (I suppose that is close enough to his underwear, and so I may not have to go all the way to cite the passage indicating that "in fact I am lying undressed in bed!" [M, 7/19:2:13].) Now turn quickly to *The Search for Truth* (1641), where Descartes, thinly disguised as *Eudoxus*, armed with sound judgment and good sense, volunteers to guide *Polyander* the-you-and-me-everyman to the gate of truth. The heuristic aim here is to help Polyander discover that he also has what Eudoxus has, namely, the "natural light of reason." Mark the motif of "hand-holding" in this inaugural passage:

> EPISTEMON:. . . The uncertainty of the Pyrrhonists. These are *deep waters*, where I think we may lose our *footing.*
> EUDOXUS: I confess that it would be dangerous for someone who does not know a ford to venture across it without a guide, and many have lost their lives in doing so. But you have nothing to fear if you follow me. Indeed, just such fears have prevented most men of letters from acquiring a body of knowledge which was firm and certain enough to deserve the name "science," . . . they have built up sand instead of digging further down to find rock or clay. So we

must not let the matter rest here. . . . The arguments I have stated . . . have already done what I desired: their chief effect has been to [1] *touch* your imagination so as to make you fear them. For this indicates that your knowledge is not so infallible as to prevent your fearing that these arguments will undermine its foundations by making you doubt everything. Consequently, it indicates that you already have these doubts, and so I have achieved my aim, which was to overturn all your learning by showing you its uncertainty. In case you should now lack the courage to proceed any further, I would advise you that these doubts, which alarmed you at the start, are like phantoms and empty images which appear at night in the uncertain glimmer of a weak light: if you flee from them, your fear will follow you, but if you approach *as if to* [2] *touch* them, you will find nothing but air and shadow and you will be more confident the next time such an encounter may occur. (S, 10:513/2:408–9, emphases and numbers added)

Descartes introduces two different kinds of touch. By "a touch" of imagination, he means, first, a movement of the accidental, the unexpected, the startling, and second, a recognition of that movement. The hand that touches becomes and stores, as Derrida observes in similar terms, "the very memory of accident."[56] The hand of the blind, at once the understanding and imagination, as we already saw in Scene 1, is an apt analogy again. An accidental touch is not a touch in the active sense of the word; rather, that is a sudden attack of the object being touched. Dreams and illusions by which we are touched involuntarily are therefore not only visual excess but tactile invasion. Nightmares are made of pointy stuff, such as "sparks of fire" (Dream 2: Thunder). That initial shock, the initial reflex, as pointed out previously, is the aim of the heuristic use of hyperbolic imagination; the subsequent, self-reflexive "solidification" of a body of knowledge through the *cogito*, as exemplified in Descartes' architectural philosophy, is then a philosophical recuperation of the mind from that initial blow. Let us examine this twofold dimension of Cartesian imagination in some detail.

The first touch of imagination, the "fortuitous course of the spirits" (Ps, 11:348/1:338, Article 26), awakens the dormant mind. "Imaginings," among the "passions of the soul," "those perceptions, sensations, or emotions of the soul which we refer particularly to it, and which are caused, maintained, and strengthened by some movement of the spirits" (Ps, 11:349/1:338, Article 27), are described as follows:

Among the perceptions caused by the body, most of them depend on the nerves. But there are some which do not and which are called "imaginings." . . . Accordingly they cannot be numbered among the actions of the soul, for they arise simply from the fact that the spirits, being agitated [*agitez*] in various different ways and coming upon the *traces of various impressions* which have preceded them in the brain, make their way by chance [*fortuitement*] through certain pores. . . . Such are the illusions of our dreams and also the day-dreams we often have when we are awake and our mind wanders idly without applying itself to anything of its own accord. Now some of these imaginings are passions of the soul [*des passions de l'ame*] . . . their cause is not so conspicuous and determinate as that of the perception. (Ps, 11:344–5/1:336, Article 21: Imaginings Which Are Caused Solely by the Body)

At this stage, the soul remains (1) passive yet responsive, "lively" and alert, and (2) most intimate to our soul, unreflected and unreflective as if in "sleep." Descartes explains the radical "passivity" (*passio*) of the passions of the soul in some neurotypographical terms. As he says elsewhere:

Sense-perception, strictly speaking, is merely passive, even though our application of the senses to objects involves action, viz. local motion; sense-perception occurs in the same way in which wax takes on an impression [imprinted figure, *figuram*] from a seal. It should not be thought that I have a mere analogy in mind here: we must think of the external shape of the sentient body as being really changed by the object in exactly the same way as the shape of the surface of the wax is altered by the seal. This is the case, we must admit, not only when we feel some body as having a shape, as being hard or rough to the touch etc., but also when we have a tactile perception of heat or cold and the like. The same is true of the other senses: thus, in the eye, the first opaque membrane receives the shape impressed upon it by multi-colored light; and in the ears. (R, 10:412/1:40, Rule 12)

The Soul has sensory awareness only in so far as it is in the brain. . . . The nerves by their motions transmit to the brain the actions of external objects which *touch* the parts of the body where the nerves are embedded. Firstly, there are various diseases which *affect* only the brain. . . . Again, sleep occurs only in the brain, yet every day it deprives us of a great part of our sensory faculties, though these are afterwards restored on waking. (P, 8A:319–320/1:283, Article no. 196, emphases added)

It is at this inaugural stage that "*the imprinting* of the ideas of various qualities in the organ of the 'common' sense and the imagination, the retention or stamping of these ideas in the memory, the internal movements of the appetites and passions" (Tm, 11:202/1:108) takes place, motivated by "the agitation by the heat of the fire burning continuously in its heart." Already at this stage, Descartes' philosophical blueprint, his visionary quest for "clear and distinct, simple ideas," begins to emerge, if not yet fully formed. The result of such "fiery" "touch" of imagination "affecting" the neurological "typography" of the brain is, Descartes says retrospectively and conclusively in the *Sixth Meditation*: "a ghost or a vision created in my brain (like those that are formed in the brain when I sleep) [added in the Fr. edition]" (M, 7:90/2:62). That famous Cartesian ghost has that tactile origin.

In the Cartesian poetics of imagination, as with Bachelard's poetics of material reverie, "only heat penetrates; heat insinuates itself"[57]; heat is "ingrained in all the fibers of being." Descartes' "wax" experiment taking place in that stove-heated room is a literal example. The Cartesian reflection uses these ingrained "passions" of the soul as its motor, as its productive matrix, as its cogitational bathtub (to recycle the metaphor introduced earlier). Then the original owner of this fire, of these passions, as the unfortunate case of Prometheus confirms, is traceable to God the original mover of Being, the originary designer of Being.

Once freshly shaken up—or heated up—this way, *res cogitans* restages the same philosophical shock, the reflex, by miming the original "imprints" or attack of ideas. The "I" of "I think" *reflects* on it; the I "approach[es] phantoms and empty images as if to touch them" again. Such is the second touch of imagination, which Descartes calls "the actions" or "volition of the soul," whose function is quite literally active rather than passive, for it is to "make the soul aware of the perceptions thus received" (Ps 11:336/1:336, Article 20). The soul, at this stage, "considers its own nature." A reflective touch is a memory enfolding a delicate gesture of imagination, "a memory of accident" that is delicate, precise, and powerful. Tactile reciprocity, the togetherness of touching and being touched, is more secure than visual reciprocity, for it involves extension, the body. It is tightly coextensive and therefore almost destroys distance: it is "airtight" (see earlier; S, 10:513/2:408–9).

Touch means security, as an act of hugging testifies. One of the effective ways to secure a relation is thereby to "impress," as exemplified in Descartes' philopoetics of somnambulism. David Hume also seems to have intuited this truth, although from the other direction. Critically questioning "the abstruse philosophy, found on a turn of the mind," that is, the "rationalist" philosophy of Cartesian kind, the impassioned empiricist says:

> It is certain that the easy and obvious philosophy will always . . . have the preference above the accurate and abstruse. . . . It *enters* more into common life; *moulds* the heart and affections; and by *touch*ing those principles which actuate them, reforms their conduct, and brings them nearer to that model of perfection which it describes. On the contrary, the abstruse philosophy, found on a turn of the mind. . . . [58]

Either Hume has not read Descartes (in detail), or his mind has irreversibly been "molded into" a prejudice. Undoubtedly, Descartes' philosophy is "found on a turn of the mind," which generates a systematized series of self-reflections. Yet this Humean objection to Cartesian rationalism misses one very important detail: The Cartesian "turn of mind" enfolds God-memory or a memory of God, which is for Descartes as intrusively tactile, especially in its dormant or incubatory state, not unlike the Humean "bundle of impressions." In fact, our abstruse rationalist does seem to know how to "mould the heart and affections," although in his own ways. Besides, as we saw earlier, he knows how to sleep well.

BE TOUCHED, LEAVING TOUCH UNTOUCHED

Although in his own way Descartes knows how to "mould the heart and affections"? Am I saying that Descartes is not only a somnambulist but a solipsist? An egotistic lunatic even? "A fanatic of rightness,"[59] whose missionary sense of righteousness has no room for any ethics or politics of self-effacement? Is he a sad, unapproachable bigot? My answer must be a resounding No.

As Gerald Bruns puts it incisively, "Cartesian doubt is methodical, not personal or ethical; it does not *touch* the whole man."[60] There is something Descartes' skeptical aggression leaves "untouched," and that is reflective intellect, "the natural light of reason," which, as the first paragraph of *Discourse* stresses famously (D, 6:2/1:111), all of us thinking—and dreaming—things share. Accordingly, we fellow moderns are encouraged to use it wisely and creatively in our own ways: "My present aim, then, is not to teach the method which everyone must follow in order to direct his reason correctly, but only to reveal how I have tried to direct my own. . . . I hope it will be useful for some without being harmful to any. . . ." (D, 6:4/1:112). Although the solitude of self-reflection is an inexplicable mystery, the intimate sense of mystery itself can be communicated. What Descartes communicates through and throughout his writings seems to be just such a philosophical experience of wonder, of wonderful awakening. More importantly, he seems to have needed as well as enjoyed such communal experiences. The Descartes I am now thinking of is the fondly remembered letter-writer (who can be sharp-tongued, when necessary):

> After acknowledging the goodness of God, the immortality of souls and the immensity of the universe, there is yet another truth that is, in my opinion, most useful to know. That is, that though each of us is a person distinct from others whose interests are accordingly in some way different from those of the rest of the world, we must still think that none of us could subsist alone and each one of us is really one of the many parts of the universe, and more particularly a part of the earth, the State, the society, the family to which we belong by our domicile, our oath of allegiance and our birth. (C, 4:293/3:266, Letter to Princess Elizabeth, September 15, 1645)

"I sleep, and I am the exterior that affects me."[61] I sleep, therefore I am "agitated," "touched," moved. The key contention of this chapter has been that Descartes' system of thinking, of hyperreflection, does not preclude this move, for the movement of Cartesian passions is primordially passive rather than active. This point of observation, stated in stronger terms, is that there is in fact an intrusion of the exterior at the heart of Cartesian landscape of thinking often characterized unfairly as self-insulated. One mode of such intrusion, which I have been exploring in this chapter, is philosophical somnambulism, and the force of such intrusion, highlighted throughout the discussion, is the divine, the infinite, the mysterious. In the presence of God (who is not necessarily "who," i.e., the Christian God, as we will see shortly), Descartes becomes a sleeping matter, a dreaming butterfly, a malleable "subject" in the passive sense of the word:

> The common feature of these states (hypnotized states) is the "stupor" or "sleep" of the individual's soul "immersed" in the "form of feeling." All these states have a hypnotic nature. But hypnotism, at best, lays bare . . . a "passive state." . . . "The diseased subject passes and remains under the power of

another subject, the magnetizer." In this state, the diseased subject is "self-less"; . . . this state is not its own.[62]

Yet the selfless slumber is a powerful sleep, powerful insofar as the sleeper is capable of dreaming, of being "magnetized" by a certain figure of the *hypnos* passing through it—called, in this case, a hypothetical skeptic. This way, the selflessness of slumber can be transformed into a promiscuous procreativity. "Narcissus satisfies himself in the dreams of the slumbering soul. But sleep is run through by a trembling. . . . Trembling is not an image; it is the rhythm of the affected soul."[63]

Descartes is contagious, affecting, and I have been "happily and lazily" led by this cogitative somnambulist. Like Descartes who concludes his *Meditations* by saying "we must acknowledge the weakness of our nature" (M, 7:90/2:62), I must acknowledge that I am now tired of following him around. Now I must go to bed again.

Cornered Reflection: With and around an Evil Genius

> I will suppose therefore that not God, who is supremely good and the source of truth, but rather some malicious demon of the utmost power and cunning has employed all his energies in order to deceive me. I shall think that the sky, the air, the earth, colours, shapes, sounds and all external things are merely the delusions of dreams which he has devised to ensnare my judgement. (M, 7:22/2:15)
>
> Does it now follow that I too do not exist? *No: if I convinced myself* [*persuasi*] *of something* [*quid*] *then I certainly existed* [*Imo certe ego eram*]. But there is a deceiver of supreme power and cunning who is deliberately and constantly deceiving me. In that case I too undoubtedly exist, if he is deceiving me; and let him deceive as much as he can, he will never bring it about that I am nothing *so long as I think I am something* [*quamdiu me aliquid esse cogitabo*]. So after considering everything very thoroughly, *I must finally conclude* [*denique statuendum sit*] that this proposition, *I am, I exist*, is necessarily true [*necessario est verum*] whenever it is put forward by me or conceived in my mind. (M, 7:25/2:16–7, emphases added)

Fables of Divine Creation: A/The; Him/It

"I don't believe in God but I miss him," says Julian Barnes.[1] "I don't believe he exists but I dislike him anyway," says Wendy Lesser.[2] While working on a project, the completion of which seems to take much longer than expected, Descartes says to his fiend Mersenne, "I too am too much in love with the fable of my *World* to give it up if God lets me live long enough to finish it; but I cannot answer for the future" (C, 1:179/3:28).

Why "but"? That is the question; explored here is a Cartesian version of those more or less same stories around God, already previewed in the previous dream story (Scene 3). In this chapter, we will focus on or rather around the three key moments, the thread of which I would formulate as follows: "I might (not) believe in God but I am still thinking of and with It/ Him." What is this affective link, of which those "I"s seem unable to let go? Whence and whither this narrative lingering around? How to understand this (dis)connective "but"? Perhaps we are no longer clear on what is meant or covered by "belief," this "need to believe." Read on.

As Julia Kristeva writes in *This Incredible Need to Believe:*

> The "God of the philosophers," need we repeat, gets reduced to the "a priori proof," which rests only on the "fact that something is possible" (Kant). From Parmenides to Leibniz and Heidegger, the "divine" gives way to *being* . . . and the *subject* thinking in it (in the being: Descartes' "I *think* therefore I *am*.").[3]

True, but let me repeat the question: How and why does the God of Descartes get reduced to what, or who, it is? What is that Cartesian "need"? And why does it matter? Or should it be not asked?

This philosophical novelist or novelistic philosopher, too, whom we have been chasing around, dwells on his complex relationship with the absent present X: "yes/no, *but* . . ." So God as "pure intelligence" (Pt, 10:218/1:5), God as "mathematical truths" (C, 1:145/3:23), or "a God, or *whatever* I may *call* him, who puts into me the thoughts I am now having . . . the author of these thoughts?" (M, 7:24/2:16, emphasis added), all characterized or inferred as such, play a part in human dramas in one way or another. God is a name for the X "out there" to which *res cogitans* returns repeatedly through various intricately networked routes, not just mathematical, poetical, or whimsical. A "God," somehow situated, passing through somewhere like an angel (Pt, 10:218/1:5), is a-part: a part of and apart from searching narratives of humanity. No one seems neutrally detached from or naturally related to God, especially the *homo novellus* who is "neither historian nor prophet" but "an explorer of existence" à la Kundera.[4] The same observation would apply, more generically, to the less exalted if equally exploratory cousin, the "*homo quarens*, the animal that asks and asks. This crowds the borders of language and image . . . in the conviction, . . . metaphysically arcane or as immediate as the cry of a child, that there is 'the other,' the 'out there.' "[5]

"If I convinced myself of something, then I certainly existed . . ." What exactly am I following here? On this occasion, I do not intend to follow any psychoanalytic route of reading, but I would like to draw on a psychoanalytic insight contained in what Kristeva says about such conviction. "Analytic experience itself is not foreign to 'belief' in the broadest sense of this term: does not the transference/countertransference establish, at the heart of the analytic cure, the conviction both affective and logical that the interpretation is well-founded?"[6] My question is then: What would be that "curative" X "out there," in which the self-doubter persuades himself to believe after all, after and through the torturous series of questioning? Descartes, too, "the first real novelist"[7] of, say, a stream of consciousness, views God, the ground zero point, in such a structurally elliptical light. God, for Descartes, is the point on which everything is to count, from which counting itself could start, and by which the new world of truth is to be accounted for. The center, double as it is, is that which stands alone, distantly, like the Sun, the source of the natural light of reason. It is the unquestionable center that generates questions, including questions about its alleged centrality or credibility. The center thus divinized *and* democratized the absolute subject position common to all thinking things, and this is what creates and controls all movements within and even outside (Newtonian) time and space. The center might be secure but does not necessarily secure—especially those incurable skeptics and neurotic infidels, thinkers of irreducible distance. Allegories, fables, and parables themselves told from such otherworldly corners, although meant to be prophetic and even comforting, "cannot answer for the future" insofar as they are about the alterities of the present, the distance of Time itself falling into time in the form of lines, existential, historical, biological, genealogical, anthropological, material. In other words, the present is unable to answer for itself, especially now. Seemingly, it disorients itself or disorientingly duplicates itself into the past that might have not been on the one hand, and the future that might not be on the other. The Cartesian present is constructed on the basis of and out of such dual failures of time, of human time-consciousness in particular, of what we call the past and the future, respectively: This is how it comes into being, in the strange persistence of the now-point.

Similarly, Descartes' narrative of a meditative existence, focused on present thoughts or the singular thoughts of necessary presence, becomes

circular on two levels that intersect, touching each other somewhat intriguingly. Sure, he finds himself "trapped"[8] there, in the corner of the
room he has just finished painting, all in black. But is he quite happily
trapped? Not quite. To begin with, as indicated earlier, for Descartes God
there is at once a part of and apart from human beings. As Arnauld and
others already articulated, this is the problem of "reasoning in a circle"
(C, 7:214/3:150). This *"aporia* of 'the circle,' "[9] this irresolvably cloistered
"criterion problem"[10] is that "we are sure that what we clearly and distinctly
perceive is true only because God exists. But we can be sure that God exists
only because we clearly and distinctly perceive this" (C, 7:214/3:150).

Upon closer inspection, we might discern the circuitry problem: "It"
and "He" are in perpetually braided, categorical conflict in the eyes and
hands of the storytelling philosopher, the God-fearing scientist. Cartesian
God, the foundational axiom of Cartesian philosophy and sciences, is seductive and sticky, inasmuch as it figures within a theological narrative.
Recall from the previous chapter on dream the sharp distinction Descartes
attempts to draw between the scripturally based "ordinary understanding"
of God and the "philosophical" notions of God conceived only "by the
mind" (Or, 8A:141/2:101–2). Seen now more clearly through the lens of the
circuitry problem, this is a distinction that does not quite hold at the end
(of the day, as it were). For Descartes, the "the natural light of reason" given
to all thinking things is not simply there but it is also "good" by definition,
like a good man who embodies good-in-itself, who takes after God. This
act of relying on the existence of God, purportedly proven by the innate
goodness and eternal perfection of It/Him, which in turn is to guarantee
the veracity of clear and distinct ideas including and especially of It/Him,
is spirally circular because, first, the former draws on the latter logically,
and second, "He" and "It" are affectively drawn to each other. "It" and "He"
as the double Pronoun of God are referentially conflated, rhetorically inter-
twined in the centrifugal system of address or attribution that is "responsorial."[11] "It" can be neither an agent nor a recipient. "It" cannot attract, call,
and recognize anything; it is the "He" in "It" that does it, just as the thinking "I," the conceptual personae, is not simply "it," an object, but a passing
figure insofar as the *res cogitans* is a conscious subject par excellence. In other
words, as "It" has to be good in itself, it is to be at least partly "He," the
embodiment of the best possible sense or intelligence. "He," a personified

figure, cannot be reduced to "It," a nonhumanized object or substance. He is impersonated, yet "He" remains impersonal. Insofar as he is simply "pure intelligence," not a human person, he is to be partly "It," just as the thinking "I" remains a thinking *thing*, an entity, a substance. So He/he becomes It/it, and It/it becomes He/he, whenever *the other* one, *the other* identity is contextually called for in place of one that is being questioned, on both macro and micro levels. For instance, the Lord, "the fear of (which) is the beginning of wisdom," is "pure intelligence" that creates. But how can one fear "it," pure intelligence? And how can "it" create? Yet it does. It has to. That is Descartes' point.

Is Descartes being confused? Yes and no. Yes, as we have already seen from the blindness chapter (Scene 1), it was Descartes himself who warned against run-of-the-mill mimetic thinking such as the identificatory conflation of light as a sensation on the one hand and light as an objective attribute on the other (C, 1:126). Also recall the feather example: The tickling feather does not contain tickling but simply produces such a sensation. By reading back into God the natural light of reason in us, the presumed source of such light, in a way that has the two cofound the intellect, Descartes does appear to make a similar bidirectional move that he himself tends to find problematic. So, yes, he is being structurally, erroneously bipolar. But no, it does not seem to be an issue for him when God is at issue. The Cartesian intellect is discriminately analytic but also sweepingly intuitive, intuition being immediate mental apprehension, "the indubitable conception of a clear and attentive mind which proceeds solely from the light of reason" (R, 10:368/1:14, Rule 3). In the Cartesian landscape of thinking, the foundational intellect itself—which not only enables but more significantly animates noticing, comparing, and contrasting things—remains covered, privileged, and actively hidden. How else is this magical transference and distribution of light to be understood if not via the world of the senses, which for Descartes is also a world of metaphoric significations, even divine revelations? From his little notebook containing early fragments perhaps not meant to be published, we find some fascinating traces of this emerging philosopher already making an exceptional case for imaginative abstractions, that is, analogical collaborations between the senses and the intellect. Under the subheading *"Olympica* (Olympian Matters)," we can see such signs and hear such pronouncements:

Just as the imagination employs figures in order to conceive of bodies, so, in order to frame ideas of spiritual things, the intellect makes use of certain bodies which are perceived through the senses, such as wind and light. By this means we may philosophize in a more exalted way, and develop the knowledge to raise our minds to lofty heights. (Pt, 10:217/1:4)

The things which are perceivable by the senses are helpful in enabling us to conceive of the Olympian matters. The wind signifies spirit; movement with the passage of time signifies life; light signifies knowledge; heat signifies love; and instantaneous activity signifies creation. (Pt, 10:218/1:5)

Man has knowledge of natural things only through their resemblance to the things which come under the senses. Indeed, our estimate of how much truth a person has achieved in his philosophizing will increase the more he has been able to propose some similarity between what he is investigation and the things known by the senses. (Pt, 10:218–219/1:5)

Such circuitous "reasoning" (Descartes) processes of "responsorial" (Marion) order of and for the Other, recursively covering the axiomatic rupture within zero-degree thinking, are "both logical and affective" (Kristeva) because they are also inseparable from the narrative impulses and nuanced jolts of the human imaginary:

"A circle" . . . requires a "guarantee" of evidence by divine "veracity." In a word, it is possible that the epistemological overtheologization characteristic of modern commentary not only raises a difficulty where there is none, but above all hides the difficulties Descartes really faced.[12]

The difficulties are elliptical. The problem comes down to the ellipsis itself geometrically built in the following question, which keeps returning to haunt the scenes of the *cogito:* How could I doubt the (source of) light that enables doubting, to begin with? *Dubito, sum.* In that formulation, I am trying to see beyond to something more and deeper than the usual logical problem of self-defeating skepticism. Let us further focus on the complex subjectivity and textuality of doubting. After all, "It" does not doubt; although he can doubt "It" while trying not to, "him" is the subject openly cloistered—covered—in both the senses and the intellect. Note the braided grammar of architectural desire for a new beginning as part of and precursor to thinking, as embodied in the flash and flesh of Cartesian intuition: irreducible thinking *for and with* as well as *of* God, the ultimate restarting point, the creative source of all things. God, to whom Augustine prays, also becomes in the eyes and hands of Descartes that of which he speaks, as Anne Hartle points out.[13] However, God, turned into an object of contemplative observation, does not necessarily erase fear from the observer. Even when rationalizing God this way, Descartes retains the structure of affective dependence on Him, knowing that God is additive, not substitutive.

"BEYOND OUR GRASP" OF THE CIRCLE

Turning toward such God, which is to say turning God into the semifaceless or peculiarly faceless external creator-author of the world as well, Descartes claims to "know" as well as fear "His greatness," if not Him per se. For Descartes, He is still "beyond our grasp" (C, 1:145/3:23): "In general we can assert that God can do everything that is within our grasp but not that he cannot do what is beyond our grasp. It would be rash to think that our imagination reaches as far as his power" (C, 1:146/3:23). "In any case, what basis have we for judging whether one infinity can be greater than another or not?" (C, 1:147/3:23). According to Descartes, we know such greatness instantly, innately, without "embracing it in one's thought," where "embracing" is hugging a mountain (which we cannot) or hugging a tree (which we can); the point is that "to know something, it is sufficient to touch it with one's thought" (C, 1:152/3:25) or be touched by the greatness of pure intelligence. While potentially fulfilling, the Cartesian prosopopoeia is positionally measured and, at least in the way I read him here, quite poetic immeasurably. What matters in itself and to us in the present context is that very confusion, that intricate grammar of fused cogitation, "where I take grammar to mean the articulate organization of perception, reflection and experience, the nerve-structure of consciousness when it communicates with itself and others."[14]

Switching back and forth between, around, and across those two levels (at least) of tightly networked reflections, Descartes on God or God in Descartes somehow freely circles around the zero point structurally doubled as such. In fact, Arnauld also spotted this Cartesian loop and, unlike some of us, found it "worrying" (C, 7:214/3:150) and "perverse" (C, 7:215/3:151), which made him feel "extremely anxious" (C, 2:215/3:151). Why? What exactly is being critically circled here?

"What exactly do you want?" (Or, 7:197/2:138); what is that "something" you are after, of which you are trying to "convince yourself"? Such is how Arnauld prefaced his letter to Mersenne, who had wanted an educated opinion, a peer review, so to speak, of the articles of faith authored by his friend Descartes who often relied on Mersenne as a messenger to the world out there as well as a sort of litmus test from whom Descartes would, therefore, "want the truth" and not praise (Pt, 10:217/1:4). "What exactly do you want?" This query, aggressively addressed to the messenger, seems in fact about the author, the philosopher of "outstanding intelligence and exceptional learning" (Or, 7:197/2:138), that man of "prudence" (Or, 7:217/2:152). What exactly does *Descartes* know (or not) and whom exactly does *he* believe (or not)? As Arnauld sensed, it is not clear on paper whether the thinker really believes or knows God as the creator, the supreme author of all beings. He is concerned with Descartes' "somewhat free style of philosophizing," especially displayed in the *First Meditation* which, he goes on to suggest, "should be furnished with a brief preface which explains that there is no serious doubt cast on these matters but that the purpose is to isolate temporarily those matters" (Or, 7:215/2:151). Descartes' reflective energy leaves things hyperbolically hanging in the air, structurally suspended, "theologically" (Or, 7:197/2:138) unclean. How can this philosopher emerge cleansed? Such is the worry aired by Arnauld who seems to understand that "unthinking, one still 'hopes to God.' The philosophical edifice of hope is that of Cartesian rationality (where, most subtly, the theological drifts, like sand in an hourglass, into the metaphysical and the scientific)."[15] What Arnauld found tricky and unnerving about Descartes' boldly rearticulated vision of God and His creatures is, quite rightly, its metaphysical driftiness, which is reflected in his "free style."

To begin with, what Descartes presents is a, not the, version; the materiality of God, let loose by a series of hyperbolic reckonings of other possibilities, cannot be restored or reconstructed by any "formal" means (Or, 7:218/7:153). This world one inhabits is a world that might, could, or should have been otherwise but would be just "it," *the* world, every fiber of which God knows, the universal creator. True, "tautologically, only God creates. But has he done so only once?"[16] What is threatening about Descartes' formulation is that it renders just that question visible, possible. With Descartes, the fable remains a fable; once upon a time, there was an/the *X*, which could go back before or beyond that time. Unlike Descartes, Arnauld needs a more linear and literal understanding of the creation story as *the* story: only once, A to Z, that's "It," and "He" made it. That level of material certainty and that kind of bodily assurance is what the theologian found wanting in the Cartesian version of God.

The "circularity-criterion" problem Arnauld points to, along with the circuitry problem of the fusion or profusion of "He" and "It," is then locatable precisely within this odd ontological tension, interdependency, and interplay between "a" versus "the," indefinite versus definite, both formal and material. The issue is that the first terms and the second terms are fundamentally interdependent, engaged in an originarily reciprocal relationship, often characterized as "viciously circular." The thinker draws—appropriates the sense of—existence from God, whose existence results from the property exchange, a kind of referential automortgaging, between God as "It" and God as "Him." This is also between "a" God whose reference remains indefinite and God to whom we would refer definitely, properly, naturally, so much so that we need not and cannot adorn it or qualify it any more by any linguistic means or with a logical step. In other words:

> It is not a formal circle; Descartes need not be seen as using the veracity of clear and distinct ideas as a premise in his argument. But he presumably uses clear and distinct perception as *a* method by which to arrive at the truth, even in the proofs of God's existence; and God's existence is then used to substantiate *that* method. . . . Descartes might try to get out of the circle.[17]

> To claim that a proposition is true, the proposition must be judged to be true in accordance with *a* criterion. One then encounters either circular reasoning or an infinite regression. That is, on the one hand, the criterion of truth requires that one knows it itself is true, meaning that one already needs to know what is true in order to specify *the* criterion, yet one already needs to know the criterion in order to recognize *the* truth. That is, because one cannot have one without the other, one is trapped in *a* circle. Alternatively, the skeptic suggests that whatever criterion of truth is advanced, the selection of *that* criterion requires *a* criterion. But the new criterion again requires *a*nother criterion, ad infinitum. . . . Descartes introduces a . . . dramatic problem . . . known as the demon hypothesis. What if, asks Descartes, our reasoning processes are systematically distorted by an all-powerful demon-deceiver?[18]

If we indeed cannot be sure of our intellect without knowing our origin, it is hard to see how we could avoid using the natural light to prove *the* very thing that is supposed to secure its trustworthiness. Perhaps the hypothesis of *a* deceiving God can be shown to be incoherent. . . . *The* circle is not avoided.[19]

When does a god become (the) God and vice versa? How does a criterion become the criterion and vice versa? The philosopher's answer above about the shift of the *cogito*'s gaze from "a" to "the" and vice versa is this: just when one is left with no other options but just one, when one needs at least one (something, "whatever I may call it/him") as one immovable and indubitable truth to rest on. This way, "one"—whether an/the ego, a god, God, a personae, or an object, whatever it is or whoever he is—remains singular in its originary ellipticality and triangular plurality, the referential aberration notwithstanding. The *cogito* argument sustains itself by shuttling between the two by always already addressing, calling upon, drawing upon the other, even in doubt: The *cogito* is that movement or names the repetition of it.

In a similar pattern, the gaze of the *cogito* that contains both the "He-moment" and the "It-moment" shuttles between the two, as if in closed circuit. To recall, "He" is not "It," but the two are braided, I said. God is not "It," but not in the way I am not an "it." Cartesian God, the absolute subject outside the dialectical chain of being and becoming, unlike myself the self-objectified self, does not have to overcome anything in order to be truly itself/himself or to become something else truer or clearer. For Descartes, God simply, purely, is. He/It has no desire to be otherwise to begin with. So rather, Cartesian God would be (the) one who would "negate" the very "negation"[20] on a wholly different level, on a holy register. How and where does it happen? By interception: by having the thinking ego intercept, or pass through, the very ellipsis of thinking, right before it is about to collapse on its own negative weight; "it may be that the *cogito* is special in the *specific way* that it is immune to the evil genius doubt, for *my* existence is directly implicated in the doubt itself."[21] In what specific way does the thinking ego become special? By blocking the evil genius's access to God, by becoming good like God, "Him." By becoming a mini-It, "it," the object of the evil genius's deception, *a* thinking thing also becomes *the* thinking thing. The repeated autoinscriptive attempts follow, in which the ego, the thinking "I," functions as the temporal glue. On my count, the evil genius, the "bad" other, tries to interrupt the smooth progression of thinking at least four times throughout the first half of the *Meditations* (M, 7:22/2:15; 7:25/2:17; 7:26/2:18; 7:36/2:25) where the key is the establishment of the dual truths prior to the solidification of them, that is, the existence of God and the immortality of the soul. So "immunity" is the other key to that special corner in Descartes' thinking room; the *cogito* becomes "special" by contrast, by depriving the evil genius, the constant security threat, of any *topos* of his or her own.

The demon, so unmasked, cannot ultimately be "it," for it will eventually disappear. Ultimately, the evil genius gets exorcized, according to Descartes' circuitously interventionist, revelatory tautology of the *cogito*, where God comes or is brought forward as the savior of that tautology, of that circle of truth. To be good, not evil: That is the only but ultimate difference between God and the evil genius, which remains "indefinite" in the sense that it is "some or a certain evil genius [*genium aliquem malignum*; Fr. *un certain mauvais génie*]" (M, 7:22/2:15),[22] not *the* evil genius that there is. The reason why this "some evil genius" is indefinite is that the theological goodness of "some God [*aliquem Deum*]" (M, 7:21/2:14)[23] automatically and ultimately wills its eradication. That is part of what God does: expunge evil. That is what God is: the essential absence of evil, the ineradicable presence of good. Strictly speaking, in terms of ontonomological "indetermination," "some God" and "some evil genius" both share the hermeneutical fate: Such an introduction of and induction into God announces "the first determination of God as indetermination itself. . . . The sole point that all of these hypotheses have in common is to be found in their very indetermination."[24] Then the difference between the two, being essentially moral, can also be grasped in terms of the strength or force of such indeterminacy. God remains definitely indefinite.

> God comes to the *ego* only hidden beneath the mask of the role (*persona*) that he has until now been playing in the theatre of the previous *Meditations*—that of an *aliquis*. In short, God appears beneath the most dissimulating mask, that of the most total indetermination.[25]

ONLY GOD CAN LIFT THE MASK IN "THE PORTRAIT OF DESCARTES' CONFUSION"

In this scenario, "only God can lift the spell. . . . The atheist, for Descartes, occupies the peculiar position of one for whom the Evil Genius hypothesis and the double engendered by it can *never* be dispelled."[26] So even if the evil genius might, could, or even should have been "the author of my being," I exist as a text of God and not the evil genius because (1) I could then become "it," namely, the object of that evil deception and (2) "it," in turn, ultimately belongs to God. Given that dual (protection of) reason, I exist. The strife is then between a firewalled, strong subjectivity and a weaker, crumbly one, from both of which my usual subjectivities derive, hence, the Olympian motto of Cartesian subjectivity *larvatus prodeo* (I come forward masked) (Pt, 10:213/1:2) or *pro deo* (toward God), as we have already seen and will see again shortly.

Descartes lets in "someone else" for and in place of himself. He does so by summarily blocking the evil genius's access to the cogitative subject by keeping invisible the face of skeptical self-effacement, by keeping visible the frame for that replacement, by keeping active the locus of that displacement. It is through this intricate narrative play of partial (self)(un)masking that (ego) *sum* is about to emerge. Who or who else? Whoever it is, *that* one only, *that* conceptual personae, akin to "a good angel" (Pt, 10:218/1:5) and close to God, "passed the idea [of God] on to him, so the idea of God which is in us must have God himself as its cause" (M, 7:15/2:11). "Before God, reverentially, and as a rarity among the metaphysicians, Descartes stands hidden—he does not keep secrets, nor does he sneak away, but hides his face before that of the infinite—*larvatus pro Deo*."[27]

What we see here is "also the portrait of Descartes' *confusion*,"[28] as Jean-Luc Nancy observes: "Since the subject was not, before coming out upon the stage where he will say 'I am,' the mask also dissimulates the confusion in which he comes unto himself (thus unto being). . . ."[29] What connects this confusion and the "blushing," "modesty," or "shame" (associated with erection, as Nancy indicates) that the "anonymous" actors are supposed to hide (Pt, 10:213–215/1:2–3)? It is the gaze of God, masculinized. It is as if the Cartesian subject had to become gender-confused in the face of God, naturally as both the subject who conceives like God and the object conceived by God. In this biblically clichéd scene, moral self-consciousness comes to function as a narrative springboard for gradational self-realization. That is, the Cartesian mask appears for a reason. It is a modern genesis, the generator of divinely buttressed subjectivity, the gendered placeholder or point of origination in the system of narrativized knowing, especially self-knowing:

> Behind the mask is no one: there is no figure for thought, if "by body I understand all that may end in some figure." There is someone beneath the mask, since masked "he" goes forward. There is someone confused with no one, since "he" resembles nothing, someone who is confused with no one (*personne*), that is, in Latin, with the role or mask with which "he" hides his shame.
>
> But this modesty is the condition of the knowledge of the subject. . . .[30]

Nancy reads that divine "person," that conceptual persona of divinity, dynamically and theatrically, writing across the hyperindeterminacy of the figure of God more readily abstracted by Marion.

The following virtual "Socratic" counterargument that highlights the moment of predatory "confusion" in Descartes' philosophical reliance on a figure of God also points to that pattern of the ego ontologically (mis)-appropriating God sightings in the theatrical production of *cogito, sum*:

SOCRATES: It seems to me, then, that you and Spinoza quite agree about pantheism.

DESCARTES: What do you mean by that?

SOCRATES: That you seem to be confusing yourself with God. Other than that minor confusion, though, I think your system passes muster . . .

DESCARTES: Wait! What do you mean, that I confuse myself with God? What a ridiculous charge!

SOCRATES: Well, in saying that "I exist" is a self-evident proposition, do you not say that its predicate is essential to its subject?

DESCARTES: Yes. That is what a self-evident proposition means.

SOCRATES: And does this not mean that you are saying that your existence, which is your predicate, is essential to your "I," which is your subject?

DESCARTES: Yes, for "existence" is my predicate and "I" is my subject.

SOCRATES: So you are saying that your existence is your essence.

DESCARTES: Oh.

SOCRATES: I thought that in your theology that was true only of God. That is why God needs no creator to give Him existence, while everything else does: His very existence is to exist, but creates need an external cause to exit.

DESCARTES: Oops.

SOCRATES: An eloquent short act of contrition!

DESCARTES: It is true that my existence is contingent, not necessary. I did not have to exist. In fact, before I was conceived, I did not exist. So my existence is *not* self-evident in this sense—only God's is. So "I am" is a self-evident proposition only for God, not for any creature.

SOCRATES: You see, now, why I said that when you begin with "I am," and declare this self-evident, you confuse your essence with God's, and your name with the name God revealed to Moses from the burning bush: "I Am."

So this is indeed a radical new beginning. Medieval man began with the divine "I Am," but you become the first truly modern man, since you begin with the human "I am."

DESCARTES: No, no, no. That would be heresy, and blasphemy, and nothing could be farther from my intention.[31]

All over again . . . it is quite clear that, as Judovitz notes, the function of the Cartesian mask is, precisely, to confuse, far from rendering X "clear and distinct":

> Descartes' use of this (theatrical) metaphor in the context of his masked authorial persona takes on specific meanings: it reflects at once his involvement with allegorical representation, with the feint and fiction that he both uses and rejects. . . . The masked ego is neither merely the figure of personal intent—of escaping religious persecution as shown by the anonymous publication of the *Discourse*, nor purely that of modesty. Rather, the mask—whether theatrical, or later autobiographical or confessional—will confuse Descartes' multiple roles as author, actor and spectacle with the actual subject of his discourse, the subject of truth.[32]

Again, Arnauld is not to be fooled. What he probably, and conclusively, sensed is the very possibility of indeed "there being no one behind the mask." He makes this one very incisive editorial suggestion on the concluding part of the *Sixth Meditation*: "following on from this point, where we find the clause 'since I did not know the author of my being,' I would suggest a substitution of the clause 'since I was pretending that I did not know'" (Or, 7:215/2:151). The addition of "since I was pretending," what value does it add? What a redemption a small phrase can generate! Arnauld is making an extremely interesting, crucial intervention, as it covers (up) the nerve center of Descartes' vision (and version) of God. His proposal is that the as-if thought, an act of hyperbole, be unambiguously renounced, expunged, by the as-is thought, an act of self-grounding at the end—hence the suggested confessional switch to "since I was pretending." Arnauld wishes to make sure that this series of hyperbolic reflections would not be really followed, and that it would, as intended, keep reorientating "even the most perverse skeptic" (Or, 7:215/2:151) to the source of light: God. Is this close to an inquisition? Was a follow-up in order?

> *Later on,* however, I had many experiences which gradually undermined all the faith I had had in the senses. *Sometimes* towers which had looked round from a distance disappeared square from close up. . . . Every sensory experience I have ever thought I was having *while* awake I can also think of myself as sometimes having *while* asleep; and since I do not believe that what I seem to perceive in sleep comes from things located outside me, I did not see why I should be any more inclined to believe this of what I think I perceive *while* awake. . . . Since I did not know the author of my being (*or at least was pretending not to*), I saw nothing to rule out the possibility that my natural constitution made me prone to error even in matters which seemed to me most true. . . .
>
> *But now,* when I am beginning to achieve a better knowledge of myself and the author of my being, although I do not think I should heedlessly accept everything I seem to have acquired from the senses, neither do I think that everything should be called into doubt.
>
> First, I know that everything which I clearly and distinctly understand is capable of being created by God so as to correspond *exactly* with my understanding of it. Hence the fact that I can clearly and distinctly understand one thing apart from another is enough to make me certain that the two things are distinct, since they are capable of being separated, at least by God. The question of what kind of power is required to bring about such a separation does not affect the judgment that the two things are distinct. Thus . . . I can infer correctly that my essence consists solely in the fact that I am a thinking thing. (7:77–8/2:53–4, emphases added)

Following the drift of Descartes' still semiperverse thinking here, I would now like to minipause and proceed to this question that seems to follow: how to "square the circle" or circle the square; what to do with such half-thinkable, half-baked thoughts that are there nonetheless, in some shape or form; how to do justice to the irreducibility of the body in time we often call "text," however indefinitely or indistinctly.

As Roland Barthes notes, "the pleasure of the text is that moment when my body pursues its own ideas—for my body does not have the same ideas I do."[33]

> Does the text have human form, is it a figure, an anagram of the body? Yes, but of our erotic body. The pleasure of the text is irreducible to physiological need.
>
> The pleasure of the text is that moment when my body pursues its own ideas. . . . How can we take pleasure in a *reported* pleasure (boredom of all narratives of dreams, of parties)? How can we read criticism? Only one way: since I am here a second-degree reader, . . . I observe clandestinely the pleasure of others, I enter perversion . . . the doubled, the trebled, the infinite perversity of the critic and of his reader.[34]

Again, at stake is the perversity, not falsity, of the skeptic: the hypercritical, the overly involved reader of *X*, for whom the issue is the tissue of certain mental sensations, affective thinking, sustaining the synaptic vitality of critical interventions. Just for instance, "He" simply feels different from "It," and vice versa. What would be "infinitely perverse," in this case, of anyone participating in this proto-Cartesian spiral of reflections is the very textured desire to touch or not to touch that circle, however passingly—again, the grammar of desire itself, ambiguous as it is.

The aporia of circular reasoning remains, returningly: Is it not all that can be "guaranteed," the name of God who calls light into being? Is it not all that can be "guaranteed," in the name of God that calls light into being? Such seems the ultimate sign of Cartesian reflection, saved around the zero point, shuttling between undifferentiated prenarrativized *logos* and *logos* that separates itself into beings in time . . . is it not what happens in the corner of your eyes, when you reflect?

Created and Cheated?—So Be It!

"SO LONG AS I THINK I AM SOMETHING," "PURE INTELLIGENCE IS GOD"

Here is a textual illustration of that tension that is one of the earliest and, in my view, most intriguing scribbles by Descartes. A Cartesian fragment or code or even Kabbalah?

"God separated the light from the darkness." This text in Genesis means that God separated the good angels from the bad angels. The text cannot be understood literally, since a privation cannot be separated from a positive state. *Pure intelligence is God.* [*Intelligentia pura est Deus.*] (Pt, 10:218/1:5, trans. modified)

The CSM version, otherwise superb, translates the last sentence, "Pure intelligence is God," as "God is pure intelligence," subtly reversing the order of cogitative origination. However, hearing the nuance of this "genetic" as well as generic reflection, one would see that God, named here, functions rather as a sign, a sticker the thinker puts *at the end*. It is not quite, or yet, the personified subject that generates or necessitates the description that follows. In fact, here, God is not in control. The one conventionally called "God" is controlled by *that* God, as it were, the real or other or another set of "alpha and omega" that is one and the same, who first and simply "posits," as in "let there be light," and who has the final say in all things in the form of the last Judgment.

Yet this does not mean that Descartes is simply a nominalist vis-à-vis the question of God—not exactly. Take Descartes' reply to Thomas Hobbes's objection to his use of the word "idea" in the *Third Meditation*, the "idea" of God in particular (Or, 7:179–181/3:126–7, Fifth). Here, Hobbes represents the position of an empiricist nominalist:

We have no idea or image corresponding to the sacred name of God. And that is why we are forbidden to worship God in the form of an image. . . . It seems, then, that there is no idea of God in us. A man born blind, who has often approached fire and felt hot, recognizes that there is something which makes him hot; and when he hears that this is called "fire" he concludes that fire exists. But he does not know what shape or color fire has, and has absolutely no idea or image of fire that comes before his mind. The same applies to a man who recognizes that there must be some cause of his images or ideas, and that this cause must have a prior cause and so on; he is finally led to the supposition of some external cause which never began to exist and hence cannot have a cause prior to itself, and he concludes that something eternal must necessarily exist. But he has no idea which he can say is the idea of that eternal being; he merely gives the name or label "God" to the thing he believes in, or acknowledges to exist. (Or, 7:180/3:127)

Using the blind as an analogical example, Hobbes is pointing to two things: (1) the fallacious inference of "something external and eternal" (God) from subjective experiences or perceptions and (2) the arbitrariness of nomenclature itself. Accordingly, Descartes' rebuttal involves a twofold clarification: turning that "something external and external" into still an innate idea, while separating such an idea itself from any systems of signification or reference:

> Here my critic wants the term "idea" to be taken to refer simply to the images of material things which are depicted in the corporeal imagination; and if this is granted, it is easy for him to prove that there can be no proper idea [*propriam ideam*] of an angel or God [*Dei*]. But I make it quite clear . . . that I am taking the word "idea" to refer to whatever [*quod*] is immediately perceived by the mind. For example, when I want something, or am afraid of something, I simultaneously perceive that I want, or am afraid. . . . I used the word "idea" because it was the standard philosophical term used to refer to the forms of perception belonging to the divine mind, even though we recognize that God does not possess any corporeal imagination. And besides, there was not any more appropriate term at my disposal. (Or, 7:181/3:127–8)

So the reason why Descartes is not simply a "rationalist nominalist" is that, for him, the "whatness" (quiddity) of the very idea of God, again "whatever it is (to be) called," remains irreducible insofar as it is reciprocally, circularly "appropriated" and shared between the senses and the intellect and, indeed, among the blind and the sighted (Scene 1). According to Descartes, it is not inductively inferred from experiences, contrary to Hobbes's view. To call It/Him "*Dei*" is primarily a result of people "agreeing to learn" or being subject to the ideologico-linguistic supremacy of "Latin" (C, 1:79/3:12). This "Polybius, citizen of the world" (Pt, 10:214/1:2), the polyglot traveler, would have no problem calling It/Him by any different name, if need be, as long as this "simple idea in the human imagination" (C, 1:81/3:13) is linguistically retained and transferrable in some ways.

The irreducible idea of God repeatedly stressed as such, which remains mysteriously "simple" or "simply" mysterious, which is differentially distant from any human acts of appellation, contains performative God who just "lets there be light," who again, whatever It/He is called, doubles It/Himself by becoming itself/himself through the human intuition—that is, "something." Cartesian God is the becoming-god or having-become-god of God. This citational departure of God from traditionally storied "God" as the figure of the ultimate Judge, this nonfigurative figure of all-in-one, is not the same as straightforward, empty abstraction. Its irreducible significance, its solar power, lies in that all are "dependent" on Him/It, coextensive with his/its directorial movements regulating every movement, human or broadly cosmic.

SEPARATING "GOD" FROM GOD "IN WHATEVER DIRECTION"

Captured in Descartes' speculative imagination vis-à-vis divine creations is, as Antonio Negri observes, such a momentous tension or vectorial "conjuncture" between finitude and infinity, that oddly immemorialized time of thinking where the originary X-factor is circuitously entertained:

> Cosmology becomes cosmogony—but only in thought. In the "imaginary spaces," adopted ironically from the Scholastic tradition, God creates a "plenitude" that extends indefinitely . . . indefinitely far beyond in all directions . . . in whatever direction.[35]

Imagine "people on some vessel in the middle of the sea," where "there is more water beyond what they see" (TI, 11:32/1:90). Imagine a ship about to sink or already wrecked. Imagine Zora Neale Hurston's seaside characters sailing out in all directions (Scene 3), searching in every direction for their God(s); "On the high seas of optical subjectivity, there is only one rule: . . . in any case, hold a steady course."[36] How does one stay "steady" here? Hold on as necessary, rather than simply tightly. Stay alert and responsive, rather than just staying put. For this autocreative, water-tight "dependency" of the eternal truths and immortal soul on God cuts both ways, carrying the seed, the weed of independence of God insofar as *that* God, often mythologized and yet conceptually self-distancing, could have willed those truths and various manifestations of eternity differently or indifferently. Curiously, what is constantly called for as a structural necessity in this foundational discourse of truth or more precisely truth-making is a certain degree of discursive fluidity rather than dead certainty, rock-solid certitude. For sequentially or concurrently, God, the ultimate author of it all, could have or will have created a world where, suddenly, all the radii of a circle become unequal (C, 1:152/1:25):

THE REASONS FOR DOUBTING EVEN MATHEMATICAL DEMONSTRATIONS

> Our doubt will also apply to other matters which we previously regarded as most certain—even the demonstrations of mathematics. . . . We have been told that there is an omnipotent God who created us. Now we do not know whether he may have wished to make us beings of the sort who are always deceived even in those matters which seem to us supremely evident; for such a constant deception seems no less a possibility than the occasional deception which . . . does occur. We may of course suppose that our existence derives not from a supremely powerful God but either from ourselves or from some other source; but in that case, the less powerful we make the author of our coming into being, the more likely it will be that we are so imperfect as to be deceived all the time. (P, 8A:6/1:194, Article 5)

Watch that difference: that multiple mutability between "God" and God becoming necessarily possible, almost impersonally. Then, the divine powers and will such as omniscience and omnipotence are to be registered in terms of sovereign arbitration rather than some extrasequential security. "It will be said that if God had established these truths he could change them as a king changes his laws. To this the answer is: Yes he can, if his will can change" (C, 1:145–6/3:23), for "in God, willing, understanding, and creating are all the same thing without one being prior to the other even conceptually" (C, 1:153/6:3:25–6). Deceptive or defective God (M, 7:21/2:14) is inconceivable, conceptually impossible, not just morally unimaginable, because such a change itself is subject to God as well. If God made human beings "the sort who are always deceived," or even if God Himself would suddenly wake up or fall asleep, as we have entertained such a scenario with Heine (Scene 3), God would not be a deceiver himself in any case but rather the creator of such deceived or deceiving beings that are both defective, epistemologically or morally.

This dualized reservation of and for God, this "*separation*" of "God" and God (or from God) is an act of turning God into a kind of ontonomological "sticker" or labeled lid, as we noted earlier. Now it is "as radical in its intensity as it is global in its extension. The affirmation of the *contingency* of essences with respect to the divine will appear to deprive the world of all reality."[37] Shortly, we will see how such "separation and the metaphysical power of the *malin* (malign, cunning) will become definitive, irremovable facts,"[38] signaling not only the contingency but the vicissitude of all cosmic performances, divine or otherwise. Again, for now we only need to register this point: What is necessary about divinity is its performative contingency or sovereign performativity; by implication, God does not have to correspond to "God." That is, "Only God can lift the spell,"[39] those scare quotes.

Cartesian God is a pure act rather than a static attribute. It/He signals something more than conceptual or nominal. He wills. He acts. He posits. When He says, inaugurally, "Let there be light," what he does is to posit truth, in which light is deposited, almost automatically. The power of God lies in Its/His time-creating or "engineering" (M, 7:14–5/2:10–11), the "objectively intricate" act (M, 7:14/2:10) of which angels and humans are also capable (P, 8A:65/1:242) to the extent that they are coextensive with and so created in the image of God, where the powers are preserved:

> The inverse path is also travelled: from the separation fixed in the metaphysical order to the separation in the historical order. The radical contingency discovered in the theological domain impinges immediately on the historical domain. The fundamental characteristics of that contingency are repeated in the social world. This should not come as a surprise. We saw how in the world of metaphor there is a sort of unitary compactness and a convergence of all the aspects of experience. Now the crisis becomes general to the precise degree to which that universe was compact. The separation is established with equal intensity in the world and in social relations. Consider how the theory of the creation of eternal truths, which grounds the radical effort to make the world contingent, is immediately exemplified. Truth is posited by God as the law of the absolute sovereign, the validity of the law is entrusted to the power that sustains it and this power is incomprehensible in both its origin and motivation.[40]

"Truth is posited by God as the law of the absolute sovereign." This is the metaphysical omnipotence of God and the radical contingency of its power, as mirrored in modern secular fragments, be they societal, cultural, historical, political, or philosophical . . . with their sovereign "truths" all individuated into the individual consciousness of them, small balls of beliefs compacted into something like "core values," however solipsistic they may sound or look. As voiced in typical Philosophy 101 classrooms, the usual sort of conversational stopper—"You are entitled to your view, and so am I, end of story"—is Cartesian in its paradigmatic individualism or subjectivism.

What is it to us that someone may make out that the perception whose truth we are so firmly convinced of may appear false to God or an angel, so that it is, absolutely speaking, false? Why should this alleged "absolute falsity" bother us, since we neither believe in it nor have even the smallest suspicion of it? For the supposition which we are making here is of a conviction so firm that it is quite incapable of being destroyed; and such a conviction is clearly the same as the most perfect certainty. (Or, 8A:145/2:103, Second Set)

As Frankfurt stresses, "Descartes' most basic and insistent preoccupation is with certainty itself, and he tends to be rather indifferent to the question of whether the certain corresponds to or fails to correspond with the real."[41] The sovereign subject, small or big, privileged as such, does not have to be right with regard to, or in correspondence to, the real; it/he only has to act as if it/he were right. The only difference between the big subject (e.g., God) and a small copy subject to its power (e.g., *res cogitans*) is that the first does not require certainty to ground Himself/Itself, whereas the second, derivative from it, does rely on such an external agency thus internalized, as if such existed; this is how the thinking thing supplements that lack, covers that distance, between itself and Pure Intelligence, namely, God.

Practically, this is also how Descartes becomes a Catholic dancing with the Protestants, a philosopher dancing with the Jesuit Fathers. That is how he moves, especially when he has to tiptoe. He convolutes that point of the independent dependency of divine cognition without missing the beat, holding on to that near eternal agitation of "as-if." Here, in this analogy, hear the Cartesian "music of thought,"[42] the "ambiguous intimacy"[43] between God "as It/He is" and God "as if It/He is": "Indeed to say that these truths are *in*dependent of God is to talk of him as if he were Jupiter or Saturn and to subject him to the Styx and the Fates" (C, 1:145/3:23, emphasis added).

AS GOD IS NEITHER JUPITER NOR SATURN BUT A/THE CONCEPTUAL PERSONA?

So again, Descartes is saying that (1) his God is not Jupiter or Saturn, or Greek or French or Latin or whatever, that is to say, neither mythological nor historicizable but still divinely transcendent, and yet (2) mathematical truths are dependent on the will of God insofar as He, as the sovereign Subject, could have made other determinations. God, for Descartes, is that figure of absolute singularity or random iningurality, where contingency and certainty must cross at least once. The other, subsequent Continental rationalists such as Nicolas Malebranche, Baruch Spinoza, and Gottfried Leibniz sought to find a way out of this conundrum of half-inferred God by progressively subjecting (even) God to *logos*, which was their way of re-orienting or reordering that traditional idea of God as independent, further insulated from the very theoretical possibility of other beginnings or endings. That is, they tried to epistemologize the divine rather than to divinize knowledge by closing the gap between God and "God," by naturalizing the second into the first; still, Descartes stays in between, shuttling. While still divinizing *logos*, ontotheologizing indubitable truths, Descartes left the content ultimately blank, *"blanche"* (white), as Jean-Luc Marion put it[44]—nothing but the whole truth? Here, Descartes, the very one who started the rationalist ball rolling by initiating an experimental separation of the *cogito* from God, remains an oddball. Again, the braided complexity in his restaging of the problem of the "the Styx and the Fates" is a riddle in point: There one sees the mythological retention of God reinforced time and again by ancient stories of time stacked upon time, the narrative impulse of which epistemological reasoning turns into the allegorical force of truths.

Theodore Adorno explains the narrative structure of this double move, this "intertwinement of history and prehistory," in terms of the Odyssean dialectic of enlightenment, where:

> the contrast between the single surviving ego and the multiplicity of fate reflects the antithesis between enlightenment and myth. The hero's peregrinations from Troy to Ithaca trace the path of the self through myths, a self infinitely weak in comparison to the force of nature and still in the process of formation as self-consciousness. The primeval world is secularized as the space he measures out; the old demons populate only the distant margins and islands of the civilized Mediterranean, retreating into the forms of rock and cave from which they had originally sprung in the face of primal dread. The adventures bestow names on each of these places, and the names give rise to a rational overview of space. The shipwrecked, tremulous navigator anticipates the work of the compass. His powerlessness, leaving no part of the sea unknown, aims to undermine the ruling powers. But, in the eyes of the man who has thus come of age, the plain untruth of the myths, the fact that sea and earth are not actually populated by demons but a magic delusion propagated by traditional popular religion, becomes something merely "aberrant" in contrast to his

unambiguous purpose of self-preservation, of returning to his homeland and fixed property.[45]

The moral of this story? Descartes' God, not exactly Descartes, is that "compass," which Descartes the thinking thing appropriates. That is the imaginary "homeland, fixed property" of utopian Cartesianism, where this Odyssean self or character, updated into a modernly roaming philosopher-scientist, is measuredly "preserved," replacing, without erasing, the mythological "space" of God traditionally reserved as such. The mystery is not lost but displaced, transferred inwardly, creating internal dramas of time and space.

Quite rightly, Marion too, who has "extensively studied the role of theology in the elaboration of Cartesian thought" precisely "in the case of the creation of the eternal truths,"[46] takes this "Jupiter, Styx, and Fate" passage seriously. Rightly again, he focuses on "the role of a poetic reference" in it, the ties between ontotheological impulses of philosophy and poetic resonances in the Cartesian meditation on God. Ferdinand Alquié, another notable commentator, partly from whom Marion draws his insight, senses in that passage the *"weakening* of the divine freedom"; on his reading, the sequential duplication of mathematical truths as the divine understanding inevitably leads to that effect.[47] Marion, in his polemical response to it, argues that "the Styx and the Fates" sequence, on the contrary, "redoubles" the first sequence or order of the divine understanding by "designating a new target for the creation of the eternal truths,"[48] which therefore strengthens the "univocity of reason, which becomes a law even for God."[49] So the effect, according to Marion, is rather a clearer demarcation of the differences between the Christian God and pagan gods or Stoic destiny.[50] For Marion, the passage represents a case of the Christian appropriation of pagan poetics for a philosophical purpose, an affirmation of mathematical naturalism, where the fixity or robustness of mathematical truths is maximally defended as part and parcel of the "naturally" given. Such is, in his view, how the tension between a god and (the) God can be resolved. I remain still skeptical, however. Should we go along with Marion's line of reading, "although the world . . . was created ready-made by God" (P, 8A:203/1:267)?

Has It/Him "unbegun"?[51] Whence and whither that "ready-made" world?

For this present reader, whose perspective too is theologically inflected but perhaps otherwise-infused, the Styx and the Fates passage rather exemplifies the creative dissonances of double-think by "the third" conceptual personae, "that someone else" who exploits precisely the inner duality of the poeticotheological imaginary. My present view on this issue of the rhetorical values of the figuration of the divine as well as the demonic in Cartesian context is closer if not identical to Alquié's, inasmuch as my analysis focuses on those moments of elastic divergences in the reasoning process of *cogito*, the recursive moments of quasi-transcendental hyperambiguation in Cartesian meditation. The second inscription of that "something that I am as long as I think," as we have seen in this section, creates precisely such a narrative edge and tension—against the backdrop already drawn.

Here, I am also reminded of *The Dream* narrative that Wilhelm Dilthey "sketched,"[52] albeit incompletely, in 1903–1904 in self-conscious imitation of Raphael's *School of Athens* (1509–1510), another crisis-inflected dream-from-the-above but much larger, longer, busier, and populated with a panoramic assemblage of philosophers from the historical past. In that other inaugural dream of philosophy branching itself out in the form of Hermeneutics, our little big Descartes, "whose delicate figure worn out by the power of thought," was seen joining the post-Renaissance modern idealists such as Kant and then swiftly "separating himself from the mathematical naturalists."[53] Again, I wonder, what does one make of this distance, these differences, among the cast of characters?

Stepping farther back, with George Steiner, I am left wondering about this, summarily:

> In what regards are theological, metaphysical and aesthetic conceptions of conception kindred or divergent? Why is it that Indo-European languages allow, indeed solicit the sentence: "God created the universe," whereas they flinch at the sentence: "God invented the universe?" The intricate play of differentiation and overlap between "creation" and "invention" has been little explored.[54]

Bursting Forth: The First Move to Sum, Squaring the Circle

<small>"I MUST FINALLY CONCLUDE" BETWEEN "CREATION AND INVENTION"</small>

How is the difference between creation and invention played out in the Cartesian context?

How does Descartes try to get out of the Cartesian circuit, his philosophical skin? When does the specter of the evil genius that "allows no distance at all,"[55] this "specter of complement entrapment,"[56] disappear? Where could I stop this seemingly interminable circus, circuit, of self-inventions? When is enough enough?

> It is clear enough that an infinite regress is impossible here, especially since I am dealing not just with the cause that produced me in the past, but also and more importantly with the cause that preserves me at the present moment. (M, 7:50/2:34)

The question is: What sort of "I" would be led to believe that "I must finally conclude that this proposition, *I am, I exist*, is necessarily true"? What is the "I" of "the present moment," the "I" "preserved" as such against all odds, against all the tricky moves by the evilly inventive genius floating out there or even lodged within me? How to stop all this, how to expunge him, how to not let myself be attracted to that pseudo-object? That is the question.

Bursting, passing, ranking . . . this is how *res cogitans* sets about coping with "the first confusion" of self-encompassment that ripples through reflective consciousness. That is how it reaches out for the first "thought" of "*cogito, sum*" that passes through, each time, singularly:

> First, the *ego* of the *cogito*, reformulated in the terms of the *Second Meditation:* "Let whoever can do so deceive me, he will never bring it about that I am nothing, so long as I continue to think I am something." Descartes here does not comment whether the conversation of this evidence into truth is valid. Would the *regula generalis* be suspended? So a number of commentators have suggested. We see no reason to admit this: rather, the whole sequence *bursts* with an almost irrepressible confidence in the truth of evidence. . . . If I think myself deceived, I am inasmuch as thinking, even if I do not think (myself) inasmuch as deceived. Here the attack provoking the *confusion* of self-perception reinforces its clarity and distinction: so for me to confuse myself, it is still *first* necessary that I exist. The ego *permits* the *regula generalis* to be put

to work—it *passes* from evidence to the rank of truth. One must not forget that the ego's existence here is not taking an inventory of the number of falsifiable evidences. . . .[57]

We are not simply psychologizing but seeking to narrativize the structurally excessive, logical forces of the evil genius argument, where the "objective reality" of God, "the sparks of knowledge" (Pt, 10:217/1:4) of It/Him, is extracted "as in a flint . . . through reason" (Pt, 10:217/1:4), wrestled out of the fiction, out of the simulacra of and by the evil genius, the other wrestler who must lose the game:

> The rhythm of wrestling is . . . that of rhetorical amplification: the emotional magniloquence, the repeated paroxysm, the exasperation of the retorts can only find their natural outcome in the most baroque confusion. Some fights, among the most successful kind, are crowned by a final charivari, a sort of unrestrained fantasia where the rules, the law of the genre, the referee's censuring and the limits of the ring are abolished, swept away by a triumphant disorder which overflows into the hall and carries off pell-mell wrestlers, seconds, referee and spectators. . . . Such a precise finality demands that wrestling should be exactly what the public expects of it. Wrestlers, who are very experienced, know perfectly how to direct the spontaneous episodes of the fight so as to make them conform to the image which the public has of the great legendary themes of its mythology. A wrestler can irritate or disgust, he never disappoints, for he always accomplishes completely, by a progressive solidification of signs, which the public expects of him. In wrestling, nothing exists except in the absolute, there is no symbol, no allusion, everything is presented exhaustively. Leaving nothing in the shade, each action discards all parasitic meanings and ceremonially offers to the public a pure and full signification, rounded like Nature. This grandiloquence is nothing but the popular and age-old image of the perfect intelligibility of reality. What is portrayed by wrestling is therefore an ideal understanding of things; it is the euphoria of men raised for a while above the constitutive ambiguity of everyday situations and placed before the panoramic view of a univocal Nature, in which signs at last correspond to causes, without obstacle, without evasion, without contradiction.[58]

The "precise finality" of the cogitative wrestler who wins—the *ego* of "*cogito, sum*"—is in its performative tautology. What the "I" of "I am thinking" discloses to itself through this process of hyperbolic autodeconstruction or self-deprivation is, as Nancy observes, "the feint's (indissociable) reverse side."[59] It is the point at which the epistemological specificity of the ego thinking, "soul-wrestling, here and now," gains an irreducible ontological weight. This point is irreducible insofar as the self-negation at this point is existentially inconsistent[60] and logically impossible to that extent. In this performatively self-contradictory statement enunciated by a person in which the same person negates his existence, what remains anchored and active is that conceptual personae, "the wrestler," as portrayed. That is, the "I" of "I am thinking" has now reached the point of triumph, of self-contradictory defeat, of strangely self-empowering exhaustion, where it can no longer pretend *not* to be—"*the point of an impossible feint or fiction*,"[61] "the farthest point of feint."[62] It is at this climatic moment of theatrical suspension and con*sum*mation that the narrative "I" and the performative "I" converge, fused together—in the eyes of God, supported by His/Its innate goodness and trustworthiness, God in waiting, for Which/Whom the "I" has been waiting.

A bit more, in slow motion?

Recall that the "I" of "I am nothing" does not yet involve the authorial intervention. Note how Descartes, the historical author of the *Meditations*, enters into—intervenes in—his own narrative by suddenly turning the narrative attention from Descartes the character in the fiction (the narrative I) to Descartes the sitter in the flesh (the authorial I). With the latter joining—breaking into—the former, sucking it in like a "blackhole"[63] that swallows universal matter only to spit back it out, the "I" of "I am now something, I exist" now includes not only the "I" referred to in the narrative but also the authorial "I" outside that narrates the very narrative.

Undeniably, such a performative self-intervention or authorial self-exposure, the kind also appearing in Laurence Sterne's *Tristram Shandy* (1759) or the *Essays* (1580)[64] of Michel de Montaigne, has a predatory streak, its quasi-schizophrenic intertextuality notwithstanding. The Cartesian self-intervention, the ego's reflective wrestle with itself, is an economized act toward self-possession, an abstract "extraction," as noted earlier with Descartes the philosopher, who does appreciate how the poets "force [the sparks of knowledge] out through the sharp blows of the imagination" (Pt, 10:217/1:4). Unlike the authorial "I" of *Tristram Shandy*, which pops up here and there through the narrative grid, the Cartesian "I" meticulously weaves its way through the text, *The Meditations,* and almost leaps out of it at one point with that "precise finality" of the winning wrestler.

GOD PINCHED, I PROCEED

Descartes' authorial intervention is neither ancillary nor accidental but topoanalytically elastic and occupationally necessary: He enters into his narrative as a self-conscious autobiographer and comes out of it as an onto-logical philosopher with "a pinch of truths" "seized" with his ink-stained three fingers—and that "pinch of truths" is composed of, if not all contain-able in, the ineradicable traces of cogitation "preserved" in this minimal propositional box, *sum,* (un)packable each time anew:

> Philosophy borrows from its two long-standing opponents: the sophists and poets. Moreover, it can also be said that it borrows from two truth procedures: mathematics, the paradigm of proof, and art, the paradigm of subjective potency. Its peculiar property is to borrow only in order to construct a categori-cal operation, which firmly fixes its locus. . . . The philosophic operation of the category of Truth lays out sorts of pincers or tongs. One of the limbs of these pincers is presented as an adjustment of the successive by the argument. The other, as a declaration at the limit. Truth links and sublimates. . . . The pincers of Truth, which link and sublimate, have a duty to seize *truths.* The relation of (philosophic) Truth to (scientific, political, artistic or amorous) truths is one of *seizing.* By "seizing," we mean capture, hold, and also seizure, astonishment. Philosophy is the locus of thinking wherein (non-philosophic) truths are seized as such, and seize us. . . . Philosophy is *a pinch of truths.*[65]

Remember how Descartes "pinches" God, like a good woman catching a good husband, to use his metaphor. Recall that narrative buildup to that point where the ego is finally head to head with the evil genius: The author-thinker enters into the character (the skeptic in the narrative), occupies his character's narrative (play)ground or dialectical field, and turns it into his own, his own ontological "ground," responding at once to the challenge from the evil genius and the call from God whom the ego must treat as "Him," the External Agent, the *Dei* of *Deus ex machina* (god from the machine), the ulti-mate rescuer or savior. By sticking to God, the ego holds water.

Again, am I nothing? No. I am something as long as I suspect that I may be nothing: That on which Descartes reflects is the event of questioning, the happening of the question. The content of the question matters less. The "No," this blocking reflex, enables and effects the return of a questioner to himself via God. Now the self-doubter shifts the focus of self-reflection from the "what" of the question to the "who" of the questioning. From there, ontological truths flow in the form of a thinker thinking of itself/himself; from here, the conceptual personae is split and solidified at once. What matters to the self-doubter at this point is not so much the burden of going forward with the question posed to himself as it is the necessity to stop to show the readers ("the public" in Barthes' text) as well as himself that it is nobody but him*self* facing the self-imposed question—that is, that it is Descartes himself who advances the question and advances with it.

With this temporally textured and layered turn of the mind to its interiority, the question becomes a hostage to the questioner, not the other way around. At play here is something like a self-cornering strategy: The thinking ego, pushed into the corner, will eventually spring back to life like a compressed spring bouncing back; this arguably most pivotal intersectional point in a philosophy rests in turn on the elastic viability of its method, its analytic mechanism. As Maurice Blanchot discerns it at the start of *The Infinite Conversation* (1969), what matters in this thought's "methodological" experimentation with itself is not a straightforward exposition or linear representation of ideas but rather the act "of describ[ing] the very movement of a research that joins thought and existence in a fundamental experience,"[66] "the bearing, the mode of holding oneself and of advancing of the one who questions [*cette méthode étant la conduite, le mode de se tenir et d'avancer de quelqu'un qui s'interroge*]."[67]

> Then the deceiving demon comes to wrap all doubts together and give them the utmost force. Little by little we are led to give up more and more of our world until there is nothing left. And it is at that point that Descartes' "solution" to the problem of the deceiving demon has the most force. Let skepticism run its course; then, if anything remains *firm* in this flux, we can *hold* on to it with the utmost confidence.[68]

What Descartes aims to demonstrate is both how self-doubt occurs affectively and naturally, not just methodologically, and how it can be overcome, if not resolved completely, through self-inscriptive remonstration. Worth noting in this regard is the opening passage of *The Passions of the Soul:*

> I note that whatever takes place or occurs is . . . a "passion" with regard to the subject to which it happens and an "action" with regard to that which makes it happen. Thus, although an agent and patient are often quite different, an action and passion must always be a single thing which has these two names on account of the two different subjects to which it may be related.
> (Ps, 11:328/1:328, Article 1)

Seen holistically this way, what matters philosophically and existentially, not just "scientifically" and "theoretically," is the constant staging taking place of critical self-interrogation; hence, the repetition as a necessary condition for habit formation, a photographic remembrance of the inaugural "event." A possible solution to the performative self-contradiction of *"dubito, sum"* he puts forward via self-demonstration is to force the self-imposed question to be finally redirected to the questioner himself. The force of reflection, of folding back, is such that there arises a need to turn the probing gaze of "the darkened intellect [*caligantis ingenii*]" (M, 7:52/2:36) from the abyss of self-doubts to the source of the "natural light of reason," the good sense that God gives, and this metaphysical need is what Descartes attempts to fulfill at this point. This point where the reflective mind strategically *averts* its gaze is a discursive point where Descartes' self-doubts become economized, punctuated.

What we witness here is the "seized" birth of the cogitational subject in a form that is acutely abstract and precisely timed, the sort often intuited by expert gamblers. Such is part of modern epistemology's narrative "games with time,"[69] as Paul Ricoeur frames it while drawing on Gérard Genette, "an interplay of interference between the time of narrating and the narrated time in the narrative itself,"[70] and more broadly "the time of life"[71] rhythmically embedded in the intensities of interstitial characters. What we have been reading is one who thinks like an alien idiot as if for the first time. What we have been following is one who first "wonders . . . without knowing whether or not the object is beneficial" (Ps, 11:373/1:350, Article 53) about something, anything, the infinite alterity of possible worlds. What we have been trying to discern is one erased through and emerging from such narrative complexity and duration of time, contrapuntally.

What we have been trying to do justice to is one living on that contradiction, in an irreducible space touchingly saved by Descartes' imagination. What we have been tracing—this allegorical leap in Descartes or Descartes as an allegorical leap—does really seem to be that transitory, "unsurpassable"[72] void *out of* which, rather than just *of* which, we might continue to speak, think, write, read . . . staying around, if not necessarily with, a certain Descartes who remains oddly anonymous.

Leaving Las Vegas?—Il faut partir . . .

"I AM LIVING IN A CORNER OF THE WORLD"

So "I am living in a corner of the world where I would manage to live quite peacefully and happily even if the verdict of the entire learned world were against me" (C, 4:217/249). In this typical Cartesian answer to stoicism, an ideal life is premised on such readiness to retreat, to depart. The old "I" out there must die, be forgotten, so that the new one over here can live on, like that famous house of Descartes under perpetual deconstruction. When he died on Feburary 11, 1650, Descartes allegedly left this as his last word: "*il faut partir*" (one must leave).[73] But depart where?

"IS THAT ALL?"

"Is that all?"

"All what, sir?"

"Are there other debts?" To this Gerald made no reply. "Other gambling debts?"

"No, sir;—not a shilling of that kind. I have never played before."

"Does it ever occur to you that going on at that rate you may very soon lose all the fortune that will ever come to you? You were not yet of age and you lost £3,400 at cards to a man whom you probably knew to be a professed gambler!" The Duke seemed to wait for a reply, but poor Gerald had not a word to say. "Can you explain to me what benefit you proposed to yourself when you played for such stakes as that?"

"I hoped to win back what I had lost."

"*Facilis descensus Averni!*" said the Duke, shaking his head. "*Noctes atque dies patet atri janua Ditis.*" No doubt he thought that as his son was at Oxford, admonitions in Latin would serve him better than in his native tongue. But Gerald, when he heard the grand hexameter rolled out in his father's grandest tone, entertained a comfortable feeling that the worst of the interview was over. "Win back what you had lost! Do you think that that is the common fortune of young gamblers when they fall among those who are more experienced than themselves?"

"One goes on, sir, without reflecting."[74]

To Be Continued . . .

PREAMBLE I: IF DESCARTES REMAINS OVERREAD AND UNDEREXPLORED . . .

1. John Cottingham, *Cartesian Reflections: Essays on Descartes' Philosophy* (Oxford: Oxford University Press, 2008), 273.

2. "Alors pourquoi ce double jeu, qui ressemble à une comédie?" Adrien Baillet, *La vie de Monsieur Des-Cartes*, 2 vols. (New York: Garland, 1691/1987), 12:305, my translation.

3. Michel de Montaigne, *The Complete Essays of Montaigne*, trans. Donald M. Frame (Stanford, Calif.: Stanford University Press, 1958), 456.

PREAMBLE II: DESCARTES NEEDS REREADING

1. John Peter Carriero, *Between Two Worlds: A Reading of Descartes's Meditations* (Princeton, N.J.: Princeton University Press, 2009), ix.

2. Susan Bordo, *The Flight to Objectivity: Essays on Cartesianism and Culture* (Albany: State University of New York Press, 1987), 14 (emphasis added).

3. Dalia Judovitz, "Philosophy and Poetry: The Difference between Them in Plato and Descartes," in *Literature and the Question of Philosophy*, ed. Anthony J. Cascardi (Baltimore: Johns Hopkins University Press, 1987), 44, 46, 48–50.

4. Richard Rorty, *Philosophy and the Mirror of Nature* (Princeton, N.J.: Princeton University Press, 1979), 17.

5. Ibid., 54 (emphases added).

6. Ibid., 66.

7. Ibid., 66, 68.

8. Ibid., 50.

9. Ibid., 69.

10. Arthur C. Danto, *What Philosophy Is: A Guide to the Elements* (New York: Harper & Row, 1968), 10.

11. Bordo, *Flight to Objectivity*, 2.

12. Ibid.

13. Ibid., 5.
14. Ibid., 3.

A STAGE SETUP: REFRAMING *"JEUX DESCARTES"*

On "Jeux Descartes" see Daniel Garber, "Foreword," in Jean-Luc Marion, *Cartesian Questions: Method and Metaphysics* (Chicago: University of Chicago Press, 1999), xi. It is also the name of a toy store in Paris, France.

1. Kirby Dick and Amy Ziering Kofman, dirs., *Derrida*, Jane Doe Films/ Zeitgeist Films (New York: Zeitgeist Video, 2003), DVD.

2. Garber, "Foreword," x.

3. Rebecca Goldstein, "Foreword," in Harry G. Frankfurt, *Demons, Dreamers, and Madmen: The Defense of Reason in Descartes's Meditations* (Princeton, N.J.: Princeton University Press, 2008), vii.

4. Thomas Henry Huxley, "On Descartes' 'Discourse Touching the Method of Using One's Reason Rightly and of Seeking Scientific Truth' (1870)," in *Collected Essays*, vol. 1: *Method and Results* (London: Elibron Classics, 2005), 167.

5. Sarah Hutton, "Women Philosophers and the Early Reception of Descartes: Anne Conway and Princess Elisabeth," in *Receptions of Descartes: Cartesianism and Anti-Cartesianism in Early Modern Europe*, ed. Tad M. Schmaltz (London: Routledge, 2005), 4.

6. Francine Prose, *Reading Like a Writer: A Guide for People Who Love Books and for Those Who Want to Write Them* (New York: HarperCollins, 2006), 74.

7. Hannah Arendt, *The Life of the Mind*, 2 vols. (New York: Harcourt Brace Jovanovich, 1978), 12, 7–12.

8. Prose, *Reading Like a Writer*, 74.

9. Roland Barthes, *Writing Degree Zero, and Elements of Semiology*, trans. Annette Lavers and Colin Smith (Boston: Beacon Press, 1970).

10. Arendt, *Life of the Mind*, 20.

11. Maurice Merleau-Ponty, *Signs*, trans. Richard C. McCleary (Evanston, Ill.: Northwestern University Press, 1964), 11.

12. Charles Adam, *Descartes: Ses amities feminines* (Paris: Boivin, 1937), 11, cited in L. Feuer, "The Dreams of Descartes," *American Imago* 20 (1963): 13.

13. Haifa Zangana, *Dreaming of Baghdad* (New York: Feminist Press at the City University of New York, 2009), 11.

14. Wendy Lesser, "On Not Writing about Hume," in *Room for Doubt* (New York: Pantheon Books, 2007), 65.

15. Gilles Deleuze and Félix Guattari, *Qu'est-ce que la philosophie?* (Paris: Éditions de Minuit, 1991), 60; *What Is Philosophy?*, trans. Hugh Tomlinson and Graham Burchell (New York: Columbia University Press, 1994), 62.

16. Deleuze and Guattari, *Qu'est-ce que la philosophie?*, 60; *What Is Philosophy?*, 62.

17. Gilles Deleuze, *Negotiations, 1972–1990*, trans. Martin Joughin (New York: Columbia University Press, 1995), 96.

18. Deleuze and Guattari, *What Is Philosophy?*, 61.

19. Ibid., 62.

20. Richard H. Popkin, *The Columbia History of Western Philosophy* (New York: Columbia University Press, 1999), 341.

21. Deleuze and Guattari, *What Is Philosophy?*, 61–62 (emphasis added).

22. Ibid., 62.

23. Ibid., 62 (emphasis added, trans. modified).

24. Ibid., 5.

25. Deleuze and Guattari, *Qu'est-ce que la philosophie?*, 63; *What Is Philosophy?*, 64 (emphasis added).

26. Deleuze and Guattari, *Qu'est-ce que la philosophie?*, 69; *What Is Philosophy?*, 67.

27. Adrien Baillet, *La vie de Monsieur Des-Cartes*, 2 vols. (New York: Garland, 1987), 81–86.

28. John Ashbery, "The Business of Falling Asleep (2)," in *Notes from the Air: Selected Later Poems* (New York: Ecco, 2007), 322.

29. Alan Gabbey and Robert E. Hall, "The Melon and the Dictionary: Reflections on Descartes's Dreams," *Journal of the History of Ideas* 59, no. 4 (1998): 661.

30. Feuer, "Dreams of Descartes," 10.

31. Gabbey and Hall, "Melon and the Dictionary," 569.

32. Hassan Melehy, *Writing Cogito: Montaigne, Descartes, and the Institution of the Modern Subject* (Albany: State University of New York Press, 1997), 110–20.

33. Arendt, *Life of the Mind*, 20.

34. Maurice Merleau-Ponty, "Philosophy and Non-Philosophy since Hegel," in *Philosophy and Non-Philosophy since Merleau-Ponty*, ed. Hugh J. Silverman (New York: Routledge, 1988), 52n85.

35. Jacques Maritain, *The Dream of Descartes, Together with Some Other Essays*, trans. Mabelle Louise Cunningham Andison (New York: Philosophical Library, 1944), 15.

36. Jonathan Bate, *The Genius of Shakespeare*, 10th anniversary ed. (Oxford: Oxford University Press, 2008), 158.

37. Maritain, *Dream of Descartes*, 15.

38. Alain Badiou and Slavoj Žižek, *Philosophy in the Present*, ed. Peter Engelmann (Malden, Mass.: Polity, 2009), 71.

39. Carlos Fuentes, "Where Is the Glory That Was France?," *New York Times*, January 14, 1996.

40. Gustave Lanson Voltaire and the Société des Textes Français Modernes (Paris France), *Lettres philosophiques*, 2nd ed. (Paris: Hachette, 1915), 83.

41. Maritain, *Dream of Descartes*, 26.

42. Antonio Negri, *The Political Descartes: Reason, Ideology, and the Bourgeois Project*, trans. Matteo Mandarini and Alberto Toscano (London: Verso, 2006), 103.

43. Gilles Deleuze, "What Is the Creative Act?," in *Two Regimes of Madness: Texts and Interviews 1975–1995*, ed. David Lapoujade (New York: Semiotext(e), 2006), 312–24.

44. Ibid., 313.

45. Ibid., 314.

46. Ibid., 315.

47. Ibid., 324.

48. Ibid.

49. Ibid.

50. Ibid., 320.

51. Goldstein, "Foreword," x.

52. Deleuze and Guattari, *What Is Philosophy?*, 83.

53. Alain Badiou, *Infinite Thought: Truth and the Return to Philosophy*, ed. Justin Clemens and Oliver Feltham (London: Continuum, 2003), 37.

54. Maritain, *Dream of Descartes*, 29.

55. Ibid., 28.

56. Jean-Luc Nancy, *The Fall of Sleep*, trans. Charlotte Mandell (New York: Fordham University Press, 2009), 23.

57. Badiou, *Infinite Thought*, 50.

58. Ibid., 3.

59. Richard Kearney, *Strangers, Gods, and Monsters: Interpreting Otherness* (London: Routledge, 2003), 189.

60. Judith Butler, *Giving an Account of Oneself* (New York: Fordham University Press, 2005), 21.

61. Emmanuel Levinas, *Otherwise Than Being: Or, Beyond Essence*, trans. Alphonso Lingis (Dordrecht, the Netherlands: Kluwer Academic, 1981), 168.

62. Deleuze and Guattari, *What Is Philosophy?*, 43.

63. Frankfurt, *Demons, Dreamers, and Madmen*, 32; 26–32.

64. Ibid., 26, 31.

65. Ibid., 31.

66. Ibid., 29–30.

67. Jean-Luc Nancy, *Corpus*, trans. Richard A. Rand (New York: Fordham University Press, 2008), 141.

68. Nancy, *Corpus*, 141.

69. Christoph Hein, *The Distant Lover*, trans. Krishna Winston (New York: Pantheon, 1989), 2.

70. Frankfurt, *Demons, Dreamers, and Madmen.*

71. John Peter Carriero, *Between Two Worlds: A Reading of Descartes's Meditations* (Princeton, N.J.: Princeton University Press, 2009); Catherine Wilson, *Descartes's Meditations: An Introduction* (Cambridge: Cambridge University Press, 2003).

72. James L. Marsh, *Post-Cartesian Meditations: An Essay in Dialectical Phenomenology* (New York: Fordham University Press, 1988).

73. Kearney, *Strangers, Gods, and Monsters.*

74. Ibid., 1.

75. Harry M. Bracken, *Descartes* (Oxford: Oneworld, 2002), 131.

76. Slavoj Žižek, *The Ticklish Subject: The Absent Centre of Political Ontology* (London: Verso, 1999), 1.

77. Ibid.

78. Popkin, *Columbia History of Western Philosophy*, 337–8.

79. Gilbert Ryle, *The Concept of Mind* (London: Hutchinson's University Library, 1949).

80. Daniel Garber, *Descartes Embodied: Reading Cartesian Philosophy through Cartesian Science* (Cambridge: Cambridge University Press, 2001).

81. Tom Sorell, *Descartes Reinvented* (Cambridge: Cambridge University Press, 2005).

82. Ronald Rubin, *Silencing the Demon's Advocate: The Strategy of Descartes' Meditations* (Palo Alto, Calif.: Stanford University Press, 2008).

83. Sorell, *Descartes Reinvented*, 104–5.

84. Frederick C. Copleston, Review of *The Concept of Mind* by Gilbert Ryle, *British Journal for the Philosophy of Science* 1, no. 4 (1951): 328–9, my insertion. Coplestone uses the word "dispose" four times.

85. Ibid., 329.

86. Lance Humphries, *Daniel Garber: Romantic Realist* (Doylestown, Penn.: James A. Michener Art Museum, 2006).

87. Ryle, *Concept of Mind*, 19.

88. Gordon P. Baker and Katherine J. Morris, *Descartes' Dualism* (London: Routledge, 2002); Joseph Almog, *Cogito?: Descartes and Thinking the World* (Oxford: Oxford University Press, 2008).

89. Margaret Dauler Wilson, *Descartes* (London: Routledge and Kegan Paul, 1982), 155–60.

90. Louis E. Loeb, "The Mind-Body Union, Interaction, and Subsumption," in *Early Modern Philosophy: Mind, Matter, and Metaphysics*, ed. Christia Mercer and Eileen O'Neill (Oxford: Oxford University Press, 2005).

91. Jean-Luc Marion, "The Originary Otherness of the Ego: A Rereading of Descartes' Second *Meditation*," in *On the Ego and on God: Further Cartesian Questions* (New York: Fordham University Press, 2007); "The Responsorial Status of the *Meditations*," in *On the Ego and on God.*

92. Deleuze and Guattari, *What Is Philosophy?*, 64.

93. Ibid.

94. Ibid.

95. Allen R. Grossman, *Descartes' Loneliness* (New York: New Directions, 2007), 3.

96. Susan McCabe, *Descartes' Nightmare* (Salt Lake City: University of Utah Press, 2008), 32–33.

97. Sorell, *Descartes Reinvented*, xx.

98. Caroline Williams, *Contemporary French Philosophy: Modernity and the Persistence of the Subject* (London: Continuum, 2005), 7.

99. Ian James, "The Persistence of the Subject: On Descartes and the Cogito," in *The Fragmentary Demand: An Introduction to the Philosophy of Jean-Luc Nancy* (Stanford, Calif.: Stanford University Press, 2006), 55.

100. Stéphane Mallarmé, "Richard Wagner: The Reverie of a French Poet," in *Divagations: The Author's 1897 Arrangement; Together with "Autobiography," and "Music and Letters"* (Cambridge, Mass.: Harvard University Press, 2007), 108.

101. Judovitz, "Philosophy and Poetry," 44, 46, 48–50.

102. Ibid., 45.

103. Žižek, *The Ticklish Subject*.

104. Françoise Dastur, *Telling Time: Sketch of a Phenomenological Chrono-Logy*, trans. Edward Bullard (London: Athlone Press, 2000), 88.

105. Merleau-Ponty, "Philosophy and Non-Philosophy," 9.

106. Maurice Merleau-Ponty, *The Visible and the Invisible*, trans. Alphonso Lingis (Evanston, Ill.: Northwestern University Press, 1968), 214–15.

107. Negri, *Political Descartes*, 175.

SCENE I. BLIND VISION: A PHOTOGRAPHIC TOUCH

1. Maurice Merleau-Ponty, "Eye and Mind," in *The Merleau-Ponty Aesthetics Reader: Philosophy and Painting*, ed. Galen A. Johnson and Michael B. Smith (Evanston, Ill.: Northwestern University Press, 1993), 130.

2. Ibid.

3. Virginia Woolf, *A Writer's Diary, Being Extracts from the Diary of Virginia Woolf* (New York: Harcourt Brace Jovanovich, 1973), 79.

4. Merleau-Ponty, "Eye and Mind," 130.

5. David Appelbaum, *The Stop* (Albany: State University of New York Press, 1995), ix.

6. Celia Wolf-Devine, *Descartes on Seeing: Epistemology and Visual Perception* (Carbondale: Southern Illinois University Press, 1993), 86.

7. Ibid.

8. Ibid.

9. Martin Jay, *Downcast Eyes: The Denigration of Vision in Twentieth-Century French Thought* (Berkeley: University of California Press, 1993), 82–83.

10. Wolf-Devine, *Descartes on Seeing*, 84–88.

11. Ibid., 92.

12. Ibid., 65, 93.

13. Ibid., 94.

14. Merleau-Ponty, "Eye and Mind," 136 (emphases added).

15. Merleau-Ponty, *The Visible and the Invisible*, trans. Alphonso Lingis (Evanston, Ill.: Northwestern University Press, 1968), 130–37.

16. Ibid., 130, 137.

17. Merleau-Ponty, "Eye and Mind," 127.

18. Merleau-Ponty, *The Visible and the Invisible*, 234–35.

19. Ibid., 171.

20. Merleau-Ponty, "Eye and Mind," 131.

21. Daniel Giovannangeli and Jacques Taminiaux, *La fiction de l'être: Lectures de la philosophie moderne* (Brussels: Le Point Philosophique, 1990), 9.

22. Merleau-Ponty, "Eye and Mind," 136.

23. Wolf-Devine, *Descartes on Seeing*, 5, 88.

24. Ibid., 87.

25. Merleau-Ponty, "Eye and Mind," 136–7 (emphases added).

26. Robert J. Sardello, *Freeing the Soul from Fear* (New York: Riverhead Books, 1999), 40–41.

27. Ibid., 137.

28. Merleau-Ponty, "Eye and Mind," 136.

29. Ibid., 122.

30. Ibid., 138.

31. Ibid., 137.

32. Ibid., 130.

33. Ibid., 137.

34. Marita Sturken and Lisa Cartwright, *Practices of Looking: An Introduction to Visual Culture*, 2nd ed. (New York: Oxford University Press, 2009), 298.

35. Merleau-Ponty, "Eye and Mind," 131.

36. Ibid., 139.

37. Amir D. Aczel, *Descartes' Secret Notebook: A True Tale of Mathematics, Mysticism, and the Quest to Understand the Universe* (New York: Broadway Books, 2005), 4.

38. Merleau-Ponty, *The Visible and the Invisible*, 234.

39. Merleau-Ponty, "Eye and Mind," 123.

40. Ibid., 130.

41. Ibid., 127 (emphasis added).

42. Ibid., 137.

43. Ibid., 122.

44. Catherine Malabou, *What Should We Do with Our Brain?*, trans. Sebastian Rand (New York: Fordham University Press, 2008).

45. Ibid., 69.

46. Ibid., 68.

47. Merleau-Ponty, "Eye and Mind," 122.

48. Ibid.

49. Ibid.

50. Ibid., 123.

51. Sturken and Cartwright, *Practices of Looking*, 281 (emphasis added).

52. Appelbaum, *The Stop*, 10.

53. Cathryn Vasseleu, *Textures of Light: Vision and Touch in Irigaray, Levinas, and Merleau-Ponty* (London: Routledge, 1998), 4.

54. Gary C. Hatfield, "Force (God) in Descartes' Physics," in *Oxford Readings in Philosophy*, ed. John Cottingham (Oxford: Oxford University Press, 1998).

55. Gilles Deleuze and Félix Guattari, *What Is Philosophy?*, trans. Hugh Tomlinson and Graham Burchell (New York: Columbia University Press, 1994), 171–2.

56. Merleau-Ponty, "Eye and Mind," 131.

57. Gary C. Hatfield and René Descartes, *Routledge Philosophy Guidebook to Descartes and the Meditations* (London: Routledge, 2003), 159.

58. Emmanuel Levinas, *Totality and Infinity: An Essay on Exteriority*, trans. Alphonso Lingis (Pittsburgh: Duquesne University Press, 1969), 87.

59. Ibid., 86 (emphasis added).

60. Ibid., 85.

61. Nancy M. Shawcross, *Roland Barthes on Photography: The Critical Tradition in Perspective* (Gainesville: University Press of Florida, 1997), 38.

62. Roland Barthes, *Camera Lucida: Reflections on Photography*, trans. Richard Howard (New York: Hill and Wang, 1981), 3.

63. Vasseleu, *Textures of Light*.

64. Emmanuel Levinas, *Existence and Existents*, trans. Alphonso Lingis (The Hague: Martinus Nijhoff, 1978), 22.

65. Estelle Jussim, *The Eternal Moment: Essays on the Photographic Image* (New York: Aperture, 1989), 12.

66. Jacques Lacan, *The Four Fundamental Concepts of Psycho-Analysis*, trans. Alan Sheridan, ed. Jacques-Alain Miller (New York: Norton, 1978), 106.

67. Susan Bordo, *The Flight to Objectivity: Essays on Cartesianism and Culture* (Albany: State University of New York Press, 1987), 33–43.

68. Appelbaum, *The Stop*, viii.

69. Ibid.

70. Maurice Merleau-Ponty, *Phenomenology of Perception*, trans. Colin Smith (London: Routledge, 1962), 398.

71. Ibid., 402–04 (emphasis added).

72. Ibid., 369.

73. Ibid., 396.

74. Ibid., 378 (emphasis added).

75. Ibid., 408 (emphasis added).

76. Ibid., 402.

77. Ibid., 403.

78. Merleau-Ponty, *The Visible and the Invisible*, 170–71.

79. Merleau-Ponty, *Phenomenology of Perception*, 242.

80. Ibid., 395.

81. Ibid.

82. Levinas, *Existence and Existents*, 68.

83. Merleau-Ponty, *Phenomenology of Perception*, 404.

84. Appelbaum, *The Stop*, 22.

85. Wolf-Devine, *Descartes on Seeing*, 63.

86. Jacques Derrida, *Margins of Philosophy*, trans. Alan Bass (Chicago: University of Chicago Press, 1982), 266–67.

87. Walter Benjamin, "The Work of Art in the Age of Its Technological Reproducibility: Third Version," in *Selected Writings*, vol. 4, *1938–1940*, ed. Marcus Paul Bullock et al. (Cambridge, Mass.: Belknap Press, 1996).

88. Merleau-Ponty, "Eye and Mind," 127.

89. David Hockney, *Secret Knowledge: Rediscovering the Lost Techniques of the Old Masters* (New York: Viking Studio, 2001).

90. Agnès Sire, Jean-Luc Nancy, and Henri Cartier-Bresson, *An Inner Silence: The Portraits of Henri Cartier-Bresson* (New York: Thames & Hudson, 2006), epigram by Cartier-Bresson, signed on January 18, 1996 (emphasis added).

91. Vilém Flusser, *Towards a Philosophy of Photography*, trans. Anthony Mathews (London: Reaktion Books, 2003), 38–39.

92. Barthes, *Camera Lucida*, 6.

93. Malabou, *What Should We Do with Our Brain?*, 68.

94. José Saramago, *Blindness: A Novel*, trans. Giovanni Pontiero (London: Harvill Press, 1997), 140.

95. Christopher Isherwood, *Goodbye to Berlin* (New York: Random House, 1939), 13.

96. Emily Dickinson, "I heard a Fly buzz—when I died [1862]," in *The Oxford Book of American Poetry*, ed. David Lehman (Oxford: Oxford University Press, 2006), 171.

97. Ibid., 170.

98. Ibid., 171.

99. Isherwood, *Goodbye to Berlin*, 13.

100. Frantz Fanon, *Black Skin, White Masks*, trans. Charles Lam Markmann (New York: Grove Press, 1967), 202.

101. Flusser, *Towards a Philosophy of Photography*, 8 (emphasis added).

102. Ibid., 23.

103. Ibid., 31.

104. Ibid., 33.

105. Merleau-Ponty, *The Visible and the Invisible*, 210.

SCENE 2. ELASTIC MADNESS: AN ALLEGORICAL COMEDY

1. In particular the first section, the first four pages of chapter 2, titled "The Great Confinement" in Michel Foucault, *Histoire de la folie à l'âge classique. Suivi de mon corps, ce papier, ce feu et la folie, L'absence d'œuvre* (Paris: Gallimard, 1972), 67–70; Michel Foucault, *History of Madness*, trans. Jonathan Murphy, ed. Jean Khalfa (London: Routledge, 2006), 44–47. This work is hereafter abbreviated as HM; for example, "HM 69–70/46" refers to pages 69–70 of the French original, and page 46 of the English translation. When the English translation suffices, that alone used and is indicated by an unpaired citation: "HM xxxi" refers to page xxxi of the English text.

2. Used here is the reprint that appeared in Michel Foucault, "Mon corps, ce papier, ce feu," in *Dits et écrits*, vol. 1: *1954–1975* (Paris: Éditions Gallimard, 1994); Michel Foucault, "My Body, This Paper, This Fire," in *The Essential Works of Foucault, 1954–1984*, vol. 2, *Aesthetics*, ed. Paul Rabinow and James D. Faubion (New York: New Press, 1997). This work is hereafter abbreviated as MT; for example, "MT 598/411–2" refers to pages 598 of the French original, and pages 411–2 of the English translation. When the English translation suffices, that alone is used and is indicated by an unpaired citation: "MT 411" refers to page 411 of the English text.

3. Jacques Derrida, "Cogito et histoire de la folie," in *L'Écriture et la différance* (Paris: Éditions du Seuil, 1967); "Cogito and the History of Madness," in *Writing and Difference* (London: Routledge & Kegan Paul, 1978/1981). This work is hereafter abbreviated as CH; for example, "CH 96–7/62–3" refers to pages 96–97 of the French original, and pages 62–62 of the English translation. When the English translation suffices, that alone is used and is indicated by an unpaired citation: "CH 62" refers to page 62 of the English text.

4. HM 69–70/46.

5. Michel Foucault, *The Hermeneutics of the Subject: Lectures at the Collège de France, 1981–1982*, trans. Graham Burchell, ed. Frédéric Gros (New York: Palgrave Macmillan, 2005), 14.

6. HM xxxi, 542–49.

7. HM xxxi.

8. HM xxxi.

9. CH 96–7/62–3.

10. Michèle Le Doeuff, *The Philosophical Imaginary*, trans. Colin Gordon (London: Continuum, 2002), 116.

11. CH 96–7/62–3.

12. CH 96–7/62–3.

13. MT 598/411–2.

14. MT 602/416.

15. MT 591/403.

16. MT 591/403ff.

17. Hassan Melehy, *Writing Cogito: Montaigne, Descartes, and the Institution of the Modern Subject* (Albany: State University of New York Press, 1997), 37–43.

18. Le Doeuff, *Philosophical Imaginary*, 122.

19. CH 52/32.

20. Jacques Derrida, "To Do Justice to Freud: History of Madness in the Age of Psychoanalysis," *Critical Inquiry* 20 (Winter 1994): 227–66; reprinted in *Resistances of Psychoanalysis*, trans. Peggy Kamuf, Pascale-Anne Brault, and Michael Naas (Stanford, Calif.; Stanford University Press, 1998), 70–118.

21. Le Doeuff, *Philosophical Imaginary*, 122.

22. Derrida, "To Do Justice to Freud," 70.

23. Ibid., 99.

24. Ibid.

25. Ibid., 71 (emphasis in original).

26. Ibid., 118–19.

27. Jacques Derrida, *Résistances de la psychoanalyse* (Paris: Galilée, 1996), 129; Derrida, "To Do Justice to Freud," 103.

28. Foucault, *Hermeneutics of the Subject*, 14.

29. Derrida, "To Do Justice to Freud," 71–72.

30. CH 96–7/62–3.

31. CH 96–7/62–3.

32. HM 69–70/46, translation modified.

33. Foucault, *Hermeneutics of the Subject*, 14.

34. Foucault, *Hermeneutics of the Subject*, xxv.

35. HM 67/44.

36. Peter Conrad and Joseph W. Schneider, *Deviance and Medicalization: From Badness to Sickness*, expanded ed. (Philadelphia: Temple University Press, 1992), 44.

37. Ibid., 57–58.

38. HM 67/44.

39. HM 70/47.

40. HM 198/147 (trans. modified).

41. HM 198/147.

42. Jeffrey Tlumak, *Classical Modern Philosophy: A Contemporary Introduction* (London: Routledge, 2006), 8.

43. Enrique D. Dussel, *Philosophy of Liberation*, trans. Aquila Martinez and Christine Morkovsky (Maryknoll, N.Y.: Orbis Books, 1985), 1–2.

44. HM 70/47.

45. HM 67–70/44–47.

46. HM 65–66/44–45.

47. HM 15–66/3–43.

48. HM 69–70/46–47 (trans. modified).

49. HM 69/46.

50. HM 237, 619.

51. HM 303/237.

52. HM 209/157.

53. HM 67/44.

54. Denis Kambouchner, "Thought versus History: Reflections on a French Problem," in *Teaching New Histories of Philosophy*, ed. J. B. Schneewind (Princeton, N.J.: Center for Human Values, Princeton University, 2004), 252.

55. HM 67/44.

56. HM 1120–1121/557–558.

57. HM 1121–1123/558–560.

58. HM 303/237.

59. HM 591/560 (trans. modified).

60. HM 1110/543.

61. Michel Foucault, *Mental Illness and Psychology*, trans. Alan Sheridan (New York: Harper & Row, 1976), 78–79.

62. Jennifer Michael Hecht, *Doubt: A History: The Great Doubters and Their Legacy of Innovation, from Socrates and Jesus to Thomas Jefferson and Emily Dickinson* (San Francisco: HarperSanFrancisco, 2003), 315.

63. Leszek Kolakowski, *Metaphysical Horror* (Oxford: Basil Blackwell, 1988), 73.

64. HM 440/542.

65. HM 440/541.

66. Jacques Derrida, "Cogito et histoire de la folie," *Revue de Metaphysique et de Morale* 68 (1963); reprinted in *L'Écriture et la différance* (Paris: Éditions du Seuil, 1967), 156–7; "Cogito and the History of Madness," in *Writing and Difference*, trans. Alan Bass (London: Routledge & Kegan Paul, 1978/1981), 106 (emphases mine, trans. modified).

67. MT 1121/558.

68. John Peter Carriero, *Between Two Worlds: A Reading of Descartes's Meditations* (Princeton, N.J.: Princeton University Press, 2009), 39–40.

69. Roland Barthes, "Writing Reading," in *The Rustle of Language*, trans. Richard Howard (Berkeley: University of California Press, 1989), 29.

70. M. A. K. Halliday, "How Do You Mean?," in *On Grammar (Collected Works of M. A. K. Halliday)* (London: Continuum, 2005), 358.

71. Ibid., 355.

72. Ibid., 353.

73. Ibid., 355.

74. Ibid., 354.

75. HM 210/158 (trans. modified).

76. Gaston Bachelard, *The Poetics of Space*, trans. Maria Jolas (New York: Orion Press, 1964), 139.

77. William T. Bluhm, "Political Theory and Ethics," in René Descartes, *Discourse on Method and Meditations on First Philosophy*, ed. David Weissman (New Haven, Conn.: Yale University Press, 1996), 308.

78. Carriero, *Between Two Worlds*, 66.

79. David Appelbaum, *The Stop* (Albany: State University of New York Press, 1995), 20.

80. Gilles Deleuze, *Différence et répétition* (Paris: Presses Universitaires de France, 1968), 182, 184; *Difference and Repetition*, trans. Paul Patton (New York: Columbia University Press, 1994), 139, 141.

81. Bachelard, *Poetics of Space*, 144–47.

82. Ibid., 147.

83. Ibid.

84. Janet Broughton, *Descartes's Method of Doubt* (Princeton, N.J.: Princeton University Press, 2002), 90.

85. Giorgio Agamben, *Idea of Prose*, trans. Michael Sullivan and Sam Whitsitt (Albany: State University of New York Press, 1995), 64.

86. Michael Naas, *Taking on the Tradition: Jacques Derrida and the Legacies of Deconstruction* (Stanford, Calif.: Stanford University Press, 2003), 57.

87. HM 370/292.

88. Vincent Carraud, "The Relevance of Cartesianism," in *Contemporary French Philosophy: Supplement to Philosophy*, ed. A. Phillips Griffiths and Pascal Engel (Cambridge: Cambridge University Press, 1987), 69.

89. Jean-Paul Sartre, "Cartesian Freedom," in *Literary and Philosophical Essays*, trans. Annette Michelson (New York: Collier Books, 1962), 185.

90. Carraud, "Relevance of Cartesianism," 75 (emphasis added).

SCENE 3. PHILOPOETIC SOMNAMBULISM: AN IMAGINARY FREEDOM

1. Philippe Ariès, *Western Attitudes toward Death: From the Middle Ages to the Present*, trans. Patricia M. Ranum (Baltimore: Johns Hopkins University Press, 1974), 104.

2. Ernst Bloch, *The Principle of Hope*, 3 vols., trans. Neville Plaice, Stephen Plaice, and Paul Knight (Cambridge, Mass.: MIT Press, 1986), 2:451.

3. Gaston Bachelard, *The Poetics of Reverie*, trans. Daniel Russell (New York: Orion Press, 1969), 154.

4. Jean-Luc Marion, "Does Thought Dream? The Three Dreams, or the Awakening of the Philosopher," in *Cartesian Questions: Method and Metaphysics* (Chicago: University of Chicago Press, 1999), 8 (emphases added).

5. Ibid.

6. L. Feuer, "The Dreams of Descartes," *American Imago* 20 (1963): 9.

7. Jacques Derrida, *Of Grammatology*, trans. Gayatri Chakravorty Spivak (Baltimore: Johns Hopkins University Press, 1976), 287.

8. Friedrich Wilhelm Nietzsche, *The Gay Science; with a Prelude in Rhymes and an Appendix of Songs*, trans. Walter Arnold Kaufmann (New York: Vintage Books, 1974), 232.

9. John R. Cole, *The Olympian Dreams and Youthful Rebellion of René Descartes* (Urbana: University of Illinois Press, 1992), 19–48.

10. Jacques Maritain, *The Dream of Descartes, Together with Some Other Essays*, trans. Mabelle Louise Cunningham Andison (New York: Philosophical Library, 1944), 189n1.

11. Ibid., 13.

12. Cole, *Olympian Dreams*, 3.

13. Ibid.

14. Sigmund Freud, *The Standard Edition of the Complete Psychological Works of Sigmund Freud*, 24 vols., ed. James Strachey et al. (London: Hogarth Press, 1953), 21:199–204.

15. Ibid.

16. Gaston Bachelard, *The Dialectic of Duration*, trans. Mary McAllester Jones (Manchester: Clinamen, 2000), 8, 23.

17. Jacques Lacan, *The Four Fundamental Concepts of Psycho-Analysis*, trans. Alan Sheridan, ed. Jacques-Alain Miller (New York: Norton, 1978), 76.

18. Gustave Cohen cited in Cole, *Olympian Dreams*, 9.

19. Bachelard, *Poetics of Space*, 144.

20. Charles Minahen, "The Turbulent Dream-Vision of Descartes's 'Olympian' Experience," in *Dreams in French Literature: The Persistent Voice*, ed. Tom Conney (Amsterdam: Rodopi, 1995), 75–77.

21. David Farrell Krell, *Of Memory, Reminiscence, and Writing: On the Verge* (Bloomington: Indiana University Press, 1990), 62; Gerald L. Bruns, *Inventions, Writing, Textuality, and Understanding in Literary History* (New Haven, Conn.: Yale University Press, 1982).

22. Catherine Clément, *Syncope: The Philosophy of Rapture*, trans. Sally O'Driscoll and Deirdre M. Mahoney (Minneapolis: University of Minnesota Press, 1994), 162.

23. Cole, *Olympian Dreams*.

24. Jacques Derrida, "Cogito and the History of Madness," in *Writing and Difference* (London: Routledge & Kegan Paul, 1978/1981).

25. Ibid., 55.

26. Susan Bordo, *The Flight to Objectivity: Essays on Cartesianism and Culture* (Albany: State University of New York Press, 1987), 20.

27. Ibid., 3.

28. Ibid., 5.

29. Zora Neale Hurston, *Their Eyes Were Watching God: A Novel* (Urbana: University of Illinois Press, 1978), 3.

30. Ibid.

31. Heinrich Heine, *Sämtliche Schriften*, vol. 3, ed. Klaus Briegleb (Munich: Carl Hanser Verlag, 1969), 136; trans. and cited in Ernst Behler, "The Theory of Irony in German Romanticism," in *Romantic Irony*, ed. Frederick Garber (Budapest: John Benjamins, 1989), 77–78.

32. Nietzsche, *Gay Science*, 283.

33. Shaun Irlam, "Showing Losses, Counting Gains: 'Scenes' from Negative Autobiography," *Modern Language Notes* 106, no. 5 (1991): 1009.

34. Ibid., 1007–09.

35. Berel Lang, *Philosophy and the Art of Writing: Studies in Philosophical and Literary Style* (Lewisburg, Penn.: Bucknell University Press, 1983), 221 (emphases both in original and added).

36. William Poundstone, *Labyrinths of Reason: Paradox, Puzzles, and the Frailty of Knowledge* (New York: Anchor Books, 1990), 8.

37. Jean-Luc Nancy, *The Fall of Sleep*, trans. Charlotte Mandell (New York: Fordham University Press, 2009), 13–14.

38. Jonathan Rée, "Descartes' Comedy," in *Philosophical Tales: An Essay on Philosophy and Literature* (London: Methuen, 1987), 20–23.

39. William T. Bluhm, "Political Theory and Ethics," in René Descartes, *Discourse on Method and Meditations on First Philosophy*, ed. David Weissman (New Haven, Conn.: Yale University Press, 1996), 308.

40. *Timaeus* 71–72. Plato, *Timaeus and Critias*, trans. Henry Desmond Pritchard Lee (Harmondsworth, U.K.: Penguin Books, 1971), 98–99.

41. Ibid., 99.

42. Nancy, *Fall of Sleep*, 1–2.

43. Lewis Carroll, *Alice's Adventures in Wonderland: A Classic Illustrated Edition*, ed. Cooper Edens (San Francisco: Chronicle Books, 2000), 2 (emphasis added).

44. Ibid.

45. Martin Heidegger, *The Fundamental Concepts of Metaphysics: World, Finitude, Solitude*, trans. William McNeill and Nicholas Walker (Bloomington: Indiana University Press, 1995), 78–168.

46. Carroll, *Alice's Adventures in Wonderland*, 2.

47. Georg Wilhelm Friedrich Hegel, *Phenomenology of Spirit*, trans. Arnold V. Miller, ed. J. N. Findlay (Oxford: Clarendon Press, 1977), 6.

48. Harvie Ferguson, *The Lure of Dreams: Sigmund Freud and the Construction of Modernity* (London: Routledge, 1996), 7.

49. Emmanuel Levinas, *Of God Who Comes to Mind*, 2nd ed., trans. Bettina Bergo (Stanford, Calif.: Stanford University Press, 1998), 120.

50. Nancy, *Fall of Sleep*, 14.

51. Emmanuel Levinas, *Totality and Infinity: An Essay on Exteriority*, trans. Alphonso Lingis (Pittsburgh: Duquesne University Press, 1969), 110 (emphasis added).

52. *Timaeus* 72–73. Plato, *Timaeus and Critias*, 100.

53. *The New Testament of Our Lord and Saviour Jesus Christ: Being the Authorised Version Set Forth in 1611, Arranged in Parallel Columns, with the Revised Version of 1881 and with the Greek Text Followed in the Revised Version* (Columbia University Press, 1896), 4.

54. Minahen, "Turbulent Dream-Vision," 75.

55. Edmund Husserl, *Die Krisis Der Europaischen Wissenschaften Und Die Transzendentale Phanomenologie*, vol. Bd. 6, *Gesammelte Werke, Husserliana* (The Hague: Martinus Nijhoff, 1954), 78, 76–78; *The Crisis of European Sciences and Transcendental Phenomenology: An Introduction to Phenomenological Philosophy*, trans. David Carr (Evanston, Ill.: Northwestern University Press, 1970), 77, 75–77.

56. Jacques Derrida, *Memoirs of the Blind: The Self-Portrait and Other Ruins*, trans. Pascale-Anne Brault and Michael Naas (Chicago: University of Chicago Press, 1993), 3, 13–16, 94–98.

57. Gaston Bachelard, *The Psychoanalysis of Fire*, trans. Alan C. M. Ross (Boston: Beacon Press, 1964), 40–41.

58. David Hume, *An Enquiry Concerning Human Understanding* (Oxford: Clarendon Press, 1888/1978), 6–7 (emphases added).

59. Jonathan Rée, *Descartes* (London: Allen Lane, 1974), 17.

60. Bruns, *Inventions, Writing, Textuality*, 77 (emphasis added).

61. Jean-Luc Nancy, "Identity and Trembling," in *The Birth to Presence*, trans. Brian Holmes et al. (Stanford: Stanford University Press, 1993), 18.

62. Ibid., 21–2.

63. Ibid., 34.

SCENE 4. CORNERED REFLECTION: WITH AND AROUND AN EVIL GENIUS

1. Julian Barnes, *Nothing to Be Frightened Of* (New York: Alfred A. Knopf, 2008), 3.

2. Wendy Lesser, *Room for Doubt* (New York: Pantheon Books, 2007), 188.

3. Julia Kristeva, *This Incredible Need to Believe*, trans Alan Sheridan (New York: Columbia University Press, 2009), 2.

4. Eva Le Grand, *Kundera, ou, la mémoire du désir* (Paris: XYZ Éditeur, 1995), 59.

5. George Steiner, *Grammars of Creation: Originating in the Gifford Lectures for 1990* (New Haven, Conn.: Yale University Press, 2001), 16.

6. Kristeva, *This Incredible Need to Believe*, 4.

7. Jonathan Rée, "Descartes' Comedy," in *Philosophical Tales: An Essay on Philosophy and Literature* (London: Methuen, 1987), 10n4.

8. Sarah Kofman, "Descartes Entrapped," in *Who Comes after the Subject?*, ed. Peter Connor and Jean-Luc Nancy, and Eduardo Cadava (London: Routledge, 1991).

9. Jean-Luc Marion, *On the Ego and on God: Further Cartesian Questions* (New York: Fordham University Press, 2007), 42.

10. Richard H. Popkin, *The Columbia History of Western Philosophy* (New York: Columbia University Press, 1999), 338.

11. Jean-Luc Marion, "The Responsorial Status of the *Meditations*," in *On the Ego and on God*, 30–41.

12. Marion, *On the Ego and on God*, 43.

13. Ann Hartle, *Death and the Disinterested Spectator: An Inquiry into the Nature of Philosophy* (New York: SUNY Press, 1986), 148, 144–52.

14. Steiner, *Grammars of Creation*, 5.

15. Ibid., 6.

16. Ibid., 20.

17. Gary C. Hatfield, "René Descartes (1596–1650)." in *The Blackwell Guide to the Modern Philosophers: from Descartes to Nietzsche*, ed. Steven M. Emmanuel (London: Wiley-Black, 2011), 11 (emphases added).

18. Popkin, *Columbia History of Western Philosophy*, 338 (emphases added).

19. Hatfield, "René Descartes," 12 (emphases added).

20. Steiner, *Grammars of Creation*, 15.

21. John Carriero, "The Cartesian Circle and the Foundations of Knowledge." In *A Companion to Descartes*, ed. Janet Broughton and John Carriero (London: John Wiley and Sons, 2010), 306 (emphasis added).

22. Jean-Luc Marion, *On Descartes' Metaphysical Prism: The Constitution and the Limits of Onto-Theo-Logy in Cartesian Thought* (Chicago: University of Chicago Press, 1999), 213.

23. Ibid., 212.

24. Ibid., 212–13.

25. Ibid., 214.

26. Susan Bordo, *The Flight to Objectivity: Essays on Cartesianism and Culture* (Albany: State University of New York Press, 1987), 21.

27. Marion, *On Descartes' Metaphysical Prism*, 276.

28. Jean-Luc Nancy, "Larvatus Pro Deo," trans. Daniel A. Brewer, *Glyph: Johns Hopkins Textual Studies* 2 (1977): 33.

29. Ibid.

30. Ibid.

31. Peter Kreeft, *Socrates Meets Descartes: The Father of Philosophy Analyzes the Father of Modern Philosophy's Discourse on Method* (San Francisco: Ignatius Press, 2007), 166–67.

32. Dalia Judovitz, *Subjectivity and Representation in Descartes: The Origins of Modernity* (Cambridge: Cambridge University Press, 1988), 34.

33. Roland Barthes, *The Pleasure of the Text*, trans. Richard Miller (New York: Hill and Wang, 1975), 17.

34. Ibid.

35. Antonio Negri, *The Political Descartes: Reason, Ideology, and the Bourgeois Project*, trans. Matteo Mandarini and Alberto Toscano (London: Verso, 2006), 133.

36. Hans Blumenberg, *Shipwreck with Spectator: Paradigm of a Metaphor for Existence*, trans. Steven Rendall (Cambridge, Mass.: MIT Press, 1997), 15.

37. Ibid., 108 (emphasis added).

38. Ibid., 149.

39. Bordo, *Flight to Objectivity*, 21.

40. Negri, *Political Descartes*, 111.

41. Harry G. Frankfurt, *Demons, Dreamers, and Madmen: The Defense of Reason in Descartes's Meditations* (Princeton, N.J.: Princeton University Press, 2008), 35.

42. Steiner, *Grammars of Creation*, 14.

43. Ibid., 12.

44. Jean-Luc Marion, *Sur la théologie blanche de Descartes: Analogie, création des vérités éternelles et fondement* (Paris: Presses Universitaires de France, 1981).

45. Max Horkheimer and Theodor W. Adorno, *Dialectic of Enlightenment: Philosophical Fragments*, trans. Edmund Jephcott, ed. Gunzelin Schmid Noerr (Stanford, Calif.: Stanford University Press, 2002), 38.

46. Jean-Luc Marion, "God, the Styx, and the Fates: The Letters to Mersenne of 1630," in *On the Ego and on God*, 103.

47. Ibid., 104 (emphasis added).

48. Ibid.

49. Ibid., 107.

50. Ibid., 107–10.

51. Steiner, *Grammars of Creation*, 15.

52. H. A. Hodges, *The Philosophy of Wilhelm Dilthey* (London: Routledge & Paul, 1952), 312.

53. Hans Meyerhoff, ed., *The Philosophy of History in Our Time* (New York: Garland, 1959/1985), 39.

54. Steiner, *Grammars of Creation*, 13.

55. Bordo, *Flight to Objectivity*, 21.

56. Ibid.

57. Marion, *On the Ego and on God*, 58 (emphases added).

58. Roland Barthes, *Mythologies*, trans. Annette Lavers (New York,: Hill and Wang, 1972), 23–5.

59. Jean-Luc Nancy, "Mundus Est Fabula," *Modern Language Notes* 93, no. 4 (1978): 649n17.

60. Jaako Hintikka, "Cogito Ergo Sum: Inference or Performance?," *Philosophical Review* 71 (1962): 56–59.

61. Nancy, "Mundus Est Fabula," 648.

62. Ibid., 651.

63. Leszek Kolakowski, *Metaphysical Horror* (Oxford: Basil Blackwell, 1988), 68.

64. Dalia Judovitz, "From Self to Subject: Montaigne to Descartes," in *Subjectivity and Representation in Descartes: The Origins of Modernity* (Cambridge: Cambridge University Press, 1988).

65. Alain Badiou, *Manifesto for Philosophy: Followed by Two Essays: "The (Re) Turn of Philosophy Itself" and "Definition of Philosophy,"* trans. Norman Madarasz (Albany: State University of New York Press, 1999), 125–26.

66. Maurice Blanchot, *L'Entretien infini* (Paris: Gallimard, 1969), 2; *The Infinite Conversation*, trans. Susan Hanson (Minneapolis: University of Minnesota Press, 1993), 3–4.

67. Blanchot, *L'Entretien infini*, 2; *Infinite Conversation*, 4.

68. Jeff Mason, *Philosophical Rhetoric: The Function of Indirection in Philosophical Writing* (London: Routledge, 1989), 55 (emphases added).

69. Paul Ricœur, *Time and Narrative*, 3 vols. (Chicago: University of Chicago Press, 1984), 2:61–99, 80, 98.

70. Ibid., 2:80.

71. Ibid., 2:81.

72. Jacques Derrida, "To Do Justice to Freud: History of Madness in the Age of Psychoanalysis," in *Resistances of Psychoanalysis*, trans. Peggy Kamuf, Pascale-Anne Brault, and Michael Naas (Stanford, Calif.: Stanford University Press, 1998), 75–76.

73. John Cottingham, *The Cambridge Companion to Descartes* (Cambridge: Cambridge University Press, 1992), 49, 252.

74. Anthony Trollope, *The Duke's Children*, vol. 3 (New York: Dodd, Mead, 1912), 3:112.

REFERENCES

Aczel, Amir D. *Descartes' Secret Notebook: A True Tale of Mathematics, Mysticism, and the Quest to Understand the Universe*. New York: Broadway Books, 2005.

Adam, Charles. *Descartes: Ses amities feminines*. Paris: Boivin, 1937.

Agamben, Giorgio. *Idea of Prose*. Translated by Michael Sullivan and Sam Whitsitt. Albany: State University of New York Press, 1995.

Almog, Joseph. *Cogito?: Descartes and Thinking the World*. New York: Oxford University Press, 2008.

Appelbaum, David. *The Stop*. Albany: State University of New York Press, 1995.

Arendt, Hannah. *The Life of the Mind*. 2 vols. New York: Harcourt Brace Jovanovich, 1978.

Ariès, Philippe. *Western Attitudes toward Death: From the Middle Ages to the Present*. Translated by Patricia M. Ranum. Baltimore: Johns Hopkins University Press, 1974.

Ashbery, John. "The Business of Falling Asleep (2)." In *Notes from the Air: Selected Later Poems*, 322–24. New York: Ecco, 2007.

Bachelard, Gaston. *The Dialectic of Duration*. Translated by Mary McAllester Jones. Manchester: Clinamen, 2000.

———. *The Poetics of Reverie*. Translated by Daniel Russell. New York: Orion Press, 1969.

———. *The Poetics of Space*. Translated by Maria Jolas. New York: Orion Press, 1964.

———. *The Psychoanalysis of Fire*. Translated by Alan C. M. Ross. Boston: Beacon Press, 1964.

Badiou, Alain. *Infinite Thought: Truth and the Return to Philosophy*. Edited by Justin Clemens and Oliver Feltham. London: Continuum, 2003.

———. *Manifesto for Philosophy: Followed by Two Essays: "The (Re)Turn of Philosophy Itself" and "Definition of Philosophy."* Translated by Norman Madarasz. Albany: State University of New York Press, 1999.

Badiou, Alain, and Slavoj Zizek. *Philosophy in the Present.* Edited by Peter Engelmann. Malden, Mass.: Polity, 2009.

Baillet, Adrien. *La vie de Monsieur Des-Cartes.* 2 vols. New York: Garland, 1987. First published 1691, Daniel Horthemels.

Baker, Gordon P., and Katherine J. Morris. *Descartes' Dualism.* New York: Routledge, 2002.

Barnes, Julian. *Nothing to Be Frightened Of.* New York: Alfred A. Knopf, 2008.

Barthes, Roland. *Camera Lucida: Reflections on Photography.* Translated by Richard Howard. York: Hill and Wang, 1981.

———. *Mythologies.* Translated by Annette Lavers. New York: Hill and Wang, 1972.

———. *The Pleasure of the Text.* Translated by Richard Miller. New York: Hill and Wang, 1975.

———. *Writing Degree Zero, and Elements of Semiology.* Translated by Annette Lavers and Colin Smith. Boston: Beacon Press, 1970.

———. "Writing Reading." In *The Rustle of Language,* 29–32. Translated by Richard Howard. Berkeley: University of California Press, 1989.

Bate, Jonathan. *The Genius of Shakespeare.* 10th anniversary ed. Oxford: Oxford University Press, 2008.

Behler, Ernst. "The Theory of Irony in German Romanticism." In *Romantic Irony,* edited by Frederick Garber, 43–81. Budapest: John Benjamins, 1989.

Benjamin, Walter. "The Work of Art in the Age of Its Technological Reproducibility: Third Version." In *Selected Writings.* Vol. 4, *1938–1940,* edited by Marcus Paul Bullock, Michael William Jennings, Howard Eiland, and Gary Smith, 251–83. Cambridge, Mass.: Belknap Press, 1996.

Blanchot, Maurice. *L'Entretien infini.* Paris: Gallimard, 1969.

———. *The Infinite Conversation.* Translated by Susan Hanson. Minneapolis: University of Minnesota Press, 1993.

Bloch, Ernst. *The Principle of Hope.* 3 vols. Translated by Neville Plaice, Stephen Plaice, and Paul Knight. Cambridge, Mass.: MIT Press, 1986.

Bluhm, William T. "Political Theory and Ethics." In René Descartes, *Discourse on Method and Meditations on First Philosophy,* edited by David Weissman, 306–29. Translated by Elizabeth S. Haldane and G. R. T. Ross. New Haven, Conn.: Yale University Press, 1996.

Blumenberg, Hans. *Shipwreck with Spectator: Paradigm of a Metaphor for Existence.* Translated by Steven Rendall. Cambridge, Mass.: MIT Press, 1997.

Bordo, Susan. *The Flight to Objectivity: Essays on Cartesianism and Culture.* Albany: State University of New York Press, 1987.

Bracken, Harry M. *Descartes.* Oxford: Oneworld, 2002.

Broughton, Janet. *Descartes's Method of Doubt.* Princeton, N.J.: Princeton University Press, 2002.

Bruns, Gerald L. *Inventions, Writing, Textuality, and Understanding in Literary History.* New Haven, Conn.: Yale University Press, 1982.

Butler, Judith. *Giving an Account of Oneself.* New York: Fordham University Press, 2005.

Carraud, Vincent. "The Relevance of Cartesianism." In *Contemporary French Philosophy: Supplement to Philosophy*, edited by A. Phillips Griffiths and Pascal Engel, 69–81. Cambridge: Cambridge University Press, 1987.

Carriero, John Peter. *Between Two Worlds: A Reading of Descartes's Meditations.* Princeton, N.J.: Princeton University Press, 2009.

———. "The Cartesian Circle and the Foundations of Knowledge." In *A Companion to Descartes*, ed. Janet Broughton and John Carriero, 302–18. London: Blackwell, 2008.

Carroll, Lewis. *Alice's Adventures in Wonderland: A Classic Illustrated Edition.* Edited by Cooper Edens. San Francisco: Chronicle Books, 2000.

Clément, Catherine. *Syncope: The Philosophy of Rapture.* Translated by Sally O'Driscoll and Deirdre M. Mahoney. Minneapolis: University of Minnesota Press, 1994.

Cole, John R. *The Olympian Dreams and Youthful Rebellion of René Descartes.* Urbana: University of Illinois Press, 1992.

Conrad, Peter, and Joseph W. Schneider. *Deviance and Medicalization: From Badness to Sickness.* Expanded ed. Philadelphia: Temple University Press, 1992.

Copleston, Frederick C. Review of *The Concept of Mind* by Gilbert Ryle. *British Journal for the Philosophy of Science* 1, no. 4 (1951): 328–32.

Cottingham, John. *The Cambridge Companion to Descartes.* New York: Cambridge University Press, 1992.

———. *Cartesian Reflections: Essays on Descartes' Philosophy.* Oxford: Oxford University Press, 2008.

Danto, Arthur C. *What Philosophy Is: A Guide to the Elements.* New York: Harper & Row, 1968.

Dastur, Françoise. *Telling Time: Sketch of a Phenomenological Chrono-Logy.* Translated by Edward Bullard. London: Athlone Press, 2000.

Descartes, René. *The Philosophical Writings of Descartes.* 3 vols. Translated by John Cottingham, Robert Stoothoff, and Dugald Murdoch. Cambridge: Cambridge University Press, 1985.

Deleuze, Gilles. *Difference and Repetition.* Translated by Paul Patton. New York: Columbia University Press, 1994.

———. *Différence et répétition.* Paris: Presses Universitaires de France, 1968.

———. *Negotiations, 1972–1990.* Translated by Martin Joughin. New York: Columbia University Press, 1995.

———. "What Is the Creative Act?" In *Two Regimes of Madness: Texts and Interviews 1975–1995*, edited by David Lapoujade, 312–24. New York: Semiotext(e), 2006.

Deleuze, Gilles, and Félix Guattari. *Qu'est-ce que la philosophie?* Paris: Éditions de Minuit, 1991.

————. *What Is Philosophy?* Translated by Hugh Tomlinson and Graham Burchell. New York: Columbia University Press, 1994.

Derrida, Jacques. "Cogito and the History of Madness." In *Writing and Difference*, 31–63. Translated by Alan Bass. London: Routledge & Kegan Paul, 1981. First published 1978.

————. "Cogito et histoire de la folie." In *L'Écriture et la différance*, 51–97. Paris: Éditions du Seuil, 1967.

————. "Cogito et histoire de la folie." *Revue de Metaphysique et de Morale* 68 (1963): 460–94.

————. *Margins of Philosophy.* Translated by Alan Bass. Chicago: University of Chicago Press, 1982.

————. *Memoirs of the Blind: The Self-Portrait and Other Ruins.* Translated by Pascale-Anne Brault and Michael Naas. Chicago: University of Chicago Press, 1993.

————. *Of Grammatology.* Translated by Gayatri Chakravorty Spivak. Baltimore: Johns Hopkins University Press, 1976.

————. *Résistances de la psychoanalyse.* Paris: Galilée, 1996.

————. "To Do Justice to Freud: History of Madness in the Age of Psychoanalysis." *Critical Inquiry* 20 (Winter 1994): 227–66. Reprinted in *Resistances of Psychoanalysis*, 70–118. Translated by Peggy Kamuf, Pascale-Anne Brault, and Michael Naas. Stanford, Calif.: Stanford University Press, 1998.

Descartes, René. *Discourse on Method, Optics, Geometry, and Meteorology.* Rev. ed. Translated by Paul J. Olscamp. Indianapolis: Hackett, 2001.

Dick, Kirby, and Amy Ziering Kofman, directors. *Derrida.* Jane Doe Films/ Zeitgeist Films. New York: Zeitgeist Video, 2003. DVD.

Dickinson, Emily. "I heard a Fly buzz—when I died [1862]." In *The Oxford Book of American Poetry*, edited by David Lehman, 170–71. Oxford: Oxford University Press, 2006.

Dussel, Enrique D. *Philosophy of Liberation.* Translated by Aquila Martinez and Christine Morkovsky. Maryknoll, N.Y.: Orbis Books, 1985.

Fanon, Frantz. *Black Skin, White Masks.* Translated by Charles Lam Markmann. New York: Grove Press, 1967.

Ferguson, Harvie. *The Lure of Dreams: Sigmund Freud and the Construction of Modernity.* London: Routledge, 1996.

Feuer, L. "The Dreams of Descartes." *American Imago* 20 (1963): 3–26.

Flusser, Vilém. *Towards a Philosophy of Photography.* Translated by Anthony Mathews. London: Reaktion Books, 2003.

Foucault, Michel. *The Hermeneutics of the Subject: Lectures at the Collège de France, 1981–1982.* Translated by Graham Burchell. Edited by Frédéric Gros. New York: Palgrave Macmillan, 2005.

————. *Histoire de la folie à l'âge classique. Suivi de mon corps, ce papier, ce feu et la folie, L'absence d'œuvre.* Paris: Gallimard, 1972.

————. *History of Madness.* Translated by Jonathan Murphy. Edited by Jean Khalfa. London: Routledge, 2006.

————. *Mental Illness and Psychology.* Translated by Alan Sheridan. New York: Harper & Row, 1976.

————. "Mon corps, ce papier, ce feu." In *Dits et écrits.* Vol. 1, *1954–1975,* 1113–36. Paris: Éditions Gallimard, 1994.

————. "My Body, This Paper, This Fire." In *The Essential Works of Foucault, 1954–1984,* vol. 2, *Aesthetics,* 393–417. Edited by Paul Rabinow, James D. Faubion. New York: New Press, 1997.

Frankfurt, Harry G. *Demons, Dreamers, and Madmen: The Defense of Reason in Descartes's Meditations.* Foreword by Rebecca Goldstein. Princeton, N.J.: Princeton University Press, 2008.

Freud, Sigmund. *The Standard Edition of the Complete Psychological Works of Sigmund Freud.* 24 vols. Edited by James Strachey, Anna Freud, Carrie Lee Rothgeb, and Angela Richards. London: Hogarth Press, 1953.

Fuentes, Carlos. "Where Is the Glory That Was France?" *New York Times,* January 14, 1996.

Gabbey, Alan, and Robert E. Hall. "The Melon and the Dictionary: Reflections on Descartes's Dreams." *Journal of the History of Ideas* 59, no. 4 (1998): 651–68.

Garber, Daniel. *Descartes Embodied: Reading Cartesian Philosophy through Cartesian Science.* Cambridge: Cambridge University Press, 2001.

Giovannangeli, Daniel, and Jacques Taminiaux. *La fiction de l'être: Lectures de la philosophie moderne.* Brussels: Le Point Philosophique, 1990.

Grossman, Allen R. *Descartes' Loneliness.* New York: New Directions, 2007.

Halliday, M. A. K. "How Do You Mean?" In *On Grammar (Collected Works of M. A. K. Halliday),* 352–68. London: Continuum, 2005.

Hartle, Ann. *Death and the Disinterested Spectator: An Inquiry into the Nature of Philosophy.* New York: SUNY Press, 1986.

Hatfield, Gary C. "Force (God) in Descartes' Physics." In *Oxford Readings in Philosophy,* ed. John Cottingham, 281–310 (Oxford: Oxford University Press, 1998).

————. "René Descartes (1596–1650)." In *The Blackwell Guide to the Modern Philosophers: from Descartes to Nietzsche,* ed. Steven M. Emmanuel, 1–27. London: Wiley-Black, 2011.

Hatfield, Gary C., and René Descartes. *Routledge Philosophy Guidebook to Descartes and the Meditations.* London: Routledge, 2003.

Hecht, Jennifer Michael. *Doubt: A History: The Great Doubters and Their Legacy of Innovation, from Socrates and Jesus to Thomas Jefferson and Emily Dickinson.* San Francisco: HarperSanFrancisco, 2003.

Hegel, Georg Wilhelm Friedrich. *Phenomenology of Spirit.* Translated by Arnold V. Miller. Edited by J. N. Findlay. Oxford: Clarendon Press, 1977.

Heidegger, Martin. *The Fundamental Concepts of Metaphysics: World, Finitude, Solitude.* Translated by William McNeill and Nicholas Walker. Bloomington: Indiana University Press, 1995.

Hein, Christoph. *The Distant Lover.* Translated by Krishna Winston. New York: Pantheon, 1989.

Heine, Heinrich. *Sämtliche Schriften.* Vol. 3. Edited by Klaus Briegleb. Munich: Carl Hanser Verlag, 1969.

Hintikka, Jaako. "Cogito Ergo Sum: Inference or Performance?" *Philosophical Review* 71 (1962): 3–32.

Hockney, David. *Secret Knowledge: Rediscovering the Lost Techniques of the Old Masters.* New York: Viking Studio, 2001.

Hodges, H. A. *The Philosophy of Wilhelm Dilthey.* London: Routledge & Paul, 1952.

Horkheimer, Max, and Theodor W. Adorno. *Dialectic of Enlightenment: Philosophical Fragments.* Translated by Edmund Jephcott. Edited by Gunzelin Schmid Noerr. Stanford, Calif.: Stanford University Press, 2002.

Hume, David. *An Enquiry Concerning Human Understanding.* Oxford: Clarendon Press, 1978. First published 1888.

Humphries, Lance. *Daniel Garber: Romantic Realist.* Doylestown, Penn.: James A. Michener Art Museum, 2006.

Hurston, Zora Neale. *Their Eyes Were Watching God: A Novel.* Urbana: University of Illinois Press, 1978.

Husserl, Edmund. *The Crisis of European Sciences and Transcendental Phenomenology: An Introduction to Phenomenological Philosophy.* Translated by David Carr. Evanston: Northwestern University Press, 1970.

———. *Die Krisis Der Europaischen Wissenschaften Und Die Transzendentale Phanomenologie.* Vol. Bd. 6, *Gesammelte Werke, Husserliana.* The Hague: Martinus Nijhoff, 1954.

Hutton, Sarah. "Women Philosophers and the Early Reception of Descartes: Anne Conway and Princess Elisabeth." In *Receptions of Descartes: Cartesianism and Anti-Cartesianism in Early Modern Europe,* edited by Tad M. Schmaltz, 3–24. London: Routledge, 2005.

Huxley, Thomas Henry. "On Descartes' 'Discourse Touching the Method of Using One's Reason Rightly and of Seeking Scientific Truth' (1870)." In *Collected Essays,* vol. 1: *Method and Results,* 166–98. London: Elibron Classics, 2005.

Irlam, Shaun. "Showing Losses, Counting Gains: 'Scenes' from Negative Autobiography." *Modern Language Notes* 106, no. 5 (1991): 997–1012.

Isherwood, Christopher. *Goodbye to Berlin.* New York: Random House, 1939.

James, Ian. "The Persistence of the Subject: On Descartes and the Cogito." In *The Fragmentary Demand: An Introduction to the Philosophy of Jean-Luc Nancy,* 26–64. Stanford, Calif.: Stanford University Press, 2006.

Jay, Martin. *Downcast Eyes: The Denigration of Vision in Twentieth-Century French Thought.* Berkeley: University of California Press, 1993.

Judovitz, Dalia. "From Self to Subject: Montaigne to Descartes." In *Subjectivity and Representation in Descartes: The Origins of Modernity,* 8–38. Cambridge: Cambridge University Press, 1988.

———. "Philosophy and Poetry: The Difference between Them in Plato and Descartes." In *Literature and the Question of Philosophy,* edited by Anthony J. Cascardi, 24–51. Baltimore: Johns Hopkins University Press, 1987.

———. *Subjectivity and Representation in Descartes: The Origins of Modernity.* Cambridge: Cambridge University Press, 1988.

Jussim, Estelle. *The Eternal Moment: Essays on the Photographic Image.* New York: Aperture, 1989.

Kambouchner, Denis. "Thought versus History: Reflections on a French Problem." In *Teaching New Histories of Philosophy,* edited by J. B. Schneewind, 235–61. Princeton, N.J.: Center for Human Values, Princeton University, 2004.

Kearney, Richard. *Strangers, Gods, and Monsters: Interpreting Otherness.* London: Routledge, 2003.

Kofman, Sarah. "Descartes Entrapped." In *Who Comes after the Subject?,* edited by Peter Connor and Jean-Luc Nancy, and Eduardo Cadava, 178–97. London: Routledge, 1991.

Kolakowski, Leszek. *Metaphysical Horror.* New York: Basil Blackwell, 1988.

Kreeft, Peter. *Socrates Meets Descartes: The Father of Philosophy Analyzes the Father of Modern Philosophy's Discourse on Method.* San Francisco: Ignatius Press, 2007.

Krell, David Farrell. *Of Memory, Reminiscence, and Writing: On the Verge.* Bloomington: Indiana University Press, 1990.

Kristeva, Julia. *This Incredible Need to Believe.* Translated by Beverly Bie Brahic. New York: Columbia University Press, 2009.

Lacan, Jacques. *The Four Fundamental Concepts of Psycho-Analysis.* Translated by Alan Sheridan. Edited by Jacques-Alain Miller. New York: Norton, 1978.

Lang, Berel. *Philosophy and the Art of Writing: Studies in Philosophical and Literary Style.* Lewisburg, Penn.: Bucknell University Press, 1983.

Le Doeuff, Michèle. *The Philosophical Imaginary.* Translated by Colin Gordon. London: Continuum, 2002.

Le Grand, Eva. *Kundera, ou, la mémoire du désir.* Paris: XYZ Éditeur, 1995.

Lesser, Wendy. "On Not Writing about Hume." In *Room for Doubt,* 59–121. New York: Pantheon Books, 2007.

———. *Room for Doubt.* New York: Pantheon Books, 2007.

Levinas, Emmanuel. *Existence and Existents.* Translated by Alphonso Lingis. The Hague: Martinus Nijhoff, 1978.

———. *Of God Who Comes to Mind.* 2nd ed. Translated by Bettina Bergo. Stanford, Calif.: Stanford University Press, 1998.

———. *Otherwise Than Being: Or, Beyond Essence.* Translated by Alphonso Lingis. Dordrecht, the Netherlands: Kluwer Academic, 1981.

———. *Totality and Infinity: An Essay on Exteriority.* Translated by Alphonso Lingis. Pittsburgh: Duquesne University Press, 1969.

Loeb, Louis E. "The Mind-Body Union, Interaction, and Subsumption." In *Early Modern Philosophy: Mind, Matter, and Metaphysics,* edited by Christia Mercer and Eileen O'Neill, 65–83. Oxford: Oxford University Press, 2005.

Malabou, Catherine. *What Should We Do with Our Brain?* Translated by Sebastian Rand. New York: Fordham University Press, 2008.

Mallarmé, Stéphane. "Richard Wagner: The Reverie of a French Poet." In *Divagations: The Author's 1897 Arrangement; Together with "Autobiography" and "Music and Letters,"* 107–16. Translated by Barbara Johnson. Cambridge, Mass.: Harvard University Press, 2007.

Marion, Jean-Luc. *Cartesian Questions: Method and Metaphysics.* Foreword by Daniel Garber. Chicago: University of Chicago Press, 1999.

———. "Does Thought Dream? The Three Dreams, or the Awakening of the Philosopher." In *Cartesian Questions: Method and Metaphysics,* 1–19. Chicago: University of Chicago Press, 1999.

———. "God, the Styx, and the Fates: The Letters to Mersenne of 1630." In *On the Ego and on God: Further Cartesian Questions,* 103–15. New York: Fordham University Press, 2007.

———. *On Descartes' Metaphysical Prism: The Constitution and the Limits of Onto-Theo-Logy in Cartesian Thought.* Chicago: University of Chicago Press, 1999.

———. *On the Ego and on God: Further Cartesian Questions.* New York: Fordham University Press, 2007.

———. "The Originary Otherness of the Ego: A Rereading of Descartes' Second *Meditation.*" In *On the Ego and on God: Further Cartesian Questions,* 3–29. New York: Fordham University Press, 2007.

———. "The Responsorial Status of the *Meditations.*" In *On the Ego and on God: Further Cartesian Questions,* 30–41. New York: Fordham University Press, 2007.

———. *Sur la théologie blanche de Descartes: Analogie, création des vérités éternelles et fondement.* Paris: Presses Universitaires de France, 1981.

Maritain, Jacques. *The Dream of Descartes, Together with Some Other Essays.* Translated by Mabelle Louise Cunningham Andison. New York: Philosophical Library, 1944.

Marsh, James L. *Post-Cartesian Meditations: An Essay in Dialectical Phenomenology.* New York: Fordham University Press, 1988.

Mason, Jeff. *Philosophical Rhetoric: The Function of Indirection in Philosophical Writing.* London: Routledge, 1989.

McCabe, Susan. *Descartes' Nightmare.* Salt Lake City: University of Utah Press, 2008.

Melehy, Hassan. *Writing Cogito: Montaigne, Descartes, and the Institution of the Modern Subject.* Albany: State University of New York Press, 1997.

Merleau-Ponty, Maurice. "Eye and Mind." In *The Merleau-Ponty Aesthetics Reader: Philosophy and Painting,* edited by Galen A. Johnson and Michael B. Smith, 121–49. Evanston, Ill.: Northwestern University Press, 1993.

———. *Phenomenology of Perception.* Translated by Colin Smith. London: Routledge, 1962.

———. "Philosophy and Non-Philosophy since Hegel." In *Philosophy and Non-Philosophy since Merleau-Ponty,* edited by Hugh J. Silverman, 9–83. New York: Routledge, 1988.

———. *Signs.* Translated by Richard C. McCleary. Evanston, Ill.: Northwestern University Press, 1964.

———. *The Visible and the Invisible.* Translated by Alphonso Lingis. Evanston, Ill.: Northwestern University Press, 1968.

Meyerhoff, Hans, ed. *The Philosophy of History in Our Time.* New York: Garland, 1985. First published 1959, Doubleday.

Minahen, Charles. "The Turbulent Dream-Vision of Descartes's 'Olympian' Experience." In *Dreams in French Literature: The Persistent Voice,* edited by Tom Conney, 65–84. Amsterdam: Rodopi, 1995.

Montaigne, Michel de. *The Complete Essays of Montaigne.* Translated by Donald M. Frame. Stanford, Calif.; Stanford University Press, 1958.

Naas, Michael. *Taking on the Tradition: Jacques Derrida and the Legacies of Deconstruction.* Stanford, Calif.: Stanford University Press, 2003.

Nancy, Jean-Luc. *Corpus.* Translated by Richard A. Rand. New York: Fordham University Press, 2008.

———. *The Fall of Sleep.* Translated by Charlotte Mandell. New York: Fordham University Press, 2009.

———. "Identity and Trembling." In *The Birth to Presence,* 9–35. Translated by Brian Holmes et al. Stanford: Stanford University Press, 1993.

———. "Larvatus Pro Deo." Translated by Daniel A. Brewer. *Glyph: Johns Hopkins Textual Studies* 2 (1977): 14–36.

———. "Mundus Est Fabula." *Modern Language Notes* 93, no. 4 (1978): 635–53.

Negri, Antonio. *The Political Descartes: Reason, Ideology, and the Bourgeois Project.* Translated by Matteo Mandarini and Alberto Toscano. London: Verso, 2006.

The New Testament of Our Lord and Saviour Jesus Christ: Being the Authorised Version Set Forth in 1611, Arranged in Parallel Columns, with the Revised Version of 1881 and with the Greek Text Followed in the Revised Version. New York: Columbia University Press, 1896.

Nietzsche, Friedrich Wilhelm. *The Gay Science; with a Prelude in Rhymes and an Appendix of Songs.* Translated by Walter Arnold Kaufmann. New York: Vintage Books, 1974.

Nye, Andrea. *The Princess and the Philosopher: Letters of Elisabeth of the Palatine to René Descartes*. Lanham, Md.: Rowman & Littlefield, 1999.

Plato. *Timaeus and Critias*. Translated by Henry Desmond Pritchard Lee. Harmondsworth, U.K.: Penguin Books, 1971.

Popkin, Richard H. *The Columbia History of Western Philosophy*. New York: Columbia University Press, 1999.

Poundstone, William. *Labyrinths of Reason: Paradox, Puzzles, and the Frailty of Knowledge*. New York: Anchor Books, 1990.

Prose, Francine. *Reading Like a Writer: A Guide for People Who Love Books and for Those Who Want to Write Them*. New York: HarperCollins, 2006.

Rée, Jonathan. *Descartes*. London: Allen Lane, 1974.

———. "Descartes' Comedy." In *Philosophical Tales: An Essay on Philosophy and Literature*. London: Methuen, 1987.

Ricoeur, Paul. *Time and Narrative*. Vol. 2. Translated by Kathleen McLaughlin and David Pellauer. Chicago: University of Chicago Press, 1984.

Rorty, Richard. *Philosophy and the Mirror of Nature*. Princeton, N.J.: Princeton University Press, 1979.

Rubin, Ronald. *Silencing the Demon's Advocate: The Strategy of Descartes' Meditations*. Palo Alto, Calif.: Stanford University Press, 2008.

Ryle, Gilbert. *The Concept of Mind*. London: Hutchinson's University Library, 1949.

Saramago, José. *Blindness: A Novel*. Translated by Giovanni Pontiero. London: Harvill Press, 1997.

Sardello, Robert J. *Freeing the Soul from Fear*. New York: Riverhead Books, 1999.

Sartre, Jean-Paul. "Cartesian Freedom." In *Literary and Philosophical Essays*, 180–97. Translated by Annette Michelson. New York: Collier Books, 1962.

Shawcross, Nancy M. *Roland Barthes on Photography: The Critical Tradition in Perspective*. Gainesville: University Press of Florida, 1997.

Sire, Agnès, Jean-Luc Nancy, and Henri Cartier-Bresson. *An Inner Silence: The Portraits of Henri Cartier-Bresson*. New York: Thames & Hudson, 2006.

Sorell, Tom. *Descartes Reinvented*. Cambridge: Cambridge University Press, 2005.

Steiner, George. *Grammars of Creation: Originating in the Gifford Lectures for 1990*. New Haven, Conn.: Yale University Press, 2001.

Sturken, Marita, and Lisa Cartwright. *Practices of Looking: An Introduction to Visual Culture*. 2nd ed. New York: Oxford University Press, 2009.

Tlumak, Jeffrey. *Classical Modern Philosophy: A Contemporary Introduction*. London: Routledge, 2006.

Trollope, Anthony. *The Duke's Children*. Vol. 3. New York: Dodd, Mead, 1912.

Vasseleu, Cathryn. *Textures of Light: Vision and Touch in Irigaray, Levinas, and Merleau-Ponty*. London: Routledge, 1998.

Voltaire, Gustave Lanson, and the Société des Textes Français Modernes. *Lettres philosophiques*. 2nd ed. Paris: Hachette, 1915.

Williams, Caroline. *Contemporary French Philosophy: Modernity and the Persistence of the Subject*. London: Continuum, 2005.

Wilson, Catherine. *Descartes's Meditations: An Introduction*. Cambridge: Cambridge University Press, 2003.

Wilson, Margaret Dauler. *Descartes*. London: Routledge and Kegan Paul, 1982.

Wolf-Devine, Celia. *Descartes on Seeing: Epistemology and Visual Perception*. Carbondale: Southern Illinois University Press, 1993.

Woolf, Virginia. *A Writer's Diary, Being Extracts from the Diary of Virginia Woolf*. New York: Harcourt Brace Jovanovich, 1973.

Zangana, Haifa. *Dreaming of Baghdad*. New York: Feminist Press at the City University of New York, 2009.

Žižek, Slavoj. *The Ticklish Subject: The Absent Centre of Political Ontology*. London: Verso, 1999.